THE BIG BOOK OF
VEGETARIAN

THE BIG
VEGET

More Than **225 RECIPES** for Breakfasts, Appetizers, Soups, Salads, Sandwiches, Main Dishes, Sides, Breads, and Desserts

BOOK OF ARIAN

by Kathy Farrell-Kingsley

CHRONICLE BOOKS

SAN FRANCISCO

Library of Congress Cataloging-in-Publication
Data available.

ISBN **0-8118-4116-2**

Manufactured in Canada.

Designed by **PJ CHMIEL**
Food styling: **DIANE SCOTT GSELL**
Photo assistant: **SARA JOHNSON**

Distributed in Canada by
RAINCOAST BOOKS
9050 Shaughnessy Street
Vancouver, British Columbia V6P 6E5

10 9 8 7 6 5 4 3 2 1

CHRONICLE BOOKS LLC
85 Second Street
San Francisco, California 94105

www.chroniclebooks.com

To David, Emma, and Caroline, for their love and patience.

CONTENTS

INTRO-
DUCTION

When I was the food editor for a leading vegetarian magazine, I would find my mailbox filled each day with the latest cookbooks and press releases about up-and-coming vegetarian chefs and hot new restaurants, as well as ideas and queries from readers or professional writers for novel meals or new twists on old dishes. Some days there were so many, I had to wonder how we could ever hope to make them all.

This constant flow of recipes got me thinking about my favorite meals, the tried-and-true recipes I reach for again and again whenever I want something wholesome and good. And I began wondering, what are the recipes no vegetarian cook should be without?

My answer to this question is in the pages of *The Big Book of Vegetarian*—more than 225 recipes designed to inspire vegetarian and nonvegetarian cooks. Whether you're looking for a classic rendition of a family favorite or a new dish to entice you, the recipes included here were developed to provide vegetarian cooks with a complete collection of great-tasting, foolproof recipes.

CHANGING TIMES

Americans have the rare opportunity to enjoy the healthiest diet in the world. Our markets are filled with wholesome foods, and there is an unprecedented depth in our understanding of which foods nourish us best. Good food is the foundation of good health, and as volumes of studies have demonstrated, vegetables, whole grains, nuts, soy products, and fruits are rich in the nutrients that can ward off such modern-day ills as heart disease, cancer, and osteoporosis.

In the last fifteen years, I have seen vegetarianism go from fringe to fashion to fact of life because it's a healthy and worthy way to live. The hippie connotation, which kept many people away, is a thing of the past. Today the American vegetarian is not just the health nut, it's the stay-at-home mom, the computer engineer, the veterinarian, the nurse, the store clerk, the neighbor across the street, and the teenager next door. They are families, individuals, and students. They live in urban areas and in suburbia, and together they represent 16 million people. You can see how health-conscious our culture has become just by taking a trip to the local grocery store, where the words "natural," "organic," and "meatless" jump out at you in every aisle.

CHOICES

Being a vegetarian means different things to different people. Some people choose to become vegetarian for health reasons, others because of animal welfare, and still others for ethical or environmental reasons. Some are transitioning toward a vegetarian diet by slowly reducing their consumption of animal products. Other vegetarians do not eat meat but will consume dairy and/or eggs. And then there are those who do not eat any animal products (red meat, poultry, pork, fish, or shellfish), dairy products, eggs, or honey. This group is known as vegan (VEE-gun), and it's the most complete of all the vegetarian lifestyles. Typically, the term "vegan" refers to more than just diet alone. Vegans are also respectful of the interconnectedness of all life and advocate harmony and empathic living by also avoiding all nonfood items made with animal products, such as leather, silk, and wool.

Some believe that vegetarianism is an evolution, starting from the typical American meat-centered diet and progressing toward the vegan ideal. Most vegetarians fall somewhere in between and are content to stay wherever they are on the continuum, while others continue to evolve and move closer to the vegan end of the spectrum. Whatever your reasons for choosing vegetarianism in any of its many forms, the choice is personal and for you alone to decide.

ORGANICS

I think it's wonderful that organic foods are finally moving into the mainstream. Studies show that foods grown organically have a higher vitamin and mineral content than their conventionally farmed counterparts. I encourage you to support organic farms and local growers, as well as markets that carry organic and locally grown produce, for the following reasons:

- Buying organic produce supports small, independently owned and operated family farms. It also supports the health of farmworkers and their families by affording them a safe work environment.

- Organic farming methods, such as the use of compost and beneficial insects, enhance rather than deplete soil fertility, prevent soil erosion, and control pests without poisons.

- Organic farming promotes biodiversity—the perpetuation of a broad variety of plant species. This simultaneously preserves consumer choice and protects our food supply over the long term.

- Organic farming techniques prevent the problem of fertilizer runoff into surface and ground water.

- Organic foods taste better.

INSIDE THIS BOOK

Many of the recipes in this book are designed to be vegan-friendly, but some use dairy products, eggs, or honey. Vegan recipes are identified as such. In the other recipes, vegans can usually use oil, soy products, and egg substitute in place of their nonvegan counterparts.

The book begins with a section on essential kitchen equipment, a guide to foods to stock the vegetarian pantry, and a glossary of ingredients and terms commonly used in vegetarian cooking. Then follow nine chapters of recipes organized by type of dish, from breakfast to dessert. At the end of the book, Chapter 10 offers menu-planning suggestions using the ample and widely varied recipes that fill the chapters before it.

It's my hope that the pages of this book become worn and dog-eared as you discover the pleasures of vegetarian cooking. I welcome your comments, ideas, and suggestions. Please visit www.vegcook.com or e-mail me at thevegcook@aol.com.

—Kathy Farrell-Kingsley

GUIDE TO KITCHEN EQUIPMENT

What comprises basic cooking gear for one cook can be completely different for another cook, depending on what they make most often. I know one person who uses a pressure cooker three times a week, and another who has never taken it out of the box. And if you like to bake, you'll use different equipment than someone who doesn't bake at all. Basic cookware is a subjective concept, but here is a list of some functional pieces, both large and small, that I feel are essential to have on hand for vegetarian cooking.

KNIVES

Good vegetarian cooking begins with good knives. Sharp, sturdy knives make easy work of chopping, slicing, and dicing. Although quality cutlery is costly, if handled properly and well maintained, knives will last a lifetime.

Every kitchen should have at least four basic knives: an 8- or 10-inch chef's knife for chopping, dicing, and slicing; a small paring knife for peeling, pitting, and seeding fruits and vegetables; a heavy cleaver for cutting dense vegetables like winter squash; and a large serrated knife, which cuts breads and tomatoes better than a chef's knife.

POTS AND PANS

You should have one or two skillets. It's good to own two, a larger one (10 to 12 inches) for making stir-fries and sautés, and a smaller one (around 7 inches) for frying up a single tofu burger or making an omelet. Those with a nonstick surface are a good way to cut down on using added fat. Keep in mind that it's always best to use either wooden or plastic utensils (especially spoons and spatulas) when cooking with nonstick pans. A wok is great for stir-frying, but any deep, slope-sided frying pan will do just as well. Chopsticks are handy for stirring in a pinch.

While nonstick skillets are great, don't feel compelled to buy the matching saucepans. It's better to buy saucepans with heavy bottoms and snug-fitting covers. A 3-quart saucepan is perfect for making small amounts of pasta, cooking stews, and boiling and steaming vegetables. A stockpot and a Dutch oven are good for soups and stews.

Here's a tip: If you have an immersion blender, use a stockpot when making puréed soups; the tall sides allow you to blend the soup right in the pan without splattering it all over the stove.

UTENSILS

Large, thick-handled wooden and metal spoons for stirring are important. Heavy, heat-resistant rubber spatulas in different sizes are essential for scraping bowls and pans.

Stainless-steel wire whisks in several sizes are good for smoothing out and mixing batters and for incorporating dry ingredients. Also useful are a pancake turner or metal spatula for flipping and serving pancakes, veggie burgers, and other flat foods; a wide, flat, flexible metal spatula for spreading, splitting, and icing cakes, turning crêpes, and prodding muffins out of tins; and a stainless-steel ladle for properly serving soups, stews, and sauces.

STEAMERS

A collapsible steamer insert will work in just about any size pot and is great for preparing crisp, flavorful, colorful vegetables.

CUTTING BOARDS

Cutting boards with either polyethylene or wooden surfaces need to be scrubbed well after using, especially between chopping onions and slicing strawberries. Some people keep one board for pungent foods and another for more delicate, odor-absorbing foods. Select a cutting board that is large enough to work on comfortably but small enough for you to lift easily. A good size is 12 by 15 inches.

BOWLS

A nesting set of three mixing bowls (small, medium, and large) saves space. Most bowls these days are stainless steel, which is preferable to aluminum, because aluminum reacts with acidic ingredients. Heavy-duty plastic bowls are adequate, but won't last as long as metal or glass. Small glass bowls are especially handy for holding small amounts of measured ingredients until you're ready to use them.

MEASURING TOOLS

Measuring is important, especially for beginners. Make sure you have a set of measuring cups for dry ingredients and a 4-cup glass measuring cup for liquids. You will also need a set of measuring spoons; those made of stainless steel or heavy plastic work fine.

OVENWARE

For baking and roasting vegetables and for making casseroles, you'll need a baking sheet, a roasting pan, and a casserole dish. Buy a casserole dish that is freezer, oven, and microwave safe.

Baking (cookie) sheets are usually flat metal pans with very low rims all around or a rim on just one end. Those without rims are designed so that cookies and the like slide off them easily onto the cooling racks. Buy heavy-duty baking sheets; thin ones will warp in the oven and cause uneven baking.

Standard loaf pans are 9 by 5 by 2¾ inches and are made of metal or glass. Mini loaf pans measure 6 by 3¼ by 2 inches. Metal loaf pans produce loaf cakes and quick breads with more evenly browned crusts; cakes and breads baked in glass loaf pans may brown before they are thoroughly baked.

Standard muffin tins have 12 cups, each holding 6 to 7 tablespoons of batter.

BLENDERS AND FOOD PROCESSORS

A blender or food processor is a big-ticket item that should go on your wish list. It is not an essential but is an extremely useful luxury. These appliances allow the cook to pulverize and purée without a lot of fuss. A mini food processor is great for chopping herbs, onions, and garlic and for grinding nuts and seeds.

Stocking Up

What do you need to have on hand for vegetarian cooking? Because tastes and budgets differ from household to household, a universal shopping list doesn't exist, but the following chart offers recommendations for basic pantry items that will make meal planning and preparations much easier.

BAKING NEEDS

unbleached all-purpose flour

whole-wheat flour

baking soda

baking powder

vanilla extract

active dry yeast

BEANS AND PEAS

garbanzo beans (chickpeas)

black beans

pinto beans

navy beans

kidney beans

Great Northern beans

brown or green lentils

green or yellow split peas

BREADS AND GRAINS

brown rice, including long-grain
    and basmati

rolled oats

barley

bulgur

couscous

cornmeal

whole-grain bread

whole-grain cereals such as muesli,
    granola, and hot cereals

whole-grain crackers

CONDIMENTS AND SEASONINGS

sea salt or coarse salt

soy sauce or tamari

light and dark misos

prepared mustards

vinegars (various kinds, such as
    balsamic, apple cider, rice)

horseradish

vegetarian Worcestershire sauce

hot pepper sauce

olives

DAIRY AND EGGS

low-fat milk

butter

low-fat soft and hard cheeses

low-fat or nonfat yogurt

eggs

DRIED FRUITS AND VEGETABLES

raisins

currants

apricots

dates

figs

prunes

mushrooms

tomatoes

DRIED HERBS AND SPICES
bay leaf
sage
whole black peppercorns
oregano
rosemary
basil
thyme
cumin
curry powder
cinnamon
nutmeg
chili powder
paprika
cayenne pepper
garlic powder
crushed red pepper flakes

NUTS AND SEEDS
almonds
walnuts
sesame seeds
sunflower seeds
tahini (sesame seed paste)

OILS
olive oil (preferably both virgin and
    extra-virgin)
canola oil
peanut oil
dark (Asian) sesame oil
vegetable oil spray

PASTA
fettuccine
linguine
penne
orzo
ramen noodles

PREPARED FOODS
ready-made pizza crust
canned tomatoes
packaged soups
tomato sauce and other pasta sauces
salsa
salad dressing
frozen vegetables and fruit
fruit-sweetened apple butter, jams,
    and preserves
vegetable stock or powder
applesauce

SOY FOODS
tofu in aseptic packages
tempeh
soymilk, both plain and flavored

SWEETENERS
pure maple syrup (grade B is all-purpose)
honey
brown rice syrup
Sucanat
barley malt syrup

GLOSSARY OF INGREDIENTS

ALL-PURPOSE FLOUR: This flour may be bleached or unbleached, but regardless of the processing it always appears bright white, and either will behave as well as the other. Which to buy is a personal preference; bleached flour is more processed than unbleached. White flour is milled from the endosperm of the wheat berry, which surrounds the center of the grain and contains no oil.

ANAHEIM CHILE: Interchangeable with the New Mexico chile, the Anaheim chile is light green with a sweet taste and just a hint of heat. Anaheim chiles are available fresh or canned and are often stuffed or used in salsas.

BAKING POWDER: A leavening powder. This mixture of alkaline and acid will leaven a batter without the addition of an acidic ingredient. Double-acting baking powder, the kind used in our recipes and also most available to the consumer, reacts first with liquid to initiate the leavening process and then again in the oven when the batter is exposed to heat.

BAKING SODA: An alkaline powder used for leavening. In order to perform its leavening magic, baking soda must react with an acid, such as sour milk, buttermilk, yogurt, citrus juice, or molasses.

BARLEY: A hardy grain, barley is larger and plumper than other grains, with the exception of corn. It is rich in protein, niacin, thiamin, and potassium. Barley with the bran layer peeled off is called pearl barley and is lower in fiber, protein, fat, and minerals than whole barley.

BARLEY MALT SYRUP: This dark sweetener is made from germinated barley and has a consistency slightly thicker than molasses. Sometimes called malted barley syrup, it can replace honey or molasses in most baked goods. Pure barley malt syrup tastes much like molasses and is about half as sweet as white sugar. It contains simple sugars, B vitamins, and protein. Refrigerate this syrup to keep it from fermenting. It is sold in natural food stores.

BROWN RICE SYRUP: A syrup used as a sugar substitute in sweets and desserts. It is also called rice malt. This thick, mild-tasting liquid sweetener is made by combining cooked brown rice with dried sprouted barley and culturing the mixture until some of the rice starch has been converted into maltose and glucose. Refrigerate brown rice syrup to prevent surface molding. Substitute it as you would barley malt syrup (see page 19). You may also find brown rice syrup powder; substitute it for refined sugar, cup for cup.

BULGUR: Parched, steamed, and dried wheat berries. This grain is popular in Middle Eastern cooking and is a good source of protein, phosphorus, and potassium.

CARDAMOM: A relative of ginger and native to India, this aromatic spice is used widely in Scandinavian and Indian cooking. It comes ground or in a pod containing small black seeds. The pods can easily be crushed with a mortar and pestle to release the spicy-sweet seeds; note that the flavor begins to diminish as soon as they are ground, so grind right before using.

CHICKPEAS: Also called garbanzo beans, these legumes are available dried, canned, and ground into flour. Dried chickpeas are notoriously hard and benefit from being soaked before cooking. They have a satisfying nutty flavor and chewy texture.

CHILE OIL: A vegetable oil infused with the flavor of chile peppers. Chile oil is orange-red in color and can be found in small bottles in Asian markets or large supermarkets. All you need is a drop to add a spicy kick to dishes.

CHINESE FIVE-SPICE POWDER: True to its name, Chinese five-spice powder is a pungent mixture of ground cinnamon, cloves, fennel seed, star anise, and Szechuan peppercorns. It is available in Asian markets and supermarkets.

CHIPOTLE CHILE: A smoked jalapeño chile pepper, great for adding a sweet, smoky flavor to foods. It is available dried and pickled, as well as canned and bottled in adobo sauce.

CORIANDER SEED: The ripe, dried fruit of the coriander plant, used as a spice. The seeds have the flavor of lemon, sage, and caraway. Whole coriander seeds are used in pickling and mulled wine; the ground spice can be found in curries, soups, and baked goods. Although the leaves of the coriander plant are known as cilantro or Chinese parsley, the seeds and leaves do not impart the same flavor.

CUMIN: An essential ingredient in most chili powder, cumin is a spice with a strong, aromatic, and slightly bitter taste. It is available whole or ground.

CURRY POWDER: A blend of numerous spices used to flavor many dishes, particularly those referred to as curries, inspired by the cooking of India. Not all curry powders are identical, but most commercially available ones include ginger, cumin, turmeric, pepper, cayenne, and coriander.

EGG REPLACER: The trademark name for a powdered combination of starches and leavening agents that bind cooked and baked foods in place of eggs. It is sold in natural food stores and large supermarkets.

FLAXSEED: Small, brown, glossy seeds that are a rich source of omega-3 fatty acids. Also called linseed, they can be ground and added to baked goods, sauces, and dressings. Flax seed is also pressed into an oil.

GARAM MASALA: A North Indian blend of dry-roasted, ground spices used to add spicy heat to dishes. Typically it includes black pepper, cinnamon, cloves, coriander, cumin, cardamom, dried chiles, fennel, mace, nutmeg, and other spices. Look for it in specialty markets or large supermarkets.

GINGER: A staple of Indian and Asian cooking, the ginger plant is grown for its aromatic, knobby root. When the root is sliced, it imparts a peppery, slightly sweet, spicy flavor that is subtle yet unmistakable. The smooth brown skin of the root is peeled before use.

HOISIN SAUCE: Used to flavor Chinese dishes, hoisin sauce is a thick, brown sauce that is both sweet and spicy. It is made from soybeans, garlic, spices, and chile peppers and is available in cans, jars, and bottles.

HUMMUS: A dip or spread made from chickpeas blended with lemon juice, garlic, olive oil, and tahini (sesame seed paste). Hummus has moved into the mainstream of American supermarkets. It is great with a vegetable platter or used on a fresh vegetable wrap.

JALAPEÑO CHILE: Of all the hot chile peppers, jalapeños may be the best known. They are smooth and dark green, 1 to 2 inches long, with a rounded tip. The seeds and stems are extremely hot and should be removed (it's best to do this wearing plastic gloves). Add a small amount to soups, stews, salsas, and chilis if like your food extra hot. Jalapeños are also available bottled in brine or pickled.

LEMONGRASS: A key ingredient in Thai cuisine, lemongrass is a long, thin, gray-green herb that has a sour-lemon flavor and fragrance. It is used to make tea and to flavor soups and other dishes and can be found fresh, dried, or bottled in Asian markets and large supermarkets.

LIQUID SMOKE: Commonly used to impart a smoky flavor to sauces, liquid smoke is bottled hickory smoke flavoring.

MAPLE SYRUP: It takes 30 to 40 gallons of maple sap containing 3 percent sucrose to produce 1 gallon of 65 percent sucrose syrup. Look for pure maple syrup; "maple-flavored" syrup consists primarily of sugar or corn syrup and usually contains artificial coloring and flavoring. Buy organic maple syrup to avoid formaldehyde and chemical antifoaming agents and mold inhibitors. Refrigerate maple syrup in a glass jar to prevent it from acquiring a metallic taste or fermenting. Highest-grade (AA or fancy) maple syrup has the sweetest, most delicate flavor and is best used as a topping.

MILLET: A tiny, round, yellow grain, millet has a slightly nutty and mild flavor. It is gluten-free, easily digestible, and contains abundant minerals, vitamins, and protein. When cooked, millet swells to a fluffy texture.

MIRIN: Sweet Japanese cooking wine made from rice that adds a subtle flavor to stir-fries. A light, sweet white wine can be substituted for mirin.

MOLASSES: The thick syrup that remains after sugar crystals are removed during the sugar-refinement process. Exceptionally dark, strong-flavored blackstrap molasses derives from the final phase of sugar extraction. About half as sweet as white sugar, it is rich in calcium, iron, and B vitamins. If not organic and unsulfured, blackstrap molasses may also contain high concentrations of pesticides and sulfur dioxide, an allergen for some people. Unsulfured molasses has a less assertive flavor than blackstrap molasses and is about two-thirds as sweet as sugar.

MUNG BEANS: These small, round beans have a dark green skin wrapped around a yellow seed; they are often sold sprouted. Native to India, mung beans are widely used in Asian cooking. They have a slightly sweet flavor and soft texture.

PESTO: There are many variations of pesto, a sauce popular in Italy, but all have the same base: fresh basil, garlic, and olive oil, often with grated Parmesan or Romano cheese and pine nuts added. Pesto is simple to make at home or can be purchased in fresh and bottled forms at most supermarkets. While pesto is most often used to flavor pasta, it is also delicious as a topping for baked potatoes and as a spread in sandwiches.

POBLANO CHILE: When stuffed with cheese and cooked in an egg batter, poblano chiles are the basis for the famous Mexican dish chiles relleños. These peppers are dark green, shiny, and curvaceous, about the size of an elongated green bell pepper, with a heat scale that is medium to hot. When dried, they are known as ancho chile peppers.

QUINOA: A quick-cooking grain native to the Andes. Its small, disk-shaped seeds are rich in calcium and protein. When cooked, it has a delicate nutlike flavor and a light texture, with a slight crunch. Readily available in health food stores and supermarkets, quinoa has been laboriously scrubbed free of saponin, a sticky substance that coats the seeds. However, it is recommended that you rinse it again thoroughly before cooking.

RICE MILK: A lightly flavored alternative to dairy milk, this beverage is made from rice and water and can be used measure for measure in place of dairy milk.

RICE VINEGAR: Common in Asian cooking, rice vinegar has a subtle, sweet flavor.

RICE WINE: Made from fermented glutinous rice, this wine is popular in Asia. Japanese rice wines are sake and mirin.

SAFFRON: The world's most expensive spice, saffron is a flavoring derived from the purple crocus. It lends a yellow color and distinctive taste to dishes. Fortunately, a little goes a long way.

SESAME OIL: Oil expressed from sesame seeds. It comes in two basic types—light and dark. Lighter varieties are good for making salad dressings and for sautéing; dark (Asian) sesame oil, which burns easily, is drizzled on Asian dishes as a flavor accent after cooking.

SHERRY VINEGAR: Vinegar made from sherry, a fortified wine originally from southern Spain. Some sherries are dry and light; others are sweeter and darker.

SOY POWDER: A ground, concentrated source of soy protein. Soy powder is an easy way to add soy to one's diet, as the powder can easily be incorporated into other foods, such as shakes or smoothies.

SOY SAUCE: A dark, salty liquid made by fermenting boiled soybeans and roasted wheat or barley. Used extensively in Asian cuisine, soy sauce flavors soups, sauces, and marinades. It comes in many varieties, ranging in color from light (weaker) to dark (stronger) and in consistencies from thin to very thick. Several brands are low in sodium.

SUCANAT: A trademark name for a sweetener made up of evaporated and granulated sugarcane and blackstrap molasses.

TAHINI: A thick paste made of ground sesame seeds, tahini is a staple of Middle Eastern cuisine.

TAMARI: A naturally brewed soy sauce that contains no sugar and is available wheat-free. It has a subtler flavor than soy sauce, but is salty.

TURMERIC: A spice with a bitter, pungent flavor and intense yellow-orange color, turmeric is the root of a tropical plant related to ginger. It is used mainly to add both flavor and color to food and is popular in East Indian cooking. It is an essential ingredient in curries.

WASABI: The Japanese version of horseradish, wasabi comes from the root of an Asian plant. It is used to make a green-colored condiment that has a fiery, pungent flavor. It comes in both paste and powdered forms.

WHEAT BERRIES: Whole grains of wheat. These need a while to cook and have a great chewy texture. The flavor will vary according to the variety.

WHEAT BRAN: The outer covering of the wheat kernel, which is separated from the wheat flour during milling. Wheat bran is a rich source of dietary fiber.

WHEAT GERM: The vitamin-, mineral-, protein-, and oil-rich embryo of the wheat berry. It has a nutty flavor and is available toasted and in its natural form.

WHOLE-WHEAT FLOUR: Made from whole, hard wheat berries, this flour contains over forty of the nutrients found in wheat. It has a rich, nutty flavor.

WHOLE-WHEAT PASTRY FLOUR: Ground and sifted wheat that is fine-textured and soft, with the high starch content needed for tender cakes and pastries. Whole-wheat pastry flour is made from whole-wheat flour, which contains the wheat germ.

WILD RICE: Not a rice at all, but a grain harvested from grass that grows in marshes along the banks of freshwater lakes. The grains are blackish in color and have a nutlike flavor and chewy texture when cooked.

WONTON SKINS: Thin sheets of dough made from flour and eggs and used to make Chinese dumplings (wontons) and egg rolls. They can be purchased in most supermarkets and Chinese markets and usually come in both square and round shapes.

WORCESTERSHIRE SAUCE: A marinade and condiment developed in India by the English. Because its ingredient list includes anchovies, it is not vegetarian, but vegetarian versions are available at natural food stores. Worcestershire sauce also contains garlic, soy sauce, tamarind, onions, molasses, lime, vinegar, and other seasonings.

GREAT
BEGINNINGS

NEWS

chapter 1

WHAT

you eat in the morning may depend on how much time you have. Unfortunately, breakfast is one of the most rushed meals of the day. But breakfast is not about quantity, it's about the quality of the foods you choose—nutritionists claim that a healthy breakfast keeps you moving efficiently for hours. For example, it makes more nutritional sense to drink a soy shake in the morning than to eat a couple of glazed doughnuts.

Breakfast items can also make excellent suppers. Whole-grain pancakes or waffles with fresh berries and soy sausage patties are a favorite any time of day. Omelets, frittatas, and poached eggs can also fill the dinner bill. And potato-vegetable hash or breakfast burritos are always easy and satisfying.

POTATO AND PEPPER FRITTATA

Frittatas are the Italian answer to the omelet, a baked egg dish that takes any number of fillings. They differ from omelets in that the filling for the frittata becomes part of the egg mixture, rather than being folded inside, as in an omelet. Serve the frittata warm or at room temperature, for breakfast or brunch.

3   tablespoons olive oil

1   large russet potato, peeled and thinly sliced

1   medium onion, thinly sliced

1   large red bell pepper, sliced

    Salt and freshly ground black pepper

1   tablespoon chopped fresh thyme, or 1 teaspoon dried

6   large eggs

½   cup grated Parmesan cheese

2   tablespoons chopped fresh parsley

2   tablespoons drained capers (optional)

In a 12-inch nonstick skillet over medium heat, warm 2 tablespoons of the oil. Layer half of the potato, onion, and bell pepper slices in the skillet. Season to taste with salt and pepper. Repeat with the remaining potato, onion, and bell pepper, and season again. Cover and cook, stirring and turning frequently with a spatula, until tender, about 20 minutes. Sprinkle the thyme over the mixture. Let cool slightly.

In a large bowl, whisk the eggs to blend. Season to taste with salt and pepper. Add the potato mixture to the eggs. Wipe the skillet clean, add the remaining 1 tablespoon oil, and warm over medium-low heat. Pour the egg mixture into the skillet; sprinkle with the cheese. Cover and cook until the eggs are just set, about 10 minutes. Slide the frittata onto a platter. Sprinkle the parsley and capers (if using) over it. Cut into wedges and serve.

SERVES 4

EGGS FLORENTINE

Named for a type of dish originating in Florence, Italy, these eggs are baked on a bed of spinach, topped with a white cheese sauce, and served over English muffins.

Preheat the oven to 350°F. Grease a 13-by-9-inch baking dish. Press the spinach into the bottom of the dish. Form six 3-inch indentations in the spinach, using the back of a spoon or the bottom of a large custard cup. Break an egg into each indentation.

In a medium saucepan, combine the flour, salt, and cayenne. Gradually add the milk, stirring with a whisk until blended. Place the milk mixture over medium heat and cook, stirring constantly, until thick, about 8 minutes. Remove from the heat and add the cheese, stirring until it melts. Pour the cheese sauce over the eggs and spinach; sprinkle with the paprika. Bake for 25 minutes, or until the egg yolks are almost set. Cut the spinach-egg mixture into 6 portions and serve each portion over 2 English muffin halves, sprinkled with black pepper to taste.

Three 10-ounce packages frozen chopped spinach, thawed, drained, and squeezed dry

6 large eggs

3 tablespoons unbleached all-purpose flour

¼ teaspoon salt

⅛ teaspoon cayenne pepper

2 cups low-fat milk

⅓ cup grated Parmesan cheese

¼ teaspoon paprika

6 English muffins, split and toasted

Freshly ground black pepper

CURRIED VEGETABLE OMELET

SERVES 2

One of the nicest things about omelets is that they can be filled with virtually anything you have in the refrigerator. The curried vegetable filling used here is good served with whole-wheat toast and freshly squeezed orange juice.

FILLING

1 cup small broccoli florets

½ cup thinly sliced peeled carrots

2 tablespoons butter

1 tablespoon olive oil

1 medium onion, thinly sliced

¼ cup finely chopped red bell pepper

1 teaspoon curry powder

¼ teaspoon ground cumin

1 clove garlic, minced

½ teaspoon salt

½ teaspoon grated lemon zest

OMELET

3 large eggs

2 teaspoons water

¼ teaspoon salt

¼ teaspoon freshly ground black pepper

1 tablespoon butter or soy margarine

Make the filling: In a medium saucepan of boiling water, cook the broccoli and carrots until crisp-tender, about 5 minutes. Drain well.

In a medium skillet over medium heat, melt the butter with the olive oil. Add the onion and bell pepper and cook, stirring often, until softened, about 5 minutes. Stir in the curry powder, cumin, garlic, salt, lemon zest, and cooked vegetables. Set aside and keep warm.

Make the omelet: In a small bowl, beat the eggs with the water, salt, and pepper. Heat an 8- to 10-inch nonstick omelet pan or skillet over medium-high heat. Melt the butter in the pan. Pour in the beaten eggs. Swirl the pan by the handle to distribute the eggs evenly over the surface. Cook without stirring until the bottom and edges begin to set, about 10 seconds. As the bottom begins to set, lift the cooked portion of the omelet with a thin spatula to let the uncooked egg mixture flow under it. Repeat until most of the omelet is set but the center is still moist and creamy.

Spoon the filling down the center of the omelet. Loosen the omelet from the pan and fold one-third from the far side toward the center. Tip the pan over a serving plate so the unfolded side begins to slide out. Flip the omelet so that it is folded into thirds. Slide the omelet onto a plate and serve right away.

VARIATION

Spinach-Mushroom Omelet: To make the filling, in a medium skillet, melt 3 tablespoons butter over medium-high heat. Add 1½ cups sliced cremini or button mushrooms and ½ cup thinly sliced red onion and cook, stirring often, until the mushrooms are lightly browned and the liquid has evaporated, about 8 minutes. Stir in ½ teaspoon dried thyme and salt and freshly ground black pepper to taste. Add 4 cups fresh spinach leaves, rinsed and patted dry, and cook, stirring, over medium heat just until the leaves are wilted, about 2 minutes. Remove from the heat.

Make the omelet as directed in the main recipe, using the spinach-mushroom filling in place of the curried vegetables.

VEGETABLE HASH WITH POACHED EGGS

Based on an old French recipe for a country supper, this dish goes well with pumpernickel toast and mugs of warm apple cider.

 SERVES 4

1 large russet potato, peeled and cut into 1-inch cubes

3 medium parsnips (8 ounces), peeled and cut into ½-inch cubes (1¼ cups)

8 ounces butternut squash, peeled and cut into ½-inch cubes (1¼ cups)

¼ cup (½ stick) butter, cut into pieces

3 shallots (6 ounces), halved lengthwise and thinly sliced crosswise (1⅓ cups)

3 cloves garlic, chopped

½ teaspoon salt

¼ teaspoon freshly ground black pepper

1½ teaspoons chopped fresh sage, or ½ teaspoon dried

4 large eggs

Bring a large saucepan of salted water to a boil. Add the cubed potato and cook until crisp-tender, about 5 minutes. Using a slotted spoon, transfer to a colander. Cook the parsnips and squash together in the same boiling water until crisp-tender, about 3 minutes, draining them in the colander.

In a large skillet over medium-high heat, melt the butter, swirling the skillet occasionally, until the foam subsides and the butter begins to brown, about 2 minutes. Add the shallots and garlic and cook, stirring occasionally, until the shallots are golden brown, about 5 minutes. Add the cooked vegetables, salt, and pepper and cook, stirring occasionally, until browned and tender, about 7 minutes. Stir in the sage.

Fill a large skillet halfway with generously salted water and bring to a boil. Reduce the heat to maintain a steady simmer. Crack the eggs, one at a time, into a custard cup, and slide them into the simmering water. Poach until the eggs are softly set, about 3 minutes.

Divide the hash among 4 plates. Using a slotted spoon, top each serving with a poached egg.

BLACKENED HASH BROWNS

SERVES 4

These hash brown potatoes are baked, not fried, giving them less fat than their counterparts but just as much flavor.

Preheat the oven to 400°F. Cook the potatoes in a medium pot of boiling salted water until almost tender, about 5 minutes. Drain well. Spread the potatoes on a large, heavy baking sheet. Sprinkle with the chili powder and paprika. Season to taste with salt. Drizzle the olive oil over the potatoes and stir to coat.

Bake for about 40 minutes, or until crisp, turning with a spatula every 10 minutes. Serve warm.

6   large red-skinned potatoes (about 2 ½ pounds), peeled and cut into ½-inch cubes

2   teaspoons chili powder

1   teaspoon paprika

Salt

¼   cup olive oil

VEGAN

BANANA-STUFFED FRENCH TOAST

Cooks in many cultures have found delicious ways to use day-old bread. But the French take first prize for their simple recipe for pain perdu or "lost bread," which Americans know as French toast. Stale bread holds together better than fresh when soaked in a mixture of egg and milk and then browned in butter. This updated version has a luscious center of banana and is served with fresh strawberries.

4   ripe bananas, peeled, each cut into 4 pieces

8   thin slices light mixed-grain bread

½   cup milk or soymilk

2   large eggs

1   teaspoon vanilla extract

    Pinch of ground cinnamon

1   tablespoon butter

    Powdered sugar for dusting

8   large strawberries

    Maple syrup for serving

Preheat the oven to 350°F. Place 4 pieces of banana on each of 4 bread slices; mash the banana on the bread. Top with the remaining 4 bread slices. In a glass pie dish, whisk together the milk, eggs, vanilla, and cinnamon. Working in batches, dip the stuffed bread in the egg mixture; let soak for 45 seconds on each side.

In a large, nonstick skillet over medium heat, melt the butter. Working in batches, add the soaked stuffed bread to the skillet and cook until golden, about 2 minutes on each side. Transfer to a baking sheet and bake for 8 minutes. Transfer to plates and dust with powdered sugar. Garnish with the strawberries. Serve with maple syrup.

SERVES 4

APPLE FRENCH TOAST

Thick slices of bread dipped in a mixture of soymilk, apple butter, vanilla, cinnamon, and flax seed makes an irresistible French toast. It's sure to beckon everyone to the table any time of day.

In a blender, combine the flax seed, apple butter, soymilk, vanilla, cinnamon, and salt and process until puréed. Pour the mixture into a shallow bowl.

In a large skillet over medium heat, warm 2 tablespoons oil. Dip 2 bread slices into the batter, coating them evenly on both sides. Cook in the skillet until lightly browned, about 2 minutes on each side. Repeat with the remaining bread slices, adding more oil to the skillet if necessary. Serve with maple syrup.

1   tablespoon flax seed

½   cup natural apple butter or applesauce

2   cups plain or vanilla soymilk

1   teaspoon vanilla extract

1   teaspoon ground cinnamon

¼   teaspoon salt

2   to 3 tablespoons vegetable oil

8   thick slices soft-crusted French bread

Maple syrup for serving

VEGAN

SCRAMBLED TOFU WITH ASPARAGUS

Scrambling is a common way to prepare tofu. The result is similar in texture to scrambled eggs. Adding fresh asparagus makes this dish truly satisfying.

1   pound firm tofu, drained
    and cut into 16 cubes

1   tablespoon vegetable oil

2   tablespoons finely chopped
    green onion (white part only)

¼   teaspoon ground turmeric

½   teaspoon salt

1   cup chopped cooked asparagus

1   tablespoon finely chopped
    fresh flat-leaf parsley

Working with one cube of tofu at a time over a sink, squeeze it gently but firmly in your hand until it crumbles slightly and water drips out. (This step is important to prevent the finished dish from being watery.) Place in a medium bowl and repeat with the remaining tofu until all the cubes have been squeezed.

In a medium skillet, heat the oil over medium heat. Add the green onion and cook, stirring often, for 30 seconds. Add the tofu to the pan. Sprinkle with the turmeric and salt and cook, stirring with a wooden spoon, until it is evenly golden and firm, 3 minutes. Add the asparagus and parsley and cook, stirring often, for 1 minute. Serve right away.

SERVES 4

TEMPEH "SAUSAGE" PATTIES

SERVES 6 TO 8

Meaty-textured tempeh combined with fresh herbs and spices makes a scrumptious vegetarian sausage. You can form patties the night before and then cook them in the morning. For best results, be sure the tempeh is very finely mashed.

In a large saucepan fitted with a steamer basket, bring 2 inches of water to a boil. Place the tempeh quarters in the basket, cover, and steam for 20 minutes.

Meanwhile, in a medium skillet over medium heat, warm 1 tablespoon of the oil. Add the onion and cook, stirring often, until it begins to soften, about 5 minutes. Add the garlic and cook, stirring often, until the onion is tender, about 2 minutes. Stir in the sun-dried tomatoes, sage, thyme, salt, and pepper. Remove from the heat.

Remove the tempeh from the steamer and let cool slightly. In a large bowl, mash the tempeh very finely with a fork. Add the onion mixture and broth and mix well. Form the mixture into 16 equal balls, then firmly press them into patties about 2 inches in diameter.

In a large, nonstick skillet over medium heat, warm the remaining 2 teaspoons oil. Add half of the patties and cook until browned, about 3 minutes on each side. Repeat with the remaining patties, adding more oil if necessary. Serve warm

Two 8-ounce packages tempeh, each cut into quarters

1 tablespoon, plus 2 teaspoons olive oil, plus more if necessary

1 medium onion, finely chopped

2 cloves garlic, minced

⅓ cup drained, chopped oil-packed sun-dried tomatoes

1 tablespoon finely chopped fresh sage, or 1 teaspoon dried

2 teaspoons finely chopped fresh thyme, or ½ teaspoon dried

1 teaspoon salt

¼ teaspoon freshly ground black pepper

¼ cup Rich Vegetable Broth (page 109), or canned broth

BREAKFAST BURRITOS

This is a homemade fast-food dish borrowed from a popular concept—you just pick it up in both hands and eat it like a sandwich. It can also be served for lunch or dinner.

VEGAN

¼ cup vegetable oil

1½ cups chopped bell peppers (preferably a mixture of red, yellow, and green)

½ cup thinly sliced onion

One 14-ounce package firm tofu, drained and cut into 1-inch cubes

2 cloves garlic, minced

2 teaspoons chili powder

2 teaspoons fresh lime juice

⅓ cup chopped fresh cilantro

Salt and freshly ground black pepper

4 flour tortillas, 8 inches in diameter

In a large skillet over medium-high heat, warm the oil. Add the bell peppers and onion and cook, stirring often, until they begin to soften, about 2 minutes. Add the tofu, garlic, and chili powder and cook, stirring often, until the peppers are soft, about 3 minutes. Stir in the lime juice and cilantro, and season to taste with salt and pepper. Remove from the heat.

Wrap the tortillas in plastic and warm on low power in a microwave. Arrange the tortillas on a work surface. Spoon one fourth of the filling into the center of each tortilla. Fold the sides over the ends of the filling; roll up to enclose the filling. Cut each burrito in half; place 2 halves on each plate.

SERVES 4

SPICED VANILLA GRANOLA

MAKES ABOUT
8 CUPS

Making granola is so easy, you will wonder why you never did it before. It's delicious served with fresh fruit and yogurt, as a topping for muffins, or just eaten plain. The granola can be made 2 weeks ahead. Store in an airtight container at room temperature.

Preheat the oven to 300°F. Grease a large baking pan. In a large bowl, mix the oats, pecans, brown sugar, salt, cinnamon, and nutmeg. In a small saucepan, combine the oil, maple syrup, and granulated sugar. Bring to a simmer over medium heat. Remove from the heat and stir in the vanilla. Pour over the hot oat mixture; stir well. Using your hands, toss the mixture until thoroughly combined.

Spread in the prepared baking pan. Bake, stirring occasionally, for about 30 minutes, or until golden brown. Transfer the pan to a rack and let cool completely.

4   cups old-fashioned rolled oats

1   cup chopped pecans

½   cup packed light brown sugar

¼   teaspoon salt

½   teaspoon ground cinnamon

¼   teaspoon ground nutmeg

⅓   cup vegetable oil

¼   cup maple syrup

2   tablespoons granulated sugar

1   tablespoon vanilla extract

VEGAN

MULTIGRAIN PANCAKES

Pancakes are at their peak when served steaming hot, right from the griddle. If you're a short-order cook, this is no problem. But many home cooks find themselves stuck in the kitchen while family and friends devour round after round of their perfect pancakes. There is another way, however: Keep the pancakes warm in the oven, loosely covered with foil, until the last batch is cooked, and then serve them all at once.

1   cup unbleached all-purpose flour

⅓   cup quick-cooking oats

⅓   cup yellow cornmeal

⅓   cup whole-wheat flour

2   teaspoons sugar

2   teaspoons baking powder

¼   teaspoon baking soda

¼   teaspoon salt

2   cups soymilk or rice milk

2   tablespoons light molasses

Fresh berries for serving

Maple syrup for serving

Preheat the oven to 200°F. In a medium bowl, combine the all-purpose flour, oats, cornmeal, whole-wheat flour, sugar, baking powder, baking soda, and salt. In a large bowl, whisk together the soymilk and molasses until blended. Add the dry ingredients; mix just until blended.

Heat a griddle or large, heavy skillet over medium-high heat until hot, or until a few drops of water sizzle on the surface. Lightly grease the griddle. For each pancake, pour about ½ cup of batter onto the hot griddle. Cook until many bubbles appear on the surface, about 2 minutes. Before turning the pancakes, lift the edge to check that the undersides are golden. Turn and cook until the second sides are golden brown, 1 to 2 minutes more. Transfer to a baking sheet, cover loosely with foil, and keep warm in the oven. Repeat with the remaining batter. Serve with berries and syrup.

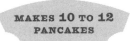

MAKES **10 TO 12** PANCAKES

LEMON WAFFLES WITH BLUEBERRIES

There's plenty of lemon flavor in these slightly sweet waffles. Fresh berries are best here, but frozen ones can be substituted. Serve the waffles with additional lemon yogurt as a topping. If you would like lighter waffles, separate the eggs, and add only the yolks to the batter. Beat the whites until they are stiff and fold them into the batter as a final step.

Preheat a waffle iron. In a small bowl, whisk together the yogurt, milk, eggs, and zest. In a large bowl, whisk together the flour, sugar, baking powder, baking soda, and salt. Add the milk mixture and whisk just until combined.

Stir in the blueberries. Lightly grease the grids of the waffle iron. Follow the manufacturer's instructions, or spoon about ⅓ cup of the batter (the amount varies with the size of the iron) onto the hot iron and spread it almost to the corners of the grids. Close the lid and cook until the waffles are golden brown, their edges look dry, and they do not stick to the grids, 1½ to 2 minutes. Transfer the waffles to a plate as they are cooked and keep them warm. Repeat with the remaining batter. Serve with maple syrup.

1 cup lemon-flavored low-fat yogurt

¾ cup milk or plain soymilk

2 large eggs, at room temperature

2 teaspoons grated lemon zest

2 cups unbleached all-purpose flour

¼ cup sugar

1½ teaspoons baking powder

½ teaspoon baking soda

½ teaspoon salt

2½ cups fresh blueberries or blackberries

Maple syrup for serving

NEW MEXICAN BLUE CORNCAKES

When developing this recipe, I was surprised by how much the flavor and grind can vary between different brands of blue cornmeal. Some had a barely perceptible corn flavor and a dusty texture, while others had a clean, pure flavor and gritty bite. For best results, use an organically grown whole-grain cornmeal.

½ cup pine nuts

1¼ cups fine blue cornmeal

¾ cup unbleached all-purpose flour

¾ teaspoon baking powder

¾ teaspoon baking soda

1 cup milk or plain soymilk

2 large eggs, at room temperature

1 tablespoon butter, melted

2 tablespoons honey, plus more for serving

MAKES 10 TO 12 PANCAKES

Preheat the oven to 200°F. In a small skillet over medium heat, toast the pine nuts, stirring often, until fragrant and golden, 2 to 3 minutes.

In a medium bowl, combine the toasted pine nuts, cornmeal, flour, baking powder, and baking soda. In a small bowl, whisk together the milk, eggs, butter, and 2 tablespoons honey. Pour into the dry ingredients, stirring just until smooth.

Heat a griddle or large, heavy skillet over medium-high heat until hot, or until a few drops of water sizzle on the surface. Lightly grease the griddle. For each pancake, pour about ¼ cup of the batter onto the hot griddle. Cook until many bubbles appear on the surface, about 2 minutes. Before turning the pancakes, lift the edge to check that the undersides are golden. Turn and cook until the second sides are golden brown, 1 to 2 minutes more. Transfer to a baking sheet, cover loosely with foil, and keep warm in the oven. Repeat with the remaining batter. Serve, passing additional honey at the table.

OAT SCONES WITH DRIED CHERRIES

These slightly sweet scones are delicious served warm with preserves or honey.
You can find oat flour in natural food stores and some well-stocked supermarkets.

Preheat the oven to 350°F. Grease a baking sheet. In a food processor, combine the oat flour, 1 tablespoon sugar, baking powder, and salt and pulse to blend. Add the ¼ cup soymilk and the applesauce and pulse on and off just until blended.

Turn the dough out onto a lightly floured surface. Knead in all but 2 tablespoon of the rolled oats and all of the dried cherries. Flatten the dough into an 8-inch disk. Transfer to the baking sheet. Brush the tops with soymilk, and sprinkle with sugar and the remaining oats. Cut into 10 wedges, but leave them in place. Bake for 12 to 15 minutes, or until firm and lightly browned. Serve warm.

1	cup oat flour
1	tablespoon sugar, plus more for sprinkling
¼	teaspoon baking powder
⅛	teaspoon salt
¼	cup vanilla soymilk, plus more for brushing
1	tablespoon natural applesauce
½	cup old-fashioned rolled oats
½	cup dried cherries

VEGAN

MAKES 10 SCONES

BANANA-PECAN MUFFINS

*Muffins are one of the fastest quick breads. With a little planning,
you can stir up a batch even on a weekday morning.*

1½ cups unbleached
    all-purpose flour

1½ teaspoons baking soda

¼ teaspoon salt

⅛ teaspoon ground nutmeg

1¼ cups mashed ripe banana
    (about 3 large)

½ cup granulated sugar

¼ cup packed dark brown sugar

2 tablespoons natural
    applesauce

¼ cup vanilla soymilk or rice milk

½ cup egg substitute

1 cup pecan pieces, toasted
    (see page 114) and chopped

Preheat the oven to 350°F. Grease a 12-cup muffin pan or line with muffin papers.

In a large bowl, mix the flour, baking soda, salt, and nutmeg. In a medium bowl, mix the banana, granulated and brown sugars, applesauce, soymilk, and egg substitute. Add to the dry ingredients, stirring just until blended. Stir in half of the nuts.

Divide the batter among the prepared muffin cups. Sprinkle the remaining nuts evenly over the batter in each cup. Bake for about 25 minutes, or until the muffins are golden brown and a tester comes out clean. Transfer to a rack and let cool.

MAKES 12 MUFFINS

SPICED PUMPKIN MUFFINS

MAKES 12 MUFFINS

Pumpkin, molasses, and spices are a popular flavor combination. Just take one taste of these warm muffins and you'll know why.

Preheat the oven to 400°F. Grease a 12-cup muffin pan or line with muffin papers.

In a medium bowl, whisk together the butter, pumpkin, buttermilk, eggs, molasses, and vanilla. In a large bowl, mix the all-purpose and whole-wheat flours, baking powder, spices, salt, and baking soda. Whisk in the brown sugar. Make a well in the center of the flour mixture and add the pumpkin mixture, stirring just until combined.

Divide the batter among the prepared muffin cups. Sprinkle the walnuts evenly over the batter in each cup. Bake for 20 to 25 minutes, until puffed and a tester comes out clean. Cool in the cups for 5 minutes and turn out onto a rack. Serve warm or at room temperature.

½ cup (1 stick) butter, melted

¾ cup canned solid-pack pumpkin

¼ cup buttermilk

2 large eggs

3 tablespoons molasses

1 teaspoon vanilla extract

1 cup unbleached all-purpose flour

1 cup whole-wheat pastry flour

1½ teaspoons baking powder

1 teaspoon ground cinnamon

½ teaspoon ground ginger

¼ teaspoon ground cloves

⅛ teaspoon freshly grated nutmeg

½ teaspoon salt

¼ teaspoon baking soda

¾ cup packed light brown sugar

¾ cup finely chopped walnuts

APPLE COFFEE CAKE

Served warm or at room temperature, this coffee cake is inviting for breakfast, but it also makes an excellent treat with mid-morning coffee or afternoon tea.

SERVES 8

2   medium tart apples
    such as Granny Smith

2   cups unbleached
    all-purpose flour

2¼ teaspoons baking powder

2   teaspoons ground cinnamon

¼   teaspoon salt

½   cup (1 stick) butter,
    at room temperature

1   cup sugar

½   cup milk or plain soymilk

2   large eggs

1½ teaspoons vanilla extract

⅓   cup apple jelly, stirred over
    low heat until smooth

Preheat the oven to 450°F. Lightly grease and flour an 8-by-3-inch springform pan. Peel, quarter, and core the apples. Cut each quarter into ½-inch-thick wedges.

In a small bowl, mix the flour, baking powder, cinnamon, and salt until blended. In a large bowl, using an electric mixer, beat the butter until smooth. Add the sugar and beat until fluffy. Beat in the milk, eggs, and vanilla. Add the flour mixture and beat on medium speed for 2 minutes, or until smooth.

Spread the batter in the prepared pan. Arrange the apple wedges, overlapping them slightly, in a circular pattern over the batter. Brush the apples with half of the apple jelly. Bake for 15 minutes. Reduce the oven temperature to 350°F. Bake for 50 to 60 minutes longer, or until a cake tester inserted near the center comes out clean. Set the pan on a wire rack to cool for 15 minutes, then remove the sides of the pan. Brush the top of the cake with the remaining apple jelly. Cool completely on a rack. Serve at room temperature.

MAPLE-GLAZED PINEAPPLE WITH MACADAMIA NUTS

SERVES 4 TO 6

This recipe not only makes for a delicious way to start the day, but is also a refreshing dessert. The quality of this dish depends on the freshness and ripeness of the pineapple. Be sure to choose fruit with a strong, sweet aroma and a rich yellow color.

Preheat the broiler. In a small bowl, mix the maple syrup, lime juice, and mint.

Put the pineapple slices on a baking sheet. Broil 4 to 6 inches from the heat source just until the edges are beginning to brown, 3 to 5 minutes.

Arrange the pineapple slices on individual plates. Pour the syrup mixture over the fruit and sprinkle with the macadamia nuts. Serve right away.

¼ cup maple syrup

2 tablespoons fresh lime juice

2 tablespoons chopped fresh mint

8 slices fresh pineapple, each ½ inch thick

¼ cup chopped, toasted macadamia nuts (see page 114)

VEGAN

PECAN STICKY BUNS

MAKES 12 BUNS

Wheat germ in the dough gives these coiled rolls a nutty flavor. If possible, use a black steel muffin pan to bake these buns; it will give them a deeper golden color.

DOUGH

1¾ cups warm milk (105° to 115°F)

1   envelope or 1 scant tablespoon active dry yeast

¼   cup sugar

⅓   cup wheat germ

4½ to 5 cups unbleached all-purpose flour, plus more as needed

¼   cup (½ stick) butter, melted

2   large egg whites, lightly beaten

¼   cup butter

¾   cup honey

½   cup chopped pecans

¼   cup sugar

2   teaspoons ground cinnamon

Make the dough: In a medium bowl, mix the milk, yeast, and ½ teaspoon of the sugar. Let stand for 10 minutes, or until foamy.

Meanwhile, in a large bowl, mix the remaining sugar, wheat germ, and 4½ cups flour. Make a well in the center of the flour mixture. Pour in the yeast mixture, melted butter, and egg whites. Stir with a wooden spoon until the flour is incorporated and a soft dough forms (the dough will pull away from the side of the bowl), adding more flour if necessary.

Turn the dough out onto a lightly floured surface. Knead for 5 to 10 minutes, or until smooth and elastic, sprinkling the surface with more flour if sticky. Clean the bowl and spray with vegetable oil spray. Put the dough in the bowl, turning to coat. Cover with plastic wrap and let rise in a warm, draft-free place for about 1 hour, or until doubled in volume.

Grease twelve 2½-inch muffin cups. Place 1 teaspoon of the butter in the bottom of each cup. Next add 1 tablespoon of the honey and 2 teaspoons of the pecans to each cup. In a small bowl, mix the sugar and cinnamon.

Punch the down dough and knead in the bowl several times. Turn out onto a lightly floured surface and roll with a rolling pin into a 21-by-12-inch rectangle. Sprinkle with the cinnamon sugar. Starting with a long side, roll the dough up tightly, jelly-roll style. Cut crosswise into 12 equal slices.

Arrange the slices, cut side down, in the prepared muffin cups. Cover lightly with a kitchen towel. Let rise in a warm, draft-free place for about 50 minutes, or until doubled in volume. Meanwhile, preheat the oven to 350°F. Place the muffin pan on a baking sheet to catch any drips. Bake for 35 to 40 minutes, or until golden brown.

Invert the muffin pan onto a baking sheet. Slowly lift the pan, allowing any excess honey to drip onto the buns. Let cool for 15 minutes. Serve warm.

FRUIT COMPOTE

Dried fruits and spices slowly cooked in a sugar syrup transform into a delicious mixture that is perfect served for breakfast or even dessert. This spice-scented compote is great served warm or at room temperature. It will keep, covered and refrigerated, for up to 1 week.

2   cups apple juice

½   cup sugar

4   strips fresh lemon zest,
    each 2½ inches by ½ inch

1   cinnamon stick, halved

3   whole cloves

10 black peppercorns, cracked

2   firm pears, peeled and cored,
    each cut into 8 wedges

½   cup dried apricots

½   cup dried tart cherries

4   dried Calimyrna figs, quartered

1   tablespoon fresh lemon juice

In a large saucepan, bring the apple juice, sugar, zest, and spices to a boil, stirring until the sugar is dissolved. Reduce the heat and simmer for 5 minutes. Add the pears and dried fruit and simmer, uncovered, stirring occasionally, until the pears are tender, about 25 minutes.

Pour the liquid through a sieve into another saucepan and boil until thickened and reduced to ½ cup. Pour back over the fruit and stir in the lemon juice. Serve warm or at room temperature.

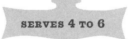

SERVES 4 TO 6

BANANA-MANGO SMOOTHIE

SERVES 2

Mango gives this smoothie a tropical flavor. It can also be made with fresh peaches or nectarines.

Arrange the mango cubes in a single layer on a baking sheet; freeze until firm (about 1 hour). Place the frozen mango and the remaining ingredients in a blender or food processor and process until smooth. Pour into tall glasses and serve.

1 cup cubed peeled ripe mango

¾ cup sliced ripe banana (about 1 medium)

⅔ cup plain or vanilla soymilk

1 teaspoon maple syrup

¼ teaspoon vanilla extract

1 tablespoon soy protein powder (optional)

VEGAN

SOY BERRY GOOD SMOOTHIE

Not only is this smoothie wonderfully delicious, it makes good nutritional sense, too. Think of this drink as a power shake to begin the day.

4	cups assorted berries, such as blueberries, strawberries, and raspberries
1½	cups plain or vanilla soymilk
½	cup fruit yogurt
4	to 5 ice cubes
1	tablespoon soy protein powder (optional)

In a blender, combine all the ingredients and process until smooth. Pour into tall glasses and serve.

SERVES
2

NUTTY TOFU BAGEL SPREAD

MAKES 2 CUPS

This bagel topping substitutes firm tofu that's been drained and pressed for the usual cream cheese. When mixed with a nut butter and some maple syrup, the result is a topping with a smooth, creamy texture and wonderful flavor.

In a blender or food processor, combine all the ingredients and process until smooth. Use right away or transfer to a container, cover tightly, and refrigerate for up to 2 weeks.

12 ounces firm tofu, drained

6 tablespoons natural nut butter such as peanut, sesame, or cashew

1 tablespoon maple syrup

2 teaspoons fresh lemon juice

½ teaspoon salt

VEGAN

chapter

2

SMALL PLEASURES

WHEN

it comes to gatherings,
whether it's a large get-together
or a small, intimate party, easy-to-make
dips, spreads, salsas, and toasts are an
irresistible way to welcome family and
friends. Bowls of marinated olives, garlicky
mushrooms, and spicy chips make any
festivity all the more successful. Just
remember that appetizers are meant
to stimulate appetites, rather than
to satiate, so plan on serving
moderate quantities of
these foods.

GREAT GUACAMOLE

The most important thing about making good guacamole is using good avocados. The two most popular market varieties are the small, rough-skinned Hass, grown primarily in California and Mexico, and the Fuerte, grown mostly in Florida. The Hass makes better guacamole; the Fuerte has a watery consistency and a fruity, sweet taste. Good guacamole also depends on the ripeness of the avocados, many of which are rock-hard when you buy them in the supermarket. This is fine, because avocados ripen off the tree; ripening can take from 2 to 5 days. An avocado is ripe when the skin turns from dark green to purple-black and the fruit yields to a gentle squeeze.

The guacamole can be covered with plastic wrap pressed directly onto the surface and refrigerated for up to 1 day. Return it to room temperature, removing the plastic wrap at the last moment, before serving.

3   ripe medium avocados, preferably Hass

2   tablespoons finely chopped onion

1   clove garlic, minced

1   small jalapeño chile, minced (wear rubber gloves)

¼   cup finely chopped cilantro

¼   teaspoon salt, plus more to taste

½   teaspoon ground cumin (optional)

2   tablespoons fresh lime juice

Halve 1 avocado, remove the pit, and the scoop the flesh into a medium bowl. Using a fork, mash the flesh lightly with the onion, garlic, jalapeño, cilantro, ¼ teaspoon salt, and cumin (if using) until just combined.

Halve and pit the remaining 2 avocados. Make criss-cross cuts in the flesh with a small knife. Gently scoop the avocado into the mashed avocado mixture.

Sprinkle the lime juice over the diced avocado and mix lightly with a fork until combined but still chunky. Adjust the seasoning with salt, if necessary, and serve.

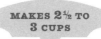

MAKES 2½ TO 3 CUPS

ROASTED EGGPLANT DIP

Middle Eastern cooks like to use roasted eggplant in many dishes, including a dip called baba ghanoush. *This recipe is very similar to baba ghanoush, except that it doesn't include tahini (sesame paste), so the flavor of the roasted eggplant can really shine through. The flavor of the dip is also brightened with garlic and lemon juice.*

When buying any kind of eggplant, look for firm, taut, shiny skin, with no shriveled or soft areas, and a bright green cap. The eggplant should feel heavy, and the flesh should bounce back slightly when gently pressed. This dip does not keep well, so plan to make it the day you want to serve it. Pita bread, black olives, tomato wedges, and cucumber slices are nice accompaniments.

VEGAN

Preheat the oven to 400°F. Pierce the eggplant several times with a fork; place on a foil-lined baking sheet, along with the shallots. Bake for 20 minutes, or until tender. Let cool slightly, then peel and coarsely chop the eggplant.

In a food processor, combine the eggplant, shallots, yogurt, lemon juice, and olive oil and process until almost smooth. Add the chives and process just until blended.

Spoon the dip into a serving bowl. Season to taste with salt and pepper. Sprinkle with paprika and garnish with the lemon wedges. Serve at room temperature, accompanied by the pita wedges.

1   medium eggplant (1 pound)

3   large shallots, peeled

3   tablespoons low-fat soy yogurt

2   tablespoons fresh lemon juice

1   tablespoon olive oil

⅓   cup chopped fresh chives

Salt and freshly ground black pepper

Paprika for sprinkling

1   lemon, cut into wedges

4   pita pocket breads, 6 inches in diameter, each cut into 8 wedges

ROASTED RED PEPPER HUMMUS

Roasted red bell pepper gives this luscious dip a slightly sweet and smoky flavor. It's ideal for snacking and also makes a delicious sandwich spread. For dipping, provide whole-wheat pita triangles, Belgian endive leaves, carrot sticks, and lightly steamed broccoli or cauliflower florets. It can be made a day ahead and refrigerated.

1   large red bell pepper

2   cups canned chickpeas, drained, ¼ cup liquid reserved

2   cloves garlic, chopped

2   tablespoons fresh lemon juice

¼   teaspoon salt

¼   teaspoon ground cumin

Preheat the broiler. Place the bell pepper on the broiler pan and broil until blistered all over, turning often with tongs, 10 to 15 minutes. Transfer to a paper bag, seal, and let steam for 10 minutes. Peel the bell pepper, discarding the skin, seeds, and stem. Set aside.

In a blender or food processor, process the chickpeas until smooth, adding enough of the reserved liquid to make a creamy mixture. Add the roasted pepper, garlic, lemon juice, salt, and cumin and purée until smooth.

Transfer the dip to a shallow serving bowl. Let stand at least for 30 minutes to let the flavors develop before serving.

MAKES 2 CUPS

SPANISH SPINACH DIP

MAKES 2 CUPS

The great flavor in this dip comes from a base of olive oil–soaked peasant bread. The spinach gives the dip a bright green color. Serve it with sliced focaccia, Belgian endive leaves, or both.

In a medium bowl, pour 2 tablespoons of the olive oil over the bread. Turn the bread to coat, then let stand until the oil is absorbed. Tear the bread into small pieces.

In a food processor, finely chop the spinach. Add the bread, lemon juice, and garlic and process until well blended. Add the remaining ¾ cup olive oil and process until smooth. Scrape the purée into a bowl and season to taste with salt and pepper. Serve at room temperature.

¾ cup, plus 2 tablespoons extra-virgin olive oil

1 slice peasant bread, about ½ inch thick and 6 inches wide

8 ounces fresh baby spinach leaves

2 tablespoons fresh lemon juice

1 clove garlic, chopped

Salt and freshly ground black pepper

VEGAN

BEAN DIP PROVENÇALE

For a pretty presentation, spoon this dip into a hollowed bell pepper or small head of red cabbage. Arrange large lettuce leaves in a shallow basket. Place the dip in the center of the basket and arrange crudités and breadsticks attractively around it.

One 19-ounce can cannellini beans, drained, ⅓ cup liquid reserved, and rinsed

¼ cup fresh basil leaves, or 1½ teaspoons dried basil

1 clove garlic, chopped

1 tablespoon extra-virgin olive oil

¼ teaspoon dried rosemary

½ cup chopped kalamata olives

Salt and freshly ground black pepper

In a blender or food processor, combine the beans, basil, garlic, olive oil, and rosemary, and process until well blended. Transfer to a medium bowl. Stir in the olives and season to taste with salt and pepper. Serve chilled or at room temperature.

MAKES 1¾ CUPS

MUSHROOM PÂTÉ

This richly flavored pâté can be made up to 3 days ahead. Cover and refrigerate, then bring to room temperature before serving. Accompany the pâté with toasted French bread slices or thin, crisp crackers.

In a large skillet over medium-high heat, melt the butter. Add the mushrooms, shallots, garlic, curry powder, and cumin and cook, stirring often, until the mixture begins to brown and all the liquid evaporates, about 12 minutes. Remove from the heat and let cool.

In a food processor, process the cashews until finely chopped. Add the olive oil and process to a coarse paste. Add the mushroom mixture and parsley and process until the mushrooms are coarsely chopped. Spoon the pâté into a bowl and season to taste with salt and pepper. Cover and chill for at least 4 hours before serving.

5 tablespoons butter

1¼ pounds cremini mushrooms, coarsely chopped

½ cup chopped shallots (about 2 large)

2 cloves garlic, chopped

1¾ teaspoons curry powder

½ teaspoon ground cumin

1 cup roasted salted cashews

2 tablespoons olive oil

2 tablespoons finely chopped fresh parsley

Salt and freshly ground black pepper

BRUSCHETTA WITH TOMATOES AND BASIL

To make perfect bruschetta, you must start with crusty country loaves that will yield large slices. As for thickness, about 1 inch provides enough heft to support weighty toppings and gives a good chew. This is the classic bruschetta, served with fresh tomatoes and basil. You can substitute other herbs for the basil, such as thyme or oregano.

VEGAN

4   ripe medium tomatoes,
    cut into ½-inch dice

⅓   cup shredded fresh
    basil leaves

    Salt and freshly ground
    black pepper

One 12-by-5-inch loaf country
    bread, sliced crosswise 1 inch
    thick, ends discarded

1   large clove garlic, peeled

3   tablespoons extra-virgin
    olive oil

Prepare a medium-hot fire in a charcoal grill, preheat a gas grill to medium, or preheat the broiler. In a medium bowl, mix the tomatoes, basil, and salt and pepper to taste. Set aside.

Grill or broil the bread until golden brown on both sides. Place on a large platter, rub the garlic over the tops, and then brush with the olive oil. Using a slotted spoon, divide the tomato mixture among the toast slices. Serve right away.

SERVES 4

POLENTA CROSTINI

The polenta for this hors d'oeuvre can be made a day ahead and reheated in the oven. Cornmeal sold as polenta will have a medium to coarse grind (similar to granulated sugar) that will cook up soft and tender. Stone-ground cornmeal is usually the right grind for making polenta. Instant or quick-cooking polenta is made of cornmeal that has been cooked and dried. Its flavor and texture are not as good as the real thing, but it's acceptable in a time crunch.

SERVES 4

Grease a 9-inch glass pie dish. In a medium saucepan, bring the broth to a boil. Gradually whisk in the cornmeal. Reduce the heat to medium and whisk constantly until the mixture thickens, about 6 minutes. Remove from the heat. Add the cheese and 3 tablespoons of the butter; stir until melted. Stir in the chopped walnuts and rosemary. Season to taste with salt and pepper. Transfer to the prepared dish, spreading it evenly. Refrigerate until the polenta is firm, at least 1 hour.

Preheat the oven to 350°F. Line a baking sheet with foil. Cut the polenta into 8 wedges. Transfer the wedges, bottom side up, to the prepared sheet. Cut the remaining 1½ tablespoons butter into small pieces and dot the polenta wedges with them. Place 1 walnut half in the center of each wedge. Bake the polenta for about 12 minutes, until heated through. Serve warm.

2½ cups Rich Vegetable Broth (page 109) or canned broth

⅔ cup yellow cornmeal

¾ cup grated Gruyère cheese

4½ tablespoons butter or soy margarine

⅓ cup walnuts, toasted (see page 114) and finely chopped, plus 8 walnut halves

1½ teaspoons chopped fresh rosemary, or ½ teaspoon dried

Salt and freshly ground black pepper

FRESH TOMATO AND CORN SALSA

For this recipe, using good-quality, fresh ingredients will make the difference between a great salsa and a good one. The easiest way to cut corn off the cob is to stand an uncooked ear of corn on its end in a shallow bowl and slice the kernels off with a sharp, thin-bladed knife.

¾   cup fresh corn kernels
     (cut from 1 large ear)

1¼ cups chopped plum tomatoes

½   cup chopped fresh cilantro

¼   cup chopped red onion

¼   cup chopped green onion

1   clove garlic, minced

¼   cup fresh lemon juice

½   teaspoon hot pepper sauce,
     or more to taste

1   teaspoon olive oil

¼   teaspoon salt

¼   teaspoon ground cumin

In a saucepan fitted with a steamer basket, bring 1 inch of water to a boil. Place corn in the basket and steam, covered, for 2 minutes. Remove from the steamer and let cool. In a large bowl, combine the corn, tomatoes, cilantro, red onion, green onion, garlic, lemon juice, hot pepper sauce, olive oil, salt, and cumin. Serve at room temperature.

MAKES **2 CUPS**

SPICY CHIPS

**MAKES
80 CHIPS**

You might be surprised at how easy it is to make your own tortilla chips. They taste so much better than the store-bought kind that you may never buy chips again. Serve them with the Fresh Tomato and Corn Salsa (facing page).

Preheat the oven to 375°F. In a small bowl, mix the paprika, thyme, garlic powder, onion powder, pepper, salt, and sugar. Coat 2 baking sheets with vegetable oil spray.

Arrange the tortilla wedges on the prepared pans. Coat with vegetable oil spray. Sprinkle the seasoning mix over the wedges. Bake for about 6 minutes, until crisp. Let cool before serving.

¾ teaspoon paprika

½ teaspoon dried thyme

¼ teaspoon garlic powder

¼ teaspoon onion powder

¼ teaspoon freshly ground black pepper

¼ teaspoon salt

¼ teaspoon sugar

10 flour tortillas, 7 to 8 inches in diameter, each cut into 8 wedges

VEGAN

NACHOS SUPREME

Be sure to serve these nachos right away so they are crisp and hot. This recipe can be increased to serve any number of hungry people as an appetizer.

32 tortilla chips

1 cup grated Monterey Jack cheese

⅓ cup drained, rinsed black beans

⅓ cup drained canned Mexican-style corn

⅓ cup chopped fresh cilantro

1 large plum tomato, seeded and chopped

2 tablespoons chopped green onion

1 generous tablespoon canned mild green chiles

¼ cup chopped green or black olives

3 tablespoons chunky mild salsa

Preheat the oven to 350°F. Arrange the tortilla chips closely together on a baking sheet. In a medium bowl, combine ½ cup of the cheese, the beans, corn, cilantro, tomato, green onion, chiles, and olives. Add the salsa and toss to mix.

Spoon the mixture over the chips. Sprinkle with the remaining ½ cup cheese. Bake for about 15 minutes, or until heated through and the cheese is melted. Serve immediately.

SERVES 4 TO 6

ROOT VEGETABLE CHIPS

**SERVES
4 TO 6**

*This recipe also works well with beets and turnips. The
vegetables are good served on their own or with an aïoli
or yogurt dressing for dipping.*

Preheat the broiler. Grease a baking sheet. Bring a large saucepan
of salted water to a boil. Add the vegetables, reduce the heat, and
simmer for 3 minutes. Drain in a colander and let cool slightly.

Transfer the vegetables to a large bowl. Add the olive oil, cornmeal, salt, and pepper, and toss to coat. Arrange the vegetables
on the baking sheet. Broil until lightly browned, 4 to 5 minutes.
Serve warm.

2   medium carrots, peeled and
    sliced diagonally ¼ inch thick

2   medium parsnips, peeled and
    sliced diagonally ¼ inch thick

1   small sweet potato, sliced
    ¼ inch thick

1   medium red-skinned potato,
    sliced ¼ inch thick

2   tablespoons olive oil

2   tablespoons yellow cornmeal

½   teaspoon salt

¼   teaspoon freshly ground
    black pepper

VEGAN

ROASTED POTATOES WITH TAPENADE

The contrast of the crispy roasted potatoes and the tangy tapenade makes these hors d'oeuvres irresistible.

24 small, red-skinned potatoes, scrubbed and patted dry

2 tablespoons olive oil

1½ teaspoons paprika

1 teaspoon garlic powder

1 teaspoon salt

TAPENADE

12 black brine-cured olives, such as kalamata, pitted

9 sun-dried tomatoes packed in oil, well drained and coarsely chopped

¼ cup chopped fresh parsley

2 tablespoons tomato paste

1 teaspoon balsamic vinegar

1 teaspoon chopped fresh thyme

1 small clove garlic, minced

Salt and freshly ground black pepper

Preheat the oven to 400°F. In a medium bowl, combine the potatoes, olive oil, paprika, garlic powder, and salt and toss to coat. Transfer to a large roasting pan and arrange in a single layer. Roast, turning occasionally with tongs, for 50 to 60 minutes, or until tender. Remove from the oven and let cool slightly.

Meanwhile, make the tapenade: In a blender or food processor, combine the olives, sun-dried tomatoes, parsley, tomato paste, vinegar, thyme, and garlic and process until finely chopped. Transfer to a small bowl. Season to taste with salt and pepper.

To serve, cut the potatoes in half and arrange on a serving tray. Spoon some of the tapenade onto the potatoes and serve.

SERVES 6 TO 8

PARMESAN TOASTS WITH ROASTED PEPPER AÏOLI

SERVES 4 TO 6

This aïoli (a Provençale garlic mayonnaise) is less bold than the traditional version because it has less garlic. The lemon juice also moderates its flavor.

Make the aïoli: Preheat the broiler. Place the bell pepper on the broiler pan and broil until blistered all over, turning often with tongs, 10 to 15 minutes. Transfer to a paper bag, seal, and let steam for 10 minutes. Peel the bell pepper, discarding the skin, seeds, and stem, and coarsely chop.

In a blender or food processor, combine the roasted pepper, mayonnaise, garlic, capers, parsley, and lemon juice and process until smooth. Season to taste with salt and pepper.

Make the toasts: Preheat the oven to 350°F. In a small bowl, mix the olive oil and garlic. Arrange the bread slices on a baking sheet. Brush the oil mixture over both sides of the bread slices. Sprinkle with the Parmesan and bake for 10 to 15 minutes, or until the bread is crisp. Arrange the toasts on a serving platter. Spoon some aïoli over each slice and serve.

ROASTED PEPPER AÏOLI

- 1 medium red bell pepper
- ½ cup soy or regular mayonnaise
- 2 cloves garlic, chopped
- 2 tablespoons drained capers
- 2 tablespoons chopped fresh flat-leaf parsley
- 1 teaspoon fresh lemon juice
  Salt and freshly ground black pepper

PARMESAN TOASTS

- 3 tablespoons olive oil
- 1 clove garlic, minced
- ½ baguette, sliced into twelve slices ½ inch thick
- ⅓ cup grated Parmesan cheese

ASPARAGUS WITH HAZELNUT VINAIGRETTE

Asparagus stems will snap off in just the right spot if you hold them correctly. Hold the asparagus about halfway down the stalk; with the other hand, hold the cut end between the thumb and index finger, about an inch or so up the stalk. Bend the stalk until it snaps. Discard the stem ends, or save them for a pot of asparagus soup.

1   shallot, minced

2   tablespoons red wine vinegar

1   tablespoon Dijon mustard

½   teaspoon sugar

⅓   cup extra-virgin olive oil

¼   cup hazelnuts, toasted, skinned, and chopped (see page 114)

    Salt and freshly ground black pepper

2   pounds thin asparagus, trimmed

In a small bowl, whisk together the shallot, vinegar, mustard, and sugar. Add the olive oil in a stream, whisking until blended. Stir in the hazelnuts. Season to taste with salt and pepper.

In a large, deep skillet, bring 1½ inches of salted water to a boil. Add the asparagus and cook until crisp-tender, 2 to 4 minutes. Using tongs, transfer the asparagus to a colander and drain.

Transfer the asparagus to a serving dish. Spoon the vinaigrette over the asparagus and serve warm or at room temperature.

 SERVES 6

CURRIED SWEET POTATO FRITTERS

These colorful and tasty pancakes are a festive way to start a dinner party. They look pretty topped with a dollop of yogurt and a sprig of fresh mint.

Preheat the oven to 350°F. Pierce the sweet potatoes with a fork. Microwave on high power until tender, about 12 minutes. Scoop out enough of the cooked potato from the skins to fill a 1-cup measure. Transfer to a medium bowl. Add the butter and mash well. Mix in the mint, salt, and curry powder, then beat in the egg. Whisk the flour, bread crumbs, and baking powder into the potato mixture to make a dough.

Pour enough oil into a heavy, medium saucepan to reach a depth of 1 inch; heat the oil to 325°F. Working in batches, drop the batter by heaping teaspoonfuls into the oil. Fry until golden brown and cooked through, about 1½ minutes per side. Using a slotted spoon, transfer the fritters to a baking sheet; place in the oven to keep warm. Repeat with the remaining batter. Serve hot.

1 pound sweet potatoes, scrubbed and patted dry

2 tablespoons butter, melted

2 tablespoons chopped fresh mint

¾ teaspoon salt

½ teaspoon curry powder

1 large egg

1 cup unbleached all-purpose flour

½ cup fresh bread crumbs

1 tablespoon baking powder

Vegetable oil for frying

CARAMELIZED ONION TARTLETS

These small tarts are made with frozen puff pastry, which you can find in the freezer section of most supermarkets. The pastry is very easy to work with, and it turns golden brown and puffy when it bakes.

MAKES 36 TARTLETS

1   sheet frozen puff pastry (from a 17¼-ounce package), thawed

3   tablespoons olive oil

1   large onion, halved and thinly sliced

2   teaspoons balsamic vinegar

1   teaspoon brown sugar

2   teaspoons chopped fresh thyme, or ½ teaspoon dried

½   teaspoon salt

¼   teaspoon freshly ground black pepper

¼   cup pitted kalamata olives, thinly sliced

Preheat the oven to 400°F. Grease 2 large baking sheets. Roll out the puff pastry on a lightly floured surface into a 12½-inch square, then trim the edges to form a 12-inch square. Prick all over with a fork. Cut into thirty-six 2-inch squares and transfer to the baking sheets, arranging them about 2 inches apart.

Bake for 12 to 15 minutes, until puffed and golden. Transfer to a rack and cool until just warm.

Meanwhile, in a large skillet over medium heat, warm 2 tablespoons of the olive oil. Add the onion and cook, stirring occasionally, for 15 to 20 minutes, or until golden brown. Stir in the vinegar, brown sugar, 1 teaspoon of the thyme (¼ teaspoon if using dried), salt, and pepper. Remove from the heat, cover, and keep warm.

Lightly brush the tops of the pastry squares with the remaining 1 tablespoon oil. Make a small indentation in the center of each square with your finger, then top each with 1 teaspoon of the onion mixture and a few olive slivers. Sprinkle the squares with the remaining 1 teaspoon thyme (remaining ¼ teaspoon if using dried) and serve.

SKILLET ANTIPASTO

SERVES 4

To make this dish especially fast and easy to prepare, you can use store-bought roasted peppers.

Preheat the broiler. Place the bell peppers on a broiler pan and broil until blistered all over, turning often with tongs, 10 to 15 minutes. Transfer to a paper bag, seal, and let steam for 10 minutes. Peel the bell peppers, discarding the skin, seeds, and stem. Cut the roasted peppers into ¾-inch-wide strips.

In a large skillet over medium heat, warm the olive oil. Add the garlic and cook, stirring often, until fragrant, about 1 minute. Add the artichoke hearts and cook, stirring often, until heated through, about 3 minutes. Stir in the roasted peppers, parsley, lemon juice, and olives. Season to taste with salt and pepper. Serve at room temperature with crusty bread.

3 medium red bell peppers

3 medium yellow bell peppers

1 tablespoon extra-virgin olive oil

2 cloves garlic, minced

Two 14-ounce cans whole artichoke hearts, drained and quartered

⅓ cup finely chopped fresh flat-leaf parsley

2 tablespoons fresh lemon juice

⅔ cup pitted brine-cured black olives such as kalamata

Salt and freshly ground black pepper

Crusty bread for serving

VEGAN

TEMPEH SATAY
WITH PEANUT DIPPING SAUCE

SERVES 6 TO 8

Tempeh is considered one of the most nutritious soy foods, offering as much as 21 grams of protein in one serving. Besides being high in protein, tempeh is also rich in vitamin B₁₂, calcium, and fiber. It has a dense, chewy texture and a rich, nutty flavor. It is sold in vacuum-packed 8-ounce packages in the refrigerated and frozen foods section of natural food stores and large supermarkets. Always check the expiration date marked on the package and select the freshest available.

¼   cup vegetable oil

1   tablespoon dark (Asian) sesame oil

¼   cup tamari or reduced-sodium soy sauce

¼   cup rice vinegar

¼   cup rice wine (mirin)

1   tablespoon minced peeled fresh ginger

1   clove garlic, minced

1   pound tempeh, cut into 1½-inch cubes

PEANUT DIPPING SAUCE

¼   cup cilantro leaves

2   cloves garlic, chopped

2   green onions, chopped

1   stalk fresh lemongrass (tender inner bulb only), chopped

¾   cup chunky peanut butter

½   cup Rich Vegetable Broth (page 109) or canned broth

3   tablespoons fresh lime juice

1   tablespoon light brown sugar

    Salt and freshly ground black pepper

In a medium bowl, mix the vegetable oil, sesame oil, tamari, rice vinegar, rice wine, ginger, and garlic until well blended. In a large skillet, arrange the tempeh in a single layer. Pour the liquid mixture over the tempeh and bring to a boil over medium-high heat. Reduce the heat to low, cover, and simmer until the liquid is almost absorbed, about 20 minutes. Remove from the heat and let cool slightly.

Meanwhile, make the dipping sauce: In a food processor, combine the cilantro, garlic, green onions, and lemongrass and process until finely chopped. Add the peanut butter, broth, lime juice, and brown sugar and process until smooth. Transfer to a bowl. Season to taste with salt and pepper.

Thread the tempeh cubes onto bamboo skewers and serve with the dipping sauce.

VEGAN

ZUCCHINI TRIANGLES

**MAKES
18 PASTRIES**

*These delicious packets can be made a day ahead.
Cover tightly with plastic and refrigerate. Bring to room
temperature before baking. Look for phyllo (filo) dough
in the freezer section of well-stocked supermarkets.*

1   medium zucchini (about 12 ounces),
    trimmed and coarsely grated

½   teaspoon salt, plus more to taste

2   tablespoons olive oil

½   cup chopped onion

⅓   cup chopped fresh basil

2   tablespoons chopped fresh parsley

1   clove garlic, minced

¼   cup dry white wine

½   cup crumbled feta cheese

⅓   cup pine nuts, toasted (see page 42)

    Freshly ground black pepper

1   large egg

6   sheets phyllo pastry, thawed if frozen

½   cup (1 stick) butter, melted

1   egg white, lightly beaten

    Sesame seeds for sprinkling

In a medium bowl, toss the zucchini with the ½ teaspoon salt. Let stand for 30 minutes. Drain well, roll in a kitchen towel, and squeeze dry.

In a large skillet over medium-high heat, warm the olive oil. Add the onion and cook, stirring often, until beginning to brown, about 6 minutes. Add the zucchini and cook, stirring often, until beginning to brown, about 5 minutes. Stir in the basil, parsley, garlic, and wine. Bring to a simmer. Reduce the heat, cover, and simmer for 3 minutes. Uncover and cook, stirring, until any remaining liquid evaporates, about 2 minutes. Transfer to a large bowl and let cool. Mix in the feta cheese, then the pine nuts. Season to taste with salt and pepper. Mix in the egg.

Grease 2 large baking sheets. Place a phyllo sheet on a work surface with 1 short end parallel to the edge of the work surface (keep the remaining phyllo covered with plastic wrap and a damp kitchen towel). Brush the sheet lightly with melted butter; cut lengthwise into 3 equal strips, each about 4 inches wide. Place 1 generous tablespoon filling at the bottom end of one strip. Fold one corner of the phyllo over the filling. Repeat this folding down the length of the strip, as you would fold a flag, brushing it twice with butter and forming a triangle. Place the pastry on a prepared baking sheet; brush with butter. Repeat with the remaining phyllo sheets and filling.

Preheat the oven to 400°F. Brush the triangles with the egg white. Sprinkle generously with sesame seeds. Bake for about 25 minutes, until golden brown. Serve warm.

VEGETABLE SPRING ROLLS WITH GINGER SAUCE

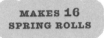

MAKES 16
SPRING ROLLS

These spring rolls are filled with cabbage, carrot, bean sprouts, bell pepper, and rice stick noodles. Rice stick noodles are available at Asian markets and in the Asian section of well-stocked supermarkets. They have already been cooked as part of their manufacturing process, so they cook very quickly in boiling water. You can also put the dried noodles into a bowl and add cold water to cover. Let soak until soft, about 30 minutes. Drain and proceed with the recipe.

GINGER SAUCE

½   cup tamari or reduced-sodium soy sauce

¼   cup rice wine (mirin)

¼   cup rice vinegar

2   green onions, (white and light green parts) finely chopped

1   tablespoon minced peeled fresh ginger

2   ounces thin rice stick noodles

1½ cups finely chopped green cabbage

¾   cup finely chopped peeled carrot

½   cup finely chopped green onion (white and light green parts)

½   cup chopped bean sprouts

½   cup finely chopped red bell pepper

2   teaspoons tamari or reduced-sodium soy sauce

    Salt and freshly ground black pepper

16 egg roll wrappers

1   large egg, lightly beaten

    Vegetable oil for frying

Make the sauce: In a small bowl, mix the tamari, rice wine, rice vinegar, green onions, and ginger until well blended.

Bring a large pot of water to a boil. Add the noodles and cook until tender, about 1 minute. Drain. Rinse with cold water. Drain well.

Coarsely chop the noodles and transfer to a large bowl. Add the cabbage, carrot, green onion, sprouts, bell pepper, and tamari. Season to taste with salt and pepper.

Place 1 egg roll wrapper on a work surface. Place ¼ cup of the filling in a 3-inch-long log down the center of the wrapper. Fold the bottom of wrapper over the filling, then fold in the sides. Brush the top edge of the wrapper with egg. Roll up tightly, pressing to seal the edge. Repeat with the remaining wrappers and filling.

Pour oil into a large, heavy skillet to a depth of 3 inches. Heat to 350°F. Working in batches, add the spring rolls to the oil and deep-fry until golden brown, about 5 minutes. Drain on paper towels. Serve with the sauce.

STEAMED TOFU AND VEGETABLE DUMPLINGS

MAKES 24 DUMPLINGS

These refreshing dumplings have a filling of tofu, mushrooms, carrots, and daikon. Daikon radishes, which look like large white carrots, are used extensively in Asian cooking. They can be found in well-stocked supermarkets and Asian markets.

8   ounces firm tofu, drained and cut into ½-inch slices

½   cup dried wood ear mushrooms (about ½ ounce)

1   cup chopped daikon radish

¾   cup shredded peeled carrot

1   tablespoon minced peeled fresh ginger

1   tablespoon minced green onion

1   teaspoon salt

2   teaspoons tamari or reduced-sodium soy sauce

½   teaspoon dark (Asian) sesame oil

1   large egg, lightly beaten

24 wonton wrappers

1   teaspoon cornstarch

DIPPING SAUCE

½   cup tamari or reduced-sodium soy sauce

1   tablespoon dark (Asian) sesame oil

2   teaspoons minced peeled fresh ginger

¼   cup water

Wrap the tofu in an absorbent dish towel. Set on a cutting board and weight it down with something heavy, like a large can of tomatoes. Rest one end of the board on a plate so that the board tilts toward the sink. The excess water will drain off and flow into the sink. Drain for about 30 minutes. Place the tofu in a large bowl and mash with a fork until smooth. Set aside.

In a small bowl, combine the mushrooms and boiling water to cover; cover and let stand for 20 minutes, or until soft. Drain. In a food processor, combine the soaked mushrooms and daikon and pulse on and off until finely chopped. Add the mushroom mixture, carrot, ginger, green onion, salt, tamari, sesame oil, and egg to the tofu and stir well.

Working with 1 wonton wrapper at a time (cover the remaining wrappers to keep them from drying), spoon 1 teaspoon of the filling into the center of the wrapper. Moisten the edges of the wrapper with water; bring 2 opposite corners to the center, pinching the points to seal. Bring the remaining 2 corners to the center, pinching the edges together to seal. Repeat with the remaining wrappers and filling. As you finish them, place the dumplings, seam sides up, on a large baking sheet sprinkled with the cornstarch (cover loosely with a towel to keep them from drying).

Arrange one-third of the dumplings in a single layer in a vegetable steamer coated with vegetable oil spray. Steam the dumplings, covered, for 15 minutes. Remove from the steamer; set aside and keep warm. Repeat the procedure with the remaining dumplings.

Meanwhile, make the sauce: In a small bowl, mix the tamari, sesame oil, ginger, and water until well blended. Serve with the dumplings.

BULGUR-STUFFED GRAPE LEAVES

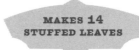

MAKES 14 STUFFED LEAVES

Stuffed grape leaves are a year-round food in Greece, enjoyed as a snack or with dinner or lunch. There are several different traditional fillings for grape leaves. In this version, bulgur, raisins, and walnuts provide a great flavor and texture. Grape leaves are available packed in jars and require soaking to remove the excess brine that preserves them. Look for them in the ethnic section of well-stocked supermarkets and at Greek or Middle Eastern groceries.

1 cup water

½ cup coarse bulgur

3 tablespoons olive oil

1 cup finely chopped red onion

¼ cup raisins

¼ cup finely chopped walnuts

¼ cup packed dried apricots, finely chopped

2 tablespoons chopped fresh mint leaves

¼ teaspoon ground cinnamon

¼ teaspoon ground allspice

 Salt and freshly ground black pepper

14 grape leaves, rinsed and dried

¼ cup fresh lemon juice

In a medium saucepan, bring the water to a boil. Stir in the bulgur. Reduce the heat, cover, and simmer until the bulgur is tender and the liquid is absorbed, about 15 minutes. Remove from the heat.

Meanwhile, in a large skillet over medium heat, warm 1 tablespoon of the olive oil. Add the onion and cook, stirring often, until softened, about 5 minutes. Remove from the heat and stir in the raisins, walnuts, apricots, mint, cinnamon, and allspice. Stir in the bulgur and season to taste with salt and pepper.

Place 1 grape leaf flat on a work surface with the veins facing upward and the stalk end nearest to you. Place 2 teaspoons of the filling in center of the leaf, near the stalk. Fold the bottom of the leaf up and the sides in to enclose the filling. Roll up firmly toward the point. Place the roll in the palm of your hand and give it a slight squeeze to form a firm shape. Repeat with the remaining filling and leaves.

Arrange the stuffed leaves, seam sides down, in a medium skillet. Add the remaining 2 tablespoons olive oil, lemon juice, and enough water to cover the leaves. Bring to a simmer. Cover and cook over low heat until tender, 1½ to 2 hours. Add more water to the skillet as necessary. Remove from the heat and let cool, covered, in the skillet. Transfer to a serving dish and refrigerate until ready to serve.

MARINATED OLIVES

Good-quality olives are now sold in most specialty food stores. Make them even more interesting with this flavorful marinade. After you drain the olives, save the oil and use it in a salad dressing or as a topping for pasta or sautéed vegetables.

1½ cups pitted green olives

3 tablespoons mixed fresh herbs such as thyme, oregano, chives, and sage, or 1 tablespoon dried

1 teaspoon finely chopped fresh rosemary, or ½ teaspoon dried

1 teaspoon fennel seed, crushed

½ teaspoon paprika

⅛ teaspoon red pepper flakes

¼ teaspoon black peppercorns

1 tablespoon coarsely chopped garlic

¼ teaspoon salt

3 bay leaves

One 1-by-3-inch piece of lemon zest

Olive oil to cover

In a medium bowl, combine the olives, mixed herbs, rosemary, fennel seed, paprika, red pepper flakes, peppercorns, garlic, and salt and mix thoroughly. Pack into a pint jar, layering with the bay leaves and tucking lemon zest in the middle. Pour the olive oil over the olives to cover, then cover tightly the jar. Refrigerate for at least 4 days, shaking occasionally.

To serve, drain the olives and remove and discard the peppercorns, bay leaves, and lemon zest. Serve at room temperature.

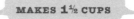

MAKES 1½ CUPS

MARINATED GARLICKY MUSHROOMS

SERVES 6

Small mushrooms are best for this recipe. Other vegetables, such as chopped zucchini, artichoke hearts, leeks, or cauliflower, can also be prepared this way.

In a large skillet over medium-low heat, warm the olive oil. Add the garlic, bay leaf, coriander, and oregano and cook, stirring occasionally, until the garlic starts to brown, about 5 minutes. Stir in the wine and lemon juice and bring to a boil. Add the mushrooms and parsley. Reduce the heat, cover, and cook for 10 minutes, shaking the pan occasionally.

Remove the pan from the heat and season to taste with salt and pepper. Using a slotted spoon, transfer the mushrooms to a serving dish. Return the skillet to the heat and bring the juices to a boil. Cook until the liquid is reduced by half, about 5 minutes. Discard the bay leaf and pour the liquid over the mushrooms. Cover and set aside to cool. If not serving right away, refrigerate and bring to room temperature before serving.

2 tablespoons olive oil

4 cloves garlic, sliced

1 bay leaf

¼ teaspoon ground coriander

1 tablespoon chopped fresh oregano, or ½ teaspoon dried

1 cup dry white wine or water

¼ cup fresh lemon juice

1¼ pounds small button mushrooms

¼ cup finely chopped fresh parsley

Salt and freshly ground black pepper

VEGAN

SOUP'S ON

chapter 3

THERE

is nothing more satisfying than a bowl of homemade soup. But don't be misled into thinking that it takes endless preparation and long, slow cooking. The recipes in this chapter use a wide range of fresh and prepared ingredients and some shortcut methods to create a selection of easy-to-prepare, flavorful soups. You can also substitute a canned vegetable broth for the homemade version. And many of the soups can be made ahead, perfect to serve for a hassle-free evening meal after a busy day.

BRAZILIAN BLACK BEAN SOUP

SERVES 6

This Latin-inspired black bean soup is served with a colorful bell pepper and lime salsa, which adds a tangy flavor. Black beans are packed with protein and are rich in vitamins and minerals. They also are a great source of fiber.

2½ cups (1 pound) dried black beans, picked over

2   tablespoons olive oil

1   cup coarsely chopped onion

1   cup coarsely chopped green bell pepper

2   cloves garlic, minced

1   teaspoon chili powder

½   teaspoon ground cumin

⅛   teaspoon cayenne pepper

3½ cups Rich Vegetable Broth (page 109) or canned broth

2   cups water

SALSA

1   large red or yellow bell pepper, finely chopped (1½ cups)

1   medium onion, finely chopped (1 cup)

1   tablespoon fresh lime juice

⅛   teaspoon salt

One 16-ounce can whole tomatoes in juice, undrained

½   cup uncooked small pasta, such as tubettini

½   teaspoon salt

Put the beans in a 2- to 3-quart saucepan (or the pot you will cook the soup in) and add water to cover by about 3 inches. Bring to a boil over high heat and boil for 2 to 3 minutes. Remove from the heat, cover, and let soak for 1 to 2 hours. Drain and rinse.

In a large pot over medium heat, warm the olive oil. Add the onion, bell pepper, and garlic and cook, stirring often, until softened, 3 to 5 minutes. Stir in the chili powder, cumin, and cayenne and cook for 30 seconds. Add the beans, broth, and 2 cups water. Cover and bring to a boil over high heat. Reduce the heat to low. Cover and simmer until the beans are tender, 70 to 80 minutes.

Meanwhile, make the salsa: In a medium bowl, mix the bell pepper, onion, lime juice, and salt. Cover with plastic wrap and refrigerate until ready to use.

Drain the juice from the canned tomatoes into the pot. Chop the tomatoes and add, along with the pasta and salt. Bring to a boil over medium-high heat, stirring occasionally. Reduce the heat to low and simmer, uncovered, stirring occasionally, until the pasta is tender, about 10 minutes. Ladle into serving bowls and garnish with a spoonful of salsa (or serve the salsa separately).

VEGAN

TUSCAN WHITE BEAN SOUP

This soup has tender, creamy beans in a broth perfumed with garlic and rosemary. For a more authentic soup, place a small slice of lightly toasted Italian bread in the bottom of each bowl and ladle the soup over it.

SERVES 6

VEGAN

1½ cups dried small white or navy beans, picked over

2 tablespoons olive oil

2 cups chopped onion

2 cloves garlic, minced

½ teaspoon dried rosemary, crumbled

¼ teaspoon dried thyme, crumbled

3½ cups Rich Vegetable Broth (page 109) or canned broth

3 cups water

3 medium russet potatoes (1 pound), peeled and cut into ½-inch dice

3 medium carrots, peeled and diced

½ teaspoon salt

¼ teaspoon freshly ground black pepper

Put the beans in a 2- to 3-quart saucepan (or the pot you will cook the soup in) and add water to cover by about 3 inches. Bring to a boil over high heat and boil for 2 to 3 minutes. Remove from the heat, cover, and let soak for 1 to 2 hours. Drain and rinse.

In a large pot over medium heat, warm the olive oil. Add the onion and garlic and cook, stirring often, until soft, about 7 minutes. Add the rosemary and thyme and cook, stirring, for 30 seconds. Add the broth, 3 cups water, and beans. Cover and bring to a boil over high heat. Reduce the heat to medium-low and simmer until the beans are nearly tender, about 40 minutes.

Add the potatoes, carrots, salt, and pepper to the pot. Bring to a boil over medium-high heat. Reduce the heat to medium-low. Cover and simmer until beans and vegetables are very tender, about 35 minutes.

Remove the pan from the heat and, with a potato masher or the back of a slotted spoon, mash some of the beans and vegetables to thicken the soup. Ladle into serving bowls.

SPICED CHICKPEA SOUP

SERVES 4 TO 6

The fragrant flavors of ground cumin, coriander, ginger, and cinnamon make this soup soothing and warming. Half the soup is puréed and half is left chunky for the best of both textures.

Put the chickpeas in a 2- to 3-quart saucepan (or the pot you will cook the soup in) and add water to cover by about 3 inches. Bring to a boil over high heat and boil for 2 to 3 minutes. Remove from the heat, cover, and let soak for 1 to 2 hours. Drain and rinse.

In a large pot, combine the chickpeas, bay leaf, and 7 cups water. Cover and bring to a boil. Reduce the heat and simmer, partially covered, until the chickpeas are almost tender, about 1½ hours.

In a medium skillet over medium heat, warm the olive oil. Add the onion, and cook, stirring often, until softened, about 5 minutes. Add the garlic, red pepper flakes, cumin, coriander, ginger, and cinnamon and cook, stirring often, until fragrant, 2 to 3 minutes. Add the onion mixture to the chickpeas and simmer until the beans are tender, about 30 minutes. Stir in the ¼ teaspoon salt.

Discard the bay leaf. Transfer half of the soup to a blender or food processor and process until smooth. Pour the purée back into the soup pot. Add additional water, if necessary, to thin the soup. Add the lemon juice and more salt, if desired. Stir in the parsley and ladle into serving bowls.

1½ cups dried chickpeas

1   bay leaf

7   cups water

2   tablespoons olive oil

2   cups chopped onion

4   cloves garlic, minced

½   teaspoon red pepper flakes

1   teaspoon ground cumin

1   teaspoon ground coriander

½   teaspoon ground ginger

½   teaspoon ground cinnamon

¼   teaspoon salt, plus more to taste

2   tablespoons fresh lemon juice

½   cup chopped fresh flat-leaf parsley

VEGAN

LENTIL SOUP WITH SPINACH

Fresh mint and oregano give this lentil soup a wonderful flavor and fragrance. Serve it with a couscous salad and whole-wheat pitas. A reheated cup of this soup also makes a great sauce for a bowl of couscous or rice.

2 tablespoons olive oil

2 cups chopped onion

½ cup chopped celery, with leaves

2 cloves garlic, minced

8 cups water

3½ cups Rich Vegetable Broth (page 109) or canned broth

2½ cups (1 pound) dried lentils, sorted and rinsed

One 16-ounce can whole tomatoes in juice, undrained

1½ teaspoons salt

½ teaspoon freshly ground black pepper

1 tablespoon chopped fresh mint, or 1 teaspoon dried

1 tablespoon chopped fresh oregano, or 1 teaspoon dried

One 10-ounce package fresh spinach leaves, stemmed and chopped

In a large pot over medium heat, warm the olive oil. Add the onion, celery, and garlic and cook, stirring often, until softened, about 8 minutes. Add the 8 cups water, broth, and lentils. Bring to a boil over high heat. Reduce the heat to low, cover, and simmer for 1 hour, or until the lentils are tender.

Drain the juice from the tomatoes into the pot. Chop and add the tomatoes, salt, pepper, mint, and oregano. Bring to a boil over medium-high heat. Reduce the heat to low and simmer, uncovered, for 5 minutes. Add the spinach and simmer, uncovered, until the spinach is heated through, 5 to 7 minutes. Ladle into serving bowls.

SERVES 8

PENNE AND CHICKPEA SOUP

SERVES 6

The satisfying combination of pasta and legumes is a staple in the Mediterranean diet, which medical researchers in recent years have called the most healthful diet in the Western world. When combined, pasta and beans form a complete protein, containing all eight of the essential amino acids. This winning combo can help fulfill your recommended daily allowance for protein.

In a large pot over medium heat, warm the olive oil. Add the garlic and rosemary sprig and cook, stirring often, until fragrant, about 2 minutes. Add the tomatoes with their liquid, whole and mashed chickpeas, 6 cups water, and 2 teaspoons salt; bring to a boil.

Reduce the heat and simmer for 10 minutes. Add the pasta and cook until tender, about 10 minutes. Remove the rosemary sprig and add chopped rosemary. Season to taste with salt and pepper. Ladle into serving bowls.

VEGAN

2   tablespoons olive oil

4   cloves garlic, chopped

1   sprig fresh rosemary, plus
    1 tablespoon chopped fresh
    rosemary leaves

Two 14½-ounce cans diced
    tomatoes in juice

Two 15½-ounce cans chickpeas,
    drained, rinsed, and half
    mashed with a fork

6   cups water

2   teaspoons salt, plus more
    to taste

8   ounces penne or other
    short pasta

    Freshly ground black pepper

RICE AND ZUCCHINI SOUP

This tempting soup gets its porridgelike consistency from short-grain Arborio rice. Because it becomes thicker as it stands, it's best served right away. To seed tomatoes, simply cut each one in half and squeeze out the seeds. This soup is also good garnished with shavings of Parmesan cheese.

1   tablespoon olive oil

1   medium onion, finely chopped

2   cloves garlic, finely chopped

4   small zucchini, quartered lengthwise, then thinly sliced crosswise

4   cups Rich Vegetable Broth (page 109) or canned broth

1¾ cups water

1   cup Arborio rice

3   medium plum tomatoes, seeded and finely diced

⅓   cup shredded fresh basil

½   teaspoon salt

½   teaspoon freshly ground black pepper

In a large saucepan over medium heat, warm the olive oil. Add the onion and garlic and cook, stirring occasionally, until softened, about 7 minutes. Add the zucchini and cook, stirring, for 1 minute. Pour in the broth and water. Stir in the rice. Bring to a boil, reduce the heat to low, and simmer until the rice is tender, 18 to 20 minutes.

Remove from the heat and let stand for 5 minutes; the soup will thicken slightly. Stir in the tomatoes, basil, salt, and pepper. Ladle into serving bowls.

SERVES 4 TO 6

ROASTED MUSHROOM BISQUE

SERVES 6

Roasting intensifies the flavor of mushrooms, giving this soup a rich, earthy flavor. Madeira is a sweet wine made in Portugal. Sherry makes an acceptable substitute.

Preheat the oven to 400°F. Line 2 large baking sheets with foil. Divide the mushrooms between the baking sheets. Drizzle the mushrooms with the olive oil. Sprinkle generously with salt and pepper; toss to coat. Cover with foil. Bake for 30 minutes. Uncover and continue baking until the mushrooms are tender and still moist, about 15 minutes longer. Cool slightly. In a blender or food processor, combine half of the mushrooms with 2 cups of the broth and process until smooth.

In a large pot over medium-high heat, melt the butter. Add the onion and garlic and cook, stirring often, until the onion is tender, about 5 minutes. Add the Madeira and simmer until almost all of the liquid evaporates, about 2 minutes. Add the flour and cook, stirring, for 2 minutes. Add the remaining 3¼ cups broth, the milk, and thyme. Stir in the remaining cooked mushroom pieces and the mushroom purée. Simmer over medium heat until slightly thickened, about 10 minutes. Season to taste with salt and pepper. Ladle into serving bowls.

1   pound portobello mushrooms, stemmed, dark gills removed, caps cut into ¾-inch pieces

1   pound fresh shiitake mushrooms, stemmed, caps cut into ¾-inch pieces

6   tablespoons olive oil

    Salt and freshly ground black pepper

5¼ cups Rich Vegetable Broth (page 109) or canned broth

1½ tablespoons butter

1   medium onion, chopped

3   cloves garlic, minced

¼   cup plus 2 tablespoons Madeira wine

3   tablespoons unbleached all-purpose flour

1   cup whole milk or plain soymilk

1   teaspoon chopped fresh thyme, or ¼ teaspoon dried

MINESTRONE SOUP

SERVES 8

Here is a signature soup from Italy combining vegetables, pasta, and beans. Each region has its own version, and this one, from Genoa, uses pesto, a pungent herb paste, as a traditional finish to the soup. To save time you can buy ready-made pesto at most large supermarkets.

1 cup dried white or red kidney beans, picked over

4 cups water

3½ cups Rich Vegetable Broth (page 109) or canned broth

One 16-ounce can whole tomatoes in juice, undrained

1 medium russet potato, peeled and chopped

3 medium onions, coarsely chopped

3 medium carrots, peeled and thinly sliced

4 ounces fresh green beans, cut into 1-inch lengths (1 cup)

1 cup uncooked elbow macaroni or small pasta shells

1 medium zucchini, quartered lengthwise, then cut crosswise into ¼-inch-thick slices

½ teaspoon salt

¼ teaspoon freshly ground black pepper

PESTO

1 cup loosely packed fresh basil leaves

2 tablespoons olive oil

1 tablespoon water

1 clove garlic

Put the beans in a 2- to 3-quart saucepan (or the pot you will cook the soup in) and add water to cover by about 3 inches. Bring to a boil over high heat and boil for 2 to 3 minutes. Remove from the heat, cover, and let soak for 1 to 2 hours. Drain and rinse.

In a large pot, combine the beans, 4 cups water, and broth. Cover and bring to a boil over high heat. Reduce the heat to medium-low and simmer, uncovered, until the beans are tender, about 55 minutes.

Drain the juice from the canned tomatoes into the pot. Chop the tomatoes and add to the pot along with the potato, onions, carrots, and green beans. Bring to a boil over medium-high heat. Reduce the heat to low and simmer, uncovered, until the vegetables are tender, about 10 minutes.

Add the macaroni, zucchini, salt, and pepper. Return to a boil, reduce the heat to low, and simmer for 10 minutes.

Meanwhile, make the pesto: In a blender or a food processor, combine the basil, olive oil, water, and garlic and process until very finely chopped.

Remove the pot from the heat and stir the pesto into the soup. Ladle into serving bowls.

VEGAN

CURRIED BUTTERNUT SQUASH SOUP

Winter squash makes a soup that's substantial on its own. Its rich, fragrant quality is nicely complemented by slices of crusty peasant bread.

SERVES 4 TO 6

VEGAN

2 butternut squash (4¾ pounds), halved lengthwise and seeded

2 tablespoons vegetable oil

2 cups thinly sliced onion

1 tablespoon light brown sugar

2 teaspoons minced peeled fresh ginger

2 cloves garlic, coarsely chopped

½ cinnamon stick

5 cups Rich Vegetable Broth (page 109) or canned broth, plus more if necessary

2 teaspoons curry powder

Salt and freshly ground black pepper

Preheat the oven to 375°F. Grease a baking sheet. Place the squash, cut side down, on the baking sheet. Bake for about 50 minutes, until the squash is very soft. Using a paring knife, remove the peel from the squash. Discard the peel and cut the squash into 2-inch pieces.

In a large pot over medium-low heat, warm the oil. Add the onion, brown sugar, ginger, garlic, and cinnamon stick. Cover and cook until the onion is softened, about 15 minutes. Add the squash and 5 cups broth. Bring to a boil. Reduce the heat to medium-low, cover, and simmer for 10 minutes. Remove and discard the cinnamon stick.

Transfer the mixture to a blender or food processor and process in batches until smooth. Return the purée to the pot. Stir in the curry powder and season to taste with salt and pepper. Bring to a simmer, thinning the soup with more broth if necessary. Ladle into bowls.

FRENCH ONION SOUP

SERVES 6

Caramelizing the onions gives this soup a wonderful rich flavor. Onions are one of the world's most pungent foods, especially when eaten raw. But when cooked a bit, they start losing their sharp flavor. And when cooked until their natural sugars caramelize, the transformation goes even further. The onions darken to a rich, golden brown and take on a delicious sweetness.

In a large pot over medium heat, melt the butter with the oil. Add the onions, sugar, and salt and cook, stirring, for 1 minute. Reduce the heat to medium-low and cook, stirring occasionally, until the onions are deep golden brown but not burned and are very soft, 20 to 25 minutes.

Add the flour and cook, stirring, for 1 minute. Stir in the broth, sherry, and thyme. Bring to a boil. Reduce the heat and simmer for 15 minutes. Season to taste with salt and pepper.

Preheat the broiler. Broil the bread slices until lightly toasted. Ladle the soup into 6 ovenproof bowls and arrange on a baking sheet. Cover with the bread slices, cutting them to fit if necessary. Sprinkle with the cheese. Broil until the cheese is melted and bubbly. Serve hot.

2 tablespoons butter

1 tablespoon vegetable oil

5 large onions, halved and thinly sliced (about 7½ cups)

1 teaspoon sugar

1 teaspoon salt, plus more to taste

2 tablespoons unbleached all-purpose flour

6 cups Rich Vegetable Broth (page 109) or canned broth

⅓ cup dry sherry

1½ teaspoons chopped fresh thyme, or ½ teaspoon dried

Freshly ground black pepper

1 loaf French bread, cut into ½-inch-thick slices

2½ cups grated Jarlsberg or Gruyère cheese

CARROT AND SWEET POTATO SOUP

The combination of sweet potatoes, carrots, and apples makes a deliciously savory and sweet soup. If you buy the carrots with the greens attached, you'll know that they're fresh and sweet. Garnish with a few croutons, if you like.

 SERVES 6

1 tablespoon olive oil

1½ pounds carrots, scrubbed and sliced

8 ounces sweet potatoes, peeled and cubed

1 large tart apple, such as Granny Smith, peeled and diced

5½ cups Rich Vegetable Broth (page 109) or canned broth

2 tablespoons long-grain rice

½ teaspoon ground coriander

1 bay leaf

2 teaspoons fresh lemon juice

Salt and freshly ground black pepper

In a large pot over medium heat, warm the olive oil. Add the carrots, sweet potatoes, and apple and cook, stirring often, for 5 minutes. Add the broth, rice, coriander, and bay leaf. Bring to a boil. Cover, reduce the heat, and simmer until the vegetables are tender, about 20 minutes.

Remove and discard the bay leaf. Transfer the mixture to a blender or food processor in batches and process until smooth. Return to the pot. Add the lemon juice and season to taste with salt and pepper. Ladle into serving bowls.

VEGAN

CREAMY TOMATO BISQUE

SERVES 6

As a kid, I was a major fan of tomato soup. But the taste of canned tomato soup just doesn't appeal to me as an adult. So I came up with this creamy version that uses rice milk, tomato paste, and capers. It's a little sophisticated but still comforting. Serve the soup with crisp breadsticks or slices of focaccia.

In a medium saucepan, combine the rice milk and tomato paste. Bring to a simmer over medium heat and cook for about 10 minutes. Whisk in the mustard; cover and remove from the heat.

In a large pot over medium heat, warm the olive oil. Add the garlic, onion, coriander, celery seed, and anise seed and cook, stirring often, for 2 minutes. Add the diced tomatoes with their liquid and the capers and cook, stirring often, for 10 minutes. Stir in the rice milk mixture and simmer for 5 minutes. Remove from the heat and cool slightly.

Transfer the mixture to a blender or food processor in batches and process until smooth. Return to the pot. Season with the salt and pepper. Ladle into serving bowls.

One 32-ounce container rice milk (4 cups)

Two 6-ounce cans tomato paste

2   tablespoons Dijon mustard

2½ teaspoons olive oil

6   cloves garlic, minced

1   large onion, chopped (1½ cups)

1   teaspoon ground coriander

1   teaspoon celery seed

½   teaspoon anise seed

One 28-ounce can diced tomatoes, undrained

2   tablespoons drained minced capers

1   teaspoon salt

½   teaspoon freshly ground black pepper

VEGAN

FRAGRANT BROCCOLI SOUP

Cumin, cloves, curry powder, and fresh ginger give this soup a heady aroma as well as an interesting flavor. If the stems on the broccoli are tough, peel them first, using a vegetable peeler.

SERVES 4 TO 6

1¼ pounds broccoli, stems and florets separated and stems chopped

5 cups Rich Vegetable Broth (page 109) or canned broth

1 cup cooked rice

1½ teaspoons salt

1 tablespoon olive oil

1 medium onion, chopped

2 cloves garlic, minced

1 teaspoon curry powder

1 teaspoon ground cumin

½ teaspoon ground cloves

2 tablespoons fresh lemon juice

1 tablespoon minced peeled fresh ginger

Pinch of cayenne pepper, or to taste

In a large pot, combine the broccoli stems, broth, cooked rice, and ½ teaspoon of the salt and bring to a boil over high heat. Reduce the heat to low, cover partially, and simmer for 10 minutes.

Meanwhile, in a large skillet over medium heat, warm the olive oil. Add the onion and cook, stirring often, until softened, about 5 minutes. Stir in the garlic, curry powder, cumin, and cloves and cook, stirring, until fragrant, about 1 minute. Add to the soup along with the broccoli florets and bring to a boil. Reduce the heat to medium-low, cover, and simmer for 15 minutes.

Remove from the heat and stir in the lemon juice, ginger, cayenne, and the remaining 1 teaspoon salt. Transfer to a blender or food processor in batches and process until smooth. Return to the pot. Cover and let stand for 15 minutes to let the flavors blend before serving.

VEGAN

CREAMY ASPARAGUS SOUP

SERVES 6

This easy-to-make soup is flavorful and creamy, yet is extremely low in fat—it has only 1 tablespoon of butter and no cream at all (except for an optional sour cream garnish).

In a large saucepan over medium heat, melt the butter. Add the onion and cook, stirring occasionally, until softened, about 5 minutes. Add the flour and cook, stirring, for 2 minutes. Gradually mix in the broth. Bring to a boil. Add the asparagus pieces and tarragon and simmer until the asparagus is very tender, about 25 minutes. Cool slightly.

With a slotted spoon, transfer the asparagus to a blender or food processor. Process the asparagus until puréed. With the machine running, gradually add ½ cup of the cooking liquid. Return to the saucepan. Season to taste with salt and pepper. Bring to a simmer. Ladle into serving bowls and top with dollops of sour cream, if desired.

1 tablespoon butter

1 small onion, chopped

1 tablespoon unbleached all-purpose flour

4 cups Rich Vegetable Broth (page 109) or canned broth

1 pound asparagus, trimmed and cut into 1-inch pieces

1 teaspoon dried tarragon or dill

Salt and freshly ground black pepper

Sour cream or plain yogurt for serving (optional)

PORTUGUESE POTATO AND KALE SOUP

Potatoes and kale are a classic combination in Portugal. Be sure to clean the kale thoroughly. The best way to do this is to plunge the leaves into a sink filled with cold water, then swish gently to dislodge the dirt. Lift the greens from the water, so the grit remains in the bottom. Repeat as needed until the water is clear.

¼   cup olive oil

1½ cups finely chopped onion

¾   cup peeled, sliced carrots

2   cloves garlic, minced

1   pound russet potatoes (about 2 large), peeled and cut into 1-inch pieces

3   cups water

3   cups Rich Vegetable Broth (page 109) or canned broth

12 ounces kale, stemmed, leaves thinly shredded (about 8 cups)

1   pound red-skinned potatoes, scrubbed and cut into 1-inch pieces

Salt and freshly ground black pepper

In a large pot over medium heat, warm the olive oil. Add the onion, carrots, and garlic and cook, stirring often, until the vegetables begin to soften, about 5 minutes. Add the russet potatoes, water, and broth. Bring to a boil. Reduce the heat, cover, and simmer until the potatoes are tender, 10 to 15 minutes.

With a slotted spoon, transfer the cooked potatoes to a blender or food processor. Add about 1½ cups of the cooking liquid and process until smooth. Stir the purée back into the pot and add the kale, red potatoes, and salt and pepper to taste. Simmer, covered, for 10 minutes, or until the potatoes are tender. Ladle into serving bowls.

SERVES 8

CORN AND POTATO CHOWDER

SERVES 6

This hearty soup has a rich, smooth texture even though it contains no cream. The flavor depends on the quality of the corn, so be sure to use the freshest and sweetest ears you can find.

In a large pot over medium heat, warm the oil. Add the carrots, celery, onion, and leek and cook, stirring often, until the vegetables are softened, about 10 minutes.

Add the corn, potatoes, broth, basil, and thyme. Bring to a simmer over medium-high heat. Reduce the heat to medium-low, cover, and simmer until the potatoes are tender and the liquid has reduced to just cover the ingredients, about 30 minutes.

Transfer the mixture to a blender or food processor in batches and process until almost smooth but still a little chunky. Return to the pot. Season to taste with salt and pepper. Ladle into serving bowls.

2   tablespoons vegetable oil

2   medium carrots, peeled and chopped

2   stalks celery, chopped

1   medium onion, chopped

1   leek (white part only), well rinsed and chopped

2   cups fresh corn kernels (cut from 4 medium ears)

2   medium russet potatoes, peeled and chopped

5   cups Rich Vegetable Broth (page 109) or canned broth

2   tablespoons chopped fresh basil, or 2 teaspoon dried

1   teaspoon chopped fresh thyme, or ¼ teaspoon dried

Salt and freshly ground black pepper

VEGAN

SPINACH MISO SOUP

To my mind, there's nothing like a bowl of miso soup: it's a warming elixir that soothes and restores the body and soul. This version of a classic Japanese soup includes shiitake mushrooms, tofu, and fresh spinach.

SERVES
4

5   cups water

1   ounce dried shiitake
    mushrooms

1   medium leek, trimmed,
    rinsed well, and chopped

One 1-inch piece fresh ginger,
    peeled and coarsely chopped

¼   cup mellow white miso

12 ounces firm tofu, drained well
    and cut into ½-inch dice

1   tablespoon rice wine

4   cups fresh spinach leaves

    Thinly sliced green onion tops
    for garnish

In a large saucepan, combine the water, mushrooms, leek, and ginger. Bring to a boil over high heat. Reduce the heat to medium and simmer for 10 minutes.

Using a slotted spoon, remove the mushrooms from the broth to a cutting board and let cool slightly. Remove and discard the mushroom stems and slice the caps. Set aside.

Strain the broth through a fine sieve into a large bowl and discard the solids. Transfer 1 cup of the broth to a small bowl and stir in the miso until well blended. Return the remaining broth to the saucepan.

Add the tofu, rice wine, reserved mushroom caps, and spinach to the broth. Simmer over medium-low heat, stirring occasionally, until the spinach is tender and the tofu is heated through, about 3 minutes. Whisk in the miso mixture until well blended. Ladle into serving bowls and garnish with the green onions.

GAZPACHO

You would be hard-pressed to find a dish that captures summer's flavor more than gazpacho. There are many variations of it, but most recipes recommend serving it well chilled. In Spain, where it originated, they traditionally serve small bowls containing extra chopped vegetables, hard-boiled eggs, and bread cubes with the soup as garnishes.

In a large bowl, mix the tomatoes, bell pepper, cucumber, onion, garlic, tomato juice, and vinegar. Cover with plastic wrap and refrigerate to chill thoroughly before serving.

To serve, ladle the chilled soup into mugs or serving bowls and garnish with a dollop of yogurt and some chopped cilantro, if desired.

2 cups seeded and finely chopped ripe tomatoes (2 large)

1½ cups finely chopped red bell pepper (1 large)

1 cup seeded and finely chopped cucumber

½ cup finely chopped red onion

2 cloves garlic, minced

One 11½-ounce can tomato-vegetable juice

2 tablespoons red wine vinegar

Plain soy yogurt for garnish (optional)

Chopped fresh cilantro for garnish (optional)

VEGAN

GARLICKY VICHYSSOISE

This version of the classic French potato soup was created by a French chef living in New York who was nostalgic for his mother's home cooking. It is the perfect choice for a summer menu because it can be prepared in advance and refrigerated until ready to serve. Although it is traditionally served cold, this soup can also be enjoyed piping hot.

2   tablespoons butter

2   cloves garlic, minced

1   pound leeks, trimmed, halved lengthwise, rinsed well, drained, and chopped (5 cups)

1   pound russet potatoes, peeled and chopped (2½ cups)

6   cups Rich Vegetable Broth (page 109) or canned broth

¼   teaspoon salt

¼   teaspoon freshly ground black pepper

1   cup half-and-half

Chopped fresh chives or green onion tops for garnish

In a large saucepan over medium-low heat, melt the butter. Add the garlic and leeks and cook, stirring often, until softened, 8 to 10 minutes. Add the potatoes, broth, salt, and pepper. Bring to a boil over high heat. Reduce the heat to medium-low. Cover and simmer, stirring occasionally, until the potatoes are tender, 15 to 20 minutes. Remove from the heat and cool slightly.

Transfer to a blender or food processor in batches and process until smooth. Pour into a bowl and stir in the half-and-half. Cover with plastic wrap and refrigerate for at least 4 hours or up to overnight.

Ladle the soup into serving bowls and garnish with chopped chives.

SERVES 8

RICH VEGETABLE BROTH

MAKES 6 CUPS

Many cooks are intimidated by the idea of making their own stock, but in fact there are few dishes that are easier to prepare. The secret to good soup is a good stock, and this is especially true for vegetarian soups. Roasting the vegetables intensifies the flavor of this basic vegetable broth.

Preheat the oven to 425°F. In a large bowl, combine the carrots, parsnips, onion, leek, celery root, and garlic and coat lightly with olive oil. Transfer to a shallow roasting pan or baking sheet with sides large enough to the hold vegetables in a single layer. Roast, stirring and turning the vegetables with a spatula every 10 minutes, for 40 minutes, until they are tender and lightly colored.

Transfer the roasted vegetables to a large pot. Add the water, salt, peppercorns, parsley, thyme, and bay leaves. Bring to a boil. Skim off any foam that rises to the top. Reduce the heat and simmer, partially covered, until the broth is well flavored, 1 to 1½ hours. Add more water as necessary to keep the vegetables covered, and skim as necessary.

Strain the broth through a fine sieve set over a large bowl, pressing on the vegetables with the back of a spoon to extract as much liquid as possible. Discard the solids. Cool the broth to room temperature, then transfer it to airtight containers and refrigerate for up to 5 days, or freeze it for up to 6 months.

4   medium carrots, peeled and cut into ½-inch-thick slices

2   medium parsnips, peeled and cut into ½-inch-thick slices

1   large onion, cut into 1-inch pieces

1   large leek (white part only), well rinsed and cut into ½-inch pieces

1   small celery root (celeriac), peeled and cut into ½-inch pieces

4   cloves garlic, peeled

    Olive oil for coating vegetables

8   cups water

1   teaspoon salt

¼   teaspoon black peppercorns

10 fresh parsley stems

6   sprigs fresh thyme

2   bay leaves

VEGAN

SUPER

SALADS

chapter 4

SALADS

have taken on a new importance
in our diet, and part of the reason
is their flexibility. They can easily feature
beans, legumes, fruits, grains, or vegetables;
can be served warm or cold; and can effortlessly
become the focal point of a meal, especially
during the warm-weather months. Most salads
are light and use fresh ingredients, making
them the spotlight of healthy eating.
And because there's such a wide
selection of ingredients available
year-round, the variations
are endless.

TABBOULEH

Tabbouleh is a Middle Eastern salad made of bulgur, which is hulled wheat that has been steamed, dried, and then cracked or ground, right? Right about the bulgur, but not about the tabbouleh. A true tabbouleh should be green, meaning that it has heaps of parsley and some fresh mint in it. The bulgur is a secondary ingredient, added to the salad to absorb the juices. I've found that the right ratio of ingredients is 5 parts parsley to 3 or 4 parts bulgur. Adding more parsley causes the wholesome goodness of the wheat to be lost, and adding less just isn't the real thing. Letting the tabbouleh mixture sit for an hour or so blends the flavors nicely, but after 5 or 6 hours the onion tends to become too strong and overpowers the other flavors, so serve it within a few hours.

½ cup fine or medium-grain bulgur

6 tablespoons fresh lemon juice

⅓ cup extra-virgin olive oil

Salt

1½ cups finely chopped fresh flat-leaf parsley

2 ripe medium tomatoes, halved, seeded, and cut into small dice

4 green onions (white and light green parts), finely chopped

2 tablespoons finely chopped fresh mint leaves

In a medium bowl, mix the bulgur with 4 tablespoons of the lemon juice and set aside until the grains are tender and fluffy, 20 to 40 minutes, depending on the type of bulgur.

In a small bowl, mix the remaining 2 tablespoons lemon juice, olive oil, and salt to taste. Add the parsley, tomatoes, green onions, and mint to the bulgur. Pour the dressing over the grain mixture and toss to combine. Cover and let stand for 1 to 2 hours to allow the flavors to blend.

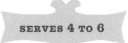

SERVES 4 TO 6

LENTIL SALAD WITH LEMON, MINT, AND FETA

SERVES 6

A humble food with ancient origins, lentils are a perfect choice for the time-challenged cook. Unlike most of the legume family, lentils cook in just 15 to 20 minutes. They make a delicious base for soup, stews, pâtés, and even salads.

In a large pot of boiling salted water, cook the lentils until just tender, about 20 minutes. Drain well. Transfer to a large bowl. Mix in the tomatoes, onion, radishes, mint, and olives.

In a medium skillet over medium heat, warm 2 tablespoons of the olive oil. Add the bell pepper and cook, stirring often, until just tender, about 5 minutes. Transfer to the bowl with the lentils. Pour the oil from the skillet into a measuring cup. Add enough additional oil to measure ½ cup. Whisk in the lemon juice. Season to taste with salt and pepper. Add the dressing to the salad, tossing to coat. Gently mix in the feta. Serve at room temperature.

1¼ cups lentils, sorted and rinsed

20 small cherry tomatoes, halved

1 cup chopped red onion

½ cup chopped radishes

¼ cup chopped fresh mint

⅓ cup chopped kalamata olives

About ½ cup extra-virgin olive oil

1 medium yellow bell pepper, chopped

3 tablespoons fresh lemon juice

Salt and freshly ground black pepper

4 ounces feta cheese, crumbled (about 1 cup)

WHEAT BERRY WALDORF

Wheat berries add a wonderful crunchy, chewy texture to this healthful apple salad. It's good served on its own, or it can be stuffed into pita pockets with some shredded lettuce for a great sandwich. To toast the nuts, heat a small, heavy skillet over medium heat. Add the nuts and toast, shaking the pan frequently, until they are fragrant, 3 to 5 minutes.

4	cups water
1	cup wheat berries, sorted and rinsed
2	medium tart apples, such as Granny Smith
1	stalk celery, chopped
2	green onions (white and light green parts), chopped
½	cup unsweetened dried cherries or cranberries
¼	cup golden raisins
¼	cup walnuts, toasted and chopped
¼	cup chopped fresh mint leaves
3	tablespoons cider vinegar
3	tablespoons orange juice
½	teaspoon grated orange zest
	Salt and freshly ground black pepper

In a large saucepan, bring the water to a boil. Stir in the wheat berries. Return to a boil. Reduce the heat, cover, and simmer until the water is absorbed and the wheat berries are tender, about 1 hour. Drain off any excess water. Spread the wheat berries out on a baking sheet to cool.

In a large bowl, combine the wheat berries, apples, celery, green onions, dried cherries, raisins, walnuts, and mint. In a measuring cup or small bowl, mix the vinegar, orange juice, and zest. Pour over the grain mixture, season to taste with salt and pepper, and toss to coat. Serve at room temperature.

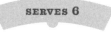

SERVES 6

CURRIED RICE SALAD

I use a technique that I call the pasta method for cooking rice for a salad. In this method you simply boil the rice in a large volume of water, just as you would pasta, until it is toothsome and cooked through but has not yet begun to fray. Then you strain the excess out. If you use this method for cooking long-grain rice, some of the starch leaches into the water and is ultimately drained off. The result is a pot of rice that is light, with grains that are separate, not sticky.

In a large pot, bring 4 quarts of water to boil. Meanwhile, heat a medium skillet over medium heat until hot, about 3 minutes. Add the rice and toast, stirring frequently, for about 5 minutes.

Add 1½ teaspoons of the salt to the boiling water and stir in the toasted rice. Return to a boil and cook, uncovered, until the rice is tender but not soft, 8 to 10 minutes for long-grain rice or about 15 minutes for basmati. Meanwhile, line a rimmed baking sheet with foil. Drain the rice in a strainer, and then spread it on the prepared baking sheet. Let cool while preparing the salad ingredients.

In a medium skillet over medium-high heat, warm the oil. Add the cauliflower, curry powder, and ½ teaspoon salt and cook, stirring constantly, for about 1 minute. Add the currants and ¼ cup water. Reduce the heat to medium and cook, stirring occasionally, until the water evaporates and the cauliflower is tender, about 3 minutes.

Transfer the cauliflower to a large bowl. Add the rice, cashews, chives, pepper, and remaining ½ teaspoon salt and toss to combine thoroughly. Let stand for 20 minutes to blend the flavors. Serve at room temperature.

1½ cups long-grain or basmati rice

2½ teaspoons salt

2 tablespoons peanut oil

½ small head cauliflower, cut into small florets (about 2 cups)

1 tablespoon curry powder

¼ cup currants

¼ cup water

½ cup raw cashews, toasted (see page 114) and chopped

3 tablespoons finely chopped chives or green onion tops

¼ teaspoon freshly ground black pepper

VEGAN

BLACK BEAN–JICAMA SALAD

Jicama (pronounced HEE-ka-mah) is often referred to as Mexican potato. It is equally good eaten raw, as in this salad, or cooked. Look for a large, bulbous root with a thin brown skin, and peel just before using. If jicama is not available, use sliced celery instead.

DRESSING

½ cup olive oil

3 tablespoons cider vinegar

2 teaspoons minced garlic

1 teaspoon ground cumin

1 teaspoon salt

1 teaspoon sugar

½ teaspoon cayenne pepper

Three 16-ounce cans black beans, drained and rinsed

2 cups diced peeled jicama

One 15-ounce can whole-kernel corn, drained

½ cup finely chopped red bell pepper

½ cup chopped fresh cilantro

Make the dressing: In a large bowl, whisk together the olive oil, vinegar, garlic, cumin, salt, sugar, and cayenne until well blended.

Add the beans, jicama, corn, bell pepper, and cilantro to the bowl and toss to mix. Cover and refrigerate for 1 hour to allow the flavors to blend. Serve chilled or at room temperature.

SERVES 4 TO 6

TUSCAN CHICKPEA SALAD

Balsamic vinegar is slightly sweeter than cider or wine vinegar. If you like a sharper bite, use 1 tablespoon red wine vinegar and 3 tablespoons balsamic vinegar. Serve with lavash (a type of cracker bread) or crusty bread.

Make the vinaigrette: In a large bowl, whisk together the olive oil, vinegar, garlic, salt, and pepper until well blended.

In a saucepan fitted with steamer basket, bring 1 inch of water to a boil. Place the green beans in the basket and steam until tender, about 10 minutes. Remove from the steamer and let cool. Add the green beans, chickpeas, olives, cucumber, tomatoes, feta cheese, and basil to the bowl with the vinaigrette and toss to mix and coat. Serve at room temperature.

BALSAMIC VINAIGRETTE

¼ cup olive oil

¼ cup balsamic vinegar

½ teaspoon minced garlic

½ teaspoon salt

¼ teaspoon freshly ground black pepper

4 ounces green beans, trimmed and cut into 1-inch lengths (1 cup)

One 16-ounce can chickpeas, drained and rinsed

12 pitted black olives, preferably kalamata

1 cup thinly sliced peeled cucumber

1½ cups diced plum tomatoes

1 cup crumbled feta cheese

¼ cup chopped fresh basil

ASIAN THREE-BEAN SALAD

Here is a light and refreshing salad that is filled with a variety of textures, including fresh soybeans, also called edamame or sweet beans. Their sweet, nutty flavor is great in salads. Edamame—both frozen and fresh, in the pod and shelled—can be found in some supermarkets, natural food stores, and Asian markets. You can also find edamame sold as whole plants at farmers' markets.

3   quarts water

1   tablespoon, plus 1 teaspoon salt

1   pound green beans, trimmed and cut into 1-inch lengths

1   pound fresh or frozen shelled edamame

8   ounces fresh bean sprouts

¼   cup Japanese pickled ginger, minced, plus 3 tablespoons liquid from the jar

2   cloves garlic, minced

2   tablespoons canola oil

2   tablespoons tamari or reduced-sodium soy sauce

2   teaspoons wasabi powder or paste

4   green onions (white and light green parts), finely chopped

In a large saucepan, bring the water to a boil over high heat. Add 1 tablespoon of the salt and the green beans and cook until crisp-tender, about 5 minutes. Add the edamame. Place the bean sprouts in a colander in the sink. When the water returns to a boil, drain the green beans and edamame over the sprouts in the colander. Rinse with cold water to stop the beans from cooking.

In a large bowl, whisk together the pickled ginger and its liquid, garlic, oil, tamari, wasabi, and the remaining 1 teaspoon salt. Add the green beans, edamame, bean sprouts, and green onions and toss well. Serve at room temperature.

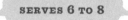

SERVES 6 TO 8

SMOKY BEAN SALAD

SERVES 4 TO 6

Molasses combines with canned chipotle chiles to give this delicious salad its smoky, robust flavor. Canned chipotle chiles packed in adobo sauce are available at Latin American markets and some supermarkets. The salad can be prepared 6 hours ahead, covered, and refrigerated. Bring it to room temperature before serving.

In a medium bowl, combine the vinegar and mustard seed and let stand at for least 1 hour and up to 4 hours.

Whisk the sun-dried tomatoes, molasses, and chiles into the vinegar mixture. Gradually whisk in the olive oil.

In a large bowl, combine the beans, red onion, and parsley. Add enough dressing to coat. Season to taste with salt and pepper. Serve at room temperature.

¼   cup white wine vinegar

1   tablespoon yellow mustard seed

¼   cup finely chopped drained oil-packed sun-dried tomatoes

3   tablespoons mild-flavored molasses

2   teaspoons finely chopped canned chipotle chiles

⅓   cup olive oil

2   cups cooked or canned Great Northern beans, drained and rinsed if canned

¾   cup finely chopped red onion

¼   cup minced fresh parsley

Salt and freshly ground black pepper

VEGAN

WARM POTATO SALAD

Potato salad once meant only the mayonnaise-based stuff served at picnics and at the deli counter, but there are many other ways to enjoy it, such as the French style. In this method you mix the potatoes with a dressing while they are still warm, giving them an extra measure of flavor. If fresh tarragon is not available, increase the parsley to 3 tablespoons and use tarragon vinegar for drizzling and in the vinaigrette. You can add about 8 ounces of blanched green beans to the salad as well.

2   pounds red-skinned potatoes
    (about 6 medium or 18 new),
    scrubbed

4   tablespoons white wine vinegar

½   teaspoon salt

½   teaspoon freshly ground
    black pepper

1   tablespoon Dijon mustard

1   medium shallot, minced

6   tablespoons olive oil

2   tablespoons finely chopped
    fresh parsley

1   tablespoon finely chopped
    fresh tarragon

Place the potatoes in a 4- to 6-quart pot and add water to cover. Bring to a boil, cover, and simmer until tender, about 20 minutes. Drain well, let the potatoes cool slightly, and peel them, if you like. Cut the potatoes (use a serrated knife if they have skins) while still warm, rinsing the knife occasionally in warm water to remove the gumminess from the starch.

Layer the warm potato slices in a medium bowl and sprinkle with 2 tablespoons of the vinegar and the salt and pepper between layers.

In a small bowl, combine the remaining 2 tablespoons vinegar, mustard, and shallot. Gradually whisk in the olive oil until well blended. Pour over the potatoes and toss to coat. Add the parsley and tarragon and toss to mix. Serve at room temperature.

SERVES 4 TO 6

NEW MEXICAN POTATO SALAD

SERVES 6

One of the great things about potato salads is that there are limitless variations on the theme. We're all familiar with the old standby featuring mayonnaise, celery, and hard-boiled eggs, but what about something a little different? This version includes jalapeños, tomatoes, cilantro, oil, and vinegar—a contemporary classic.

Place the potatoes in a 4- to 6-quart pot and add water to cover. Bring to a boil, cover, and simmer until tender, 10 to 15 minutes. Drain and rinse under cold water until slightly cooled. Cut the potatoes in half, put into a large bowl, and while still warm, gently toss with 1 tablespoon of the vinegar.

In a small bowl, mix the tomatoes, jalapeños, cilantro, shallot, garlic, olive oil, and the remaining 3 tablespoons vinegar. Add to the potatoes, toss, and serve at room temperature.

4   pounds small red-skinned or new potatoes

4   tablespoons cider vinegar

¾   cup chopped plum tomatoes

2   jalapeño chiles, seeded and minced (wear rubber gloves)

1   cup chopped fresh cilantro

2   tablespoons finely chopped shallot

1   clove garlic, minced

¼   cup extra-virgin olive oil

VEGAN

POTATO AND BEET SALAD NIÇOISE

This delicious beet-and-potato salad gets extra goodness from dill and sour cream. To get a head start, you can cook the vegetables and make the dressing a day ahead.

SERVES 4

1   pound small beets (about 8)

4   ounces haricots verts or thin green beans

1   pound small red-skinned potatoes

2   tablespoons minced shallot

2   tablespoons prepared horseradish

2   tablespoons sherry vinegar

2   tablespoons reduced-fat sour cream

1   teaspoon Dijon mustard

¼   cup extra-virgin olive oil

    Salt and freshly ground black pepper

1   tablespoon chopped fresh dill

6   hard-boiled eggs, quartered lengthwise

12 cherry tomatoes, halved

Preheat the oven to 425°F. Wrap the beets in foil and bake until tender when pierced, about 1 hour. Set aside to cool. Peel the beets and cut into 2-by-½-inch matchsticks or small wedges.

Bring a medium saucepan of lightly salted water to a boil. Add the beans and cook until tender, about 4 minutes. Using a slotted spoon, transfer the beans to a colander and rinse under cold running water; pat dry with paper towels. Pour off all but 2 inches of the water from the pan and place a steamer basket inside. Add the potatoes, cover, and steam until tender, about 18 minutes. Let cool slightly, then cut the potatoes into quarters.

In a medium bowl, combine the shallot, horseradish, vinegar, sour cream, and mustard. Slowly whisk in the olive oil until emulsified. Season to taste with salt and pepper.

Just before serving, stir the dill into the dressing. In a large bowl, toss the beets, beans, and potatoes with ¼ cup of the dressing. Mound the salad on plates and garnish with the eggs and tomatoes. Pass the remaining dressing separately.

MEDITERRANEAN COUSCOUS SALAD

SERVES 6

*Lightness and fluffiness are the charms of this couscous salad.
Look for couscous in the rice section of large supermarkets.*

In a medium saucepan, bring the broth to a boil. Add the couscous. Remove from the heat, cover, and let stand for 5 minutes. Transfer to a large bowl. Fluff with a fork and let cool.

Add the green onion, tomatoes, basil, olive oil, vinegar, and red pepper flakes to the couscous and toss to mix. Season to taste with salt and pepper. Serve at room temperature.

2¼ cups Rich Vegetable Broth (page 109) or canned broth

One 10-ounce box couscous

1 cup chopped green onion (white and light green parts)

1 cup diced plum tomatoes

⅓ cup thinly sliced fresh basil

½ cup extra-virgin olive oil

¼ cup balsamic vinegar

¼ teaspoon red pepper flakes

Salt and freshly ground black pepper

VEGAN

COLD SESAME NOODLES

The nutty flavor and chewy texture of buckwheat (soba) noodles are highlighted in this light and refreshing salad. It's guaranteed to perk you up on a hot summer day.

SERVES 6

12 ounces dried buckwheat noodles (soba)

2 cups peeled and julienned carrots

2 cups julienned snow peas, strings and ends removed

1½ cups julienned red bell pepper

½ cup tamari or reduced-sodium soy sauce

6 tablespoons rice vinegar

¼ cup dark (Asian) sesame oil

3 tablespoons chopped green onion (white and light green parts)

2 tablespoons rice wine (mirin)

2 tablespoons sugar

1½ tablespoons minced peeled fresh ginger

In a large pot, bring 2½ quarts of water to a boil. Add the noodles, stir gently, and reduce the heat to medium. Simmer until tender but still firm to the bite (al dente), about 6 minutes. Drain well, rinse under cold running water, and drain again. Transfer to a large, shallow serving bowl.

Add the carrots, snow peas, and bell pepper to the noodles. In a small bowl, combine the tamari, vinegar, sesame oil, green onion, rice wine, sugar, and ginger. Stir until the sugar is dissolved. Pour over the noodles and vegetables and toss to coat. Serve at room temperature.

MINT CUCUMBER SALAD

SERVES 4

Cucumber salads are refreshing and offer a cooling note to many spicy meals. But more often than not, by the time you eat a cucumber salad the cucumbers have gone soft and watery, losing their appealing crunch and diluting the dressing. The standard method for ridding watery vegetables, such as cucumbers, of unwanted moisture is to salt them. The salt draws out the liquid from the vegetable, leaving it crisp.

Peel the cucumbers, halve them lengthwise, and scoop out the seeds. Stack the halves flat side down and slice diagonally ¼ inch thick. Toss with the 1 tablespoon salt in a strainer set over bowl; weight with a water-filled, gallon-sized zipper-lock freezer bag, sealed tight. Drain for at least 1 hour and up to 3 hours.

In a medium bowl, whisk the yogurt, olive oil, mint, garlic, cumin, and salt and pepper to taste. Add the drained cucumbers and toss to coat. Serve chilled, adjusting the seasonings if necessary.

3 medium cucumbers

1 tablespoon salt, plus more to taste

1 cup plain low-fat yogurt

2 tablespoons extra-virgin olive oil

¼ cup finely chopped fresh mint

1 clove garlic, minced

½ teaspoon ground cumin

Freshly ground black pepper

CAESAR SALAD

SERVES 4 TO 6

A traditional Caesar salad contains coddled (partly cooked) eggs. However, I wanted a rich and creamy Caesar salad that's easy to prepare and doesn't use eggs—or anchovies. This recipe relies on soft tofu instead of raw or coddled eggs. The tofu lends a wonderfully creamy texture and mellow flavor to the dressing. You must use soft tofu for the best results, and be sure to drain it well. To do this, simply pour off the water that the tofu is packed in, then wrap it in a cloth or paper towel and let it sit on toweling to force out the excess water. This step is important so the tofu won't dilute the dressing. For a special treat, you can omit the croutons and use toasted walnuts instead. Their sweetness is a perfect foil to the tangy dressing.

GARLIC CROUTONS

2   cloves garlic, minced

¼   teaspoon salt

2   cups cubed white bread from a baguette (½-inch cubes)

3   tablespoons extra-virgin olive oil

⅓   cup soft tofu, well drained

3   tablespoons fresh lemon juice

1   teaspoon vegetarian Worcestershire sauce

¼   teaspoon salt

8   grinds black pepper

1   clove garlic, minced

⅓   cup extra-virgin olive oil

2   medium heads romaine lettuce, large outer leaves removed, torn into 1½-inch pieces (about 10 cups, lightly packed)

⅓   cup grated Parmesan cheese

Make the croutons: Preheat the oven to 350°F. In a small bowl, mix the garlic and salt and let stand for 20 minutes. Spread the bread cubes in a single layer on a baking sheet. Drizzle the olive oil evenly over the bread and toss to coat. Bake for 12 minutes, or until golden. Cool on the baking sheet to room temperature.

In a food processor, combine the tofu, lemon juice, Worcestershire sauce, salt, pepper, and garlic and process until well blended, scraping down the sides of the bowl as needed. With the motor running, add the olive oil in a slow, steady stream, processing until smooth.

Place the lettuce in a large bowl. Drizzle with half of the dressing, then toss to coat lightly. Sprinkle with the cheese, remaining dressing, and croutons, and toss to coat well. Divide among individual plates; serve immediately.

ITALIAN BREAD AND TOMATO SALAD

Panzanella, as this classic Italian dish is called, is a time-honored way to use up stale bread, but fresh bread works, too.

1 small loaf crusty Italian bread (about 12 ounces), sliced ½ inch thick

½ cup extra-virgin olive oil

¼ cup red wine vinegar

1 clove garlic, minced

1½ teaspoons salt

½ teaspoon freshly ground black pepper

2¾ pounds firm ripe tomatoes (about 8 medium), cut into large chunks

½ cup thinly sliced red onion

1 cup thinly sliced fresh basil

Put the bread slices in a large bowl. Add cold water to cover. Let soak for 10 minutes. In another large bowl, whisk together the olive oil, vinegar, garlic, salt, and pepper until well blended.

Drain the bread and press out the excess water. Tear into small pieces and add to the oil and vinegar mixture. Add the tomatoes and onion. Toss to mix. Let stand at room temperature for at least 30 minutes. Stir in the sliced basil just before serving.

 SERVES 8

ARUGULA AND PEAR SALAD

SERVES 8

In this salad, the peppery taste of arugula contrasts nicely with the creamy butteriness of the pears. I like to mix arugula with milder-tasting greens, such as butter lettuce. But you could use only arugula here, if you prefer.

In a small bowl, whisk together the shallot, olive oil, broth, vinegar, mustard, salt, and pepper.

Place the pear slices in a large bowl. Spoon 1 tablespoon of the dressing over the pears and toss to coat. Add the remaining dressing, arugula, and lettuce and toss to coat. Divide the salad among 8 serving plates. Top each with some of the walnuts.

2   tablespoons minced shallot

3   tablespoons extra-virgin olive oil

3   tablespoons Rich Vegetable Broth (page 109) or canned broth

1½ tablespoons balsamic vinegar

½   teaspoon Dijon mustard

¼   teaspoon salt

¼   teaspoon freshly ground black pepper

2   firm, ripe Bosc or Anjou pears, each cut lengthwise into 16 slices

4   cups arugula, tough stems removed

1   head butter lettuce, torn into bite-size pieces

½   cup chopped walnuts, toasted (see page 114)

VEGAN

WILTED SPINACH SALAD

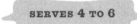

SERVES 4 TO 6

5   ounces fresh baby spinach leaves (about 6 cups)

3   tablespoons extra-virgin olive oil

2   tablespoons minced shallot

1   clove garlic, minced

¼   teaspoon dried oregano

¼   teaspoon salt

⅛   teaspoon freshly ground black pepper

⅛   teaspoon sugar

1   tablespoon fresh lemon juice

¼   cup feta cheese, crumbled

2   tablespoons thinly sliced black olives

To make a good spinach salad, it's essential to start with good greens. The quality of spinach can vary. Mostly it is sold in plastic bags because it keeps better, but this prepackaged stuff is often tired and can have a strong taste. Once you've tasted fresh, healthy spinach, it's hard to go back to bags. So when buying spinach, look for bins or bushels filled with loose spinach leaves, or those tied into bundles. Make sure the leaves are stiff and fresh look-ing—not watery or limp—with no signs of deterioration.

Tossing fresh spinach leaves in a hot vinaigrette really brings out their flavor. But nothing can devastate a spinach salad more thoroughly than gritty greens, so be sure to follow the steps for properly cleaning them (facing page).

Place the spinach in a large bowl. In a small skillet over medium heat, warm the olive oil. Add the shallot, garlic, oregano, salt, pepper, and sugar and cook, stirring often, until the shallot is slightly softened, 2 to 3 minutes. Stir in the lemon juice.

Pour the warm dressing over the spinach. Add the feta and olives and toss gently until the spinach is wilted. Serve right away.

CLEANING SPINACH

Fine sand, which is hard to see, often clings to fresh spinach leaves, so it's important to wash them thoroughly. Remove and discard any bruised or wilted leaves. Fill the sink two thirds full with cold water. Tear off the stems and the thicker ribs from the leaves and place them in the sink without crowding. Gently swish the leaves around in the sink to loosen the grit and dirt. Allow the spinach to sit for 5 to 10 minutes, depending on how dirty or dehydrated the leaves are. Place a large colander over a kitchen towel. Lift the greens from the sink to the colander and let drain for 5 minutes. Make sure the leaves are clean by tasting a few.

FRESH FRUIT SALAD WITH LIME-GINGER DRESSING

This salad is simple to prepare, light, and colorful. Be sure to use the freshest fruit you can get your hands on for the best possible flavor.

½   cup plain low-fat yogurt

¼   cup honey

¼   cup fresh lime juice

1   teaspoon grated lime zest

1   tablespoon grated peeled fresh ginger

2   cups diced cantaloupe

2   cups diced honeydew melon

2   cups seedless red or green grapes

2   cups diced pineapple

1½ cups diced papaya

1   cup halved hulled strawberries

In a small bowl, mix the yogurt, honey, lime juice, lime zest, and ginger. In a large bowl, combine all of the fruit with the dressing and toss to mix. Let stand for 15 minutes to blend the flavors.

If not serving right away, cover the dressing and fruit separately and chill for up to 6 hours. When ready to serve, add the dressing to the fruit and mix gently.

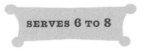

SERVES 6 TO 8

ROASTED GARLIC AND BASIL DRESSING

MAKES 1¼ CUPS

This dressing is great over blanched fresh vegetables or pasta served at room temperature.

Preheat the oven to 350°F. Place the garlic in a small baking pan and brush with 1 teaspoon of the olive oil. Roast until golden and soft, about 15 minutes. Set aside to cool.

Peel the garlic and transfer to a blender or food processor. Add the remaining olive oil, green onions, tomatoes, basil, lemon juice, and vinegar and process until well blended. Use right away or store, covered, in the refrigerator for up to 5 days.

3   to 4 large cloves garlic, unpeeled

¼   cup extra-virgin olive oil

3   green onions (white part only), chopped

2   medium tomatoes, chopped and excess liquid drained

⅓   cup chopped fresh basil

3   tablespoons fresh lemon juice

2   tablespoons white wine vinegar

VEGAN

TOMATO BALSAMIC DRESSING

This dressing is a treasure to have in the refrigerator for quick salad making. As a general rule, figure on 2 tablespoons of dressing for each salad serving.

¼ cup balsamic vinegar

¼ cup red wine vinegar

3 tablespoons tomato paste

1 tablespoon Dijon mustard

1 tablespoon sugar

1 clove garlic, minced

½ teaspoon salt

¼ teaspoon freshly ground black pepper

1 cup olive oil

In a blender or food processor, combine the vinegars, tomato paste, mustard, sugar, garlic, salt, and pepper and process until smooth. With the machine running, add the olive oil in a slow, steady stream until well blended and thickened. Use right away or store, covered, in the refrigerator for up to 5 days. If chilled, bring to room temperature and stir well before using.

MAKES ABOUT 2 CUPS

CREAMY ROASTED RED PEPPER DRESSING

MAKES ABOUT 2½ CUPS

Try this on a salad of new potatoes, green peas, and sweet onions, or with a combination of chilled green beans and chickpeas.

In a blender or food processor, combine the roasted peppers, egg substitute, vinegar, green onions, salt, and basil and process until smooth. With the motor running, add the olive oil in a slow, steady stream until smooth and thickened. Use right away or store, covered, in the refrigerator for up to 5 days. If chilled, bring to room temperature and stir well before using.

One 7-ounce jar roasted red peppers, drained and patted dry

¼ cup egg substitute

2 tablespoons red wine vinegar

2 green onions (white and light green parts), chopped

½ teaspoon salt

½ teaspoon dried basil

1½ cups extra-virgin olive oil

VEGAN

LEMON TOFU DRESSING

This dressing is wonderfully rich and creamy due to the tofu and tahini; it also gets a nice tang from the lemon juice. Extremely versatile, it's great on a simple green salad or as a dipping sauce for crudités.

One 10-ounce package firm silken tofu, well drained

¼ cup fresh lemon juice

¼ cup tamari or reduced-sodium soy sauce

¼ cup tahini (sesame paste)

¼ cup canola oil

¼ cup packed chopped fresh flat-leaf parsley

In a blender or food processor, combine the tofu, lemon juice, tamari, tahini, oil, and parsley and process until smooth and creamy. Use right away or store, covered, in the refrigerator for up to 5 days. If chilled, bring to room temperature and stir well before using.

**MAKES ABOUT
2 CUPS**

FRESH ORANGE DRESSING

MAKES ABOUT 1¼ CUPS

Not only is this dressing great on a tossed salad, it's also tasty drizzled over steamed or grilled vegetables.

In a blender or food processor, combine the oil, orange juice, vinegar, parsley, orange zest, sugar, paprika, and Worcestershire sauce and process until well blended. Season to taste with salt and pepper. Use right away or store, covered, in the refrigerator for up to 5 days. If chilled, bring to room temperature and stir well before using.

½ cup vegetable oil

⅓ cup fresh orange juice

¼ cup white wine vinegar

1 tablespoon chopped fresh parsley

1 teaspoon grated orange zest

1 teaspoon sugar

½ teaspoon paprika

¼ teaspoon vegetarian Worcestershire sauce

Salt and freshly ground black pepper

VEGAN

chapter

5

SENSATIONAL SANDWICHES

THERE'S

almost no place or time
that you cannot enjoy a sandwich:
at your desk, in the car, on a picnic
blanket, at the beach, or during a
meeting. And sandwiches are more
than just hand-held meals; these
recipes add health to the mix to
create culinary stars that are
as easy to make as they
are to eat.

TANDOORI LENTIL BURGERS WITH RAITA

SERVES 6

These burgers can be served on a bun or with couscous and steamed cauliflower for a simple dinner. If you have some raita left over, it's great served with any kind of curry dish.

RAITA

1   medium cucumber, well chilled

1   cup plain nonfat yogurt

2   tablespoons finely chopped fresh mint

1   medium jalapeño chile, seeded and minced (wear rubber gloves)

Salt and freshly ground black pepper

BURGERS

2   cups water

¾   cup dried red lentils, sorted and rinsed

¾   teaspoon salt

1   cup chopped onion

½   cup finely diced peeled carrot

3   cloves garlic, chopped

2   cups chopped button or cremini mushrooms

1   teaspoon dried marjoram

¼   teaspoon freshly ground black pepper

⅓   cup dried bread crumbs

1   tablespoon fresh lemon juice

2   large egg whites

1   tablespoon vegetable oil

6   hamburger buns

Curly lettuce leaves

6   slices tomato, ¼ inch thick

Make the raita: Peel the cucumber and cut in half lengthwise. Using a spoon, remove the seeds and pulp. Slice thinly. In a small bowl, combine the cucumber, yogurt, mint, and jalapeño. Season to taste with salt and pepper. Cover and refrigerate until ready to use.

Make the burgers: In a medium saucepan, combine the water, lentils, and ¼ teaspoon of the salt. Bring to a boil. Cover, reduce the heat to medium-low, and simmer until the lentils are tender, about 20 minutes. Drain and set aside.

Heat a large, nonstick skillet coated with vegetable oil spray over medium-high heat. Add the onion, carrot, and garlic and cook, stirring occasionally, for 3 minutes. Add the remaining ½ teaspoon salt, mushrooms, marjoram, and pepper and cook for 3 minutes. Transfer to a large bowl and let stand for 5 minutes. Add the lentils, bread crumbs, lemon juice, and egg whites and mix well. Cover and chill for 30 minutes to firm up the mixture.

Divide the lentil mixture into 6 equal portions, shaping each into a ½-inch-thick patty. In a nonstick skillet over medium heat, warm the vegetable oil. Add the lentil patties and cook until golden brown, about 5 minutes on each side.

Line the bottom half of each bun with lettuce and top each with a burger, 1 tablespoon raita, 1 tomato slice, and the top half of the bun. Serve immediately.

TOFU-WALNUT BURGERS

Tofu and nuts turn these humble burgers into a protein powerhouse. Keep in mind that even the best sandwiches are only as good as the bread that holds them. Fortunately, good bread is getting easier to find. Supermarket shelves now overflow with whole-grain breads and rolls. The burgers can be made 4 up to hours ahead; cover and chill.

One 12-ounce package firm tofu, drained, patted dry, and cut into 1-inch-thick slices

2 teaspoons vegetable oil

½ cup grated peeled carrot

½ cup thinly sliced green onion (white and light green parts)

2 teaspoons minced peeled fresh ginger

1 clove garlic, minced

½ cup walnuts, toasted (page 114) and finely chopped

1 large egg white, lightly beaten

4 teaspoons tamari or reduced-sodium soy sauce

1 teaspoon dark (Asian) sesame oil

Salt and freshly ground black pepper

4 sesame seed buns, toasted

1 cup alfalfa sprouts

Wrap the tofu in a doubled dish towel. Place on a work surface. Weigh down with a board topped with food cans or weights for 1 hour. Squeeze the towel-wrapped tofu to extract as much liquid as possible. Transfer to a medium bowl. Using a fork, mash into small pieces.

In a medium nonstick skillet over medium heat, warm the vegetable oil. Add the carrot, green onion, ginger, and garlic and cook, stirring often, until slightly softened, about 3 minutes. Remove from the heat and let cool. Add the carrot mixture, walnuts, egg white, tamari, and sesame oil to the tofu, mixing to blend. Season to taste with salt and pepper. Shape the mixture into four ½-inch-thick patties.

If grilling, coat a grill rack with vegetable oil spray, then preheat the grill to medium heat. If sautéing, coat a large, nonstick skillet with vegetable oil spray and heat over medium heat. Lightly coat the patties on both sides with vegetable oil spray. Place on the grill or in the skillet and cook until golden brown, 3 to 4 minutes per side. Place 1 burger on each bun bottom. Top each with some sprouts and the bun top and serve.

SERVES 4

PAN BAGNA

A Provençale specialty, pan bagna might be one of the world's best sandwiches. The words translate as "bathed bread." The sandwich is made by splitting open crusty French bread and then filling it with a salade Niçoise of sorts, whose delicious olive oil dressing seeps into, or "bathes," the bread. It's a great sandwich to pack for a picnic.

Slice the baguette in half horizontally. Remove some of the interior of the bread to create a hollow space for the vegetables. Transfer the crumbs to a blender or food processor and process until finely chopped; set aside.

In a large bowl, whisk together the lemon juice, olive oil, and garlic. Stir in the reserved bread crumbs, tomato, bell pepper, green onions, olives, capers, and thyme. Season to taste with salt and pepper. Spoon over the bottom half of the loaf. Cover with the top half. Slice and serve.

1	French baguette, about 16 inches long
¼	cup fresh lemon juice
1	tablespoon olive oil
1	clove garlic, minced
1	large, ripe tomato, chopped
1	red bell pepper, chopped
2	green onions (white and light green parts), chopped
2	tablespoons chopped black olives, preferably kalamata
1	tablespoon drained capers
1	teaspoon chopped fresh thyme, or ¼ teaspoon dried
	Salt and freshly ground black pepper

VEGAN

CHICKPEA BURGERS WITH TAHINI SAUCE

SERVES 8

Cumin, garlic, parsley, and mint give these chickpeas burgers the flavor of the Middle East. A lively dressing of sesame and lemon adds a nice flavor boost.

TAHINI SAUCE

½ cup tahini

¼ cup fresh lemon juice

2 green onions (white and light green parts), finely chopped

¼ cup water

Salt and freshly ground black pepper

Pinch of cayenne pepper

Two 16-ounce cans chickpeas, rinsed and well drained

3 tablespoons olive oil, plus more for brushing

1½ teaspoons salt

¼ teaspoon freshly ground black pepper

1 tablespoon grated lemon zest

¼ cup finely chopped fresh parsley

¼ cup finely chopped fresh mint

2 tablespoons tamari or reduced-sodium soy sauce

1 cup finely chopped red onion

1½ teaspoons ground cumin

3 cloves garlic, minced

⅓ cup unbleached all-purpose flour

8 pita pocket breads

2 cups shredded lettuce

Make the tahini sauce: In a blender or food processor, combine the tahini, lemon juice, green onions, water, salt and pepper to taste, and cayenne. Process until smooth. If the sauce is too thick, thin with a little more water or lemon juice. Set aside.

In a food processor, combine the chickpeas, 2 tablespoons of the olive oil, 1 teaspoon of the salt, and the black pepper, and process until finely ground. Add the lemon zest, parsley, mint, and tamari and process until just blended. Transfer to a medium bowl.

In a large, nonstick skillet over medium heat, warm the remaining 1 tablespoon of oil. Add the onion and cook, stirring often, until softened, about 5 minutes. Reduce the heat to medium-low. Add the cumin, remaining ½ teaspoon salt, and garlic and cook, stirring often, for 5 minutes. Add the onion mixture and flour to the chickpea mixture and mix well.

Divide the mixture into 8 equal portions, shaping each into a ½-inch-thick patty. If grilling, coat the grill rack with vegetable oil spray, then preheat the grill to medium. If sautéing, coat a large, nonstick skillet with vegetable spray and heat over medium heat. Lightly coat the patties on both sides with vegetable oil spray. Place the burgers on the grill or in the skillet and cook until golden brown and heated through, about 5 minutes per side. Fill the pita pockets with lettuce and a burger, drizzle with tahini sauce, and serve.

VEGAN

NO-EGG SALAD PITAS

Tahini, sweet pickle relish, bell pepper, and onion transform tofu into a delicious sandwich filling that is reminiscent of egg salad.

½ cup firm tofu, drained

2 tablespoons tahini

2 teaspoons tamari or reduced-sodium soy sauce

1 teaspoon cider vinegar

1 green onion (white and light green parts), chopped

⅓ cup chopped red bell pepper

2 tablespoons chopped sweet pickle relish

4 whole-wheat pita pocket breads

1 cup shredded lettuce

Place the tofu in a medium bowl and mash coarsely with a fork. Add the tahini, tamari, and vinegar and mix well. Stir in the green onion, bell pepper, and relish. Fill the pita pockets with the tofu mixture and lettuce. Serve right away.

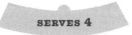

SERVES 4

"SAUSAGE" AND PEPPER SANDWICHES

SERVES 4 TO 6

Inspired by the classic Italian dish, these hot sandwiches make a great supper on a busy weeknight. Serve with a tossed salad.

In a large skillet over medium heat, warm the olive oil. Add the "sausage" and cook, turning often, until golden, about 5 minutes. Add the onion, bell peppers, and garlic and cook, stirring often, until the vegetables are softened, about 10 minutes. Add the tomatoes, parsley, oregano, and salt and pepper to taste and mix well.

Cover and cook until the flavors are blended, about 5 minutes. Split the rolls. Spoon the "sausage" and pepper mixture into the rolls and serve.

VEGAN

1   tablespoon olive oil

1   pound soy Italian "sausage" links, cut into thirds

1   large onion, quartered and thinly sliced

6   medium bell peppers (3 each green and red), cut into thin strips

2   cloves garlic, minced

1   cup chopped plum tomatoes

3   tablespoons finely chopped fresh parsley

½   teaspoon dried oregano

    Salt and freshly ground black pepper

4   to 6 kaiser rolls

BULGUR-STUFFED PITAS

I consider bulgur the perfect food: thoroughly versatile, delicious, filling, low in fat, and packed with nutrients. Besides having a wide range of B vitamins, grains provide ample iron, calcium, phosphorous, potassium, magnesium, and zinc.

1½ cups water

1 cup fine or medium-grain bulgur

1 teaspoon curry powder

1 teaspoon balsamic vinegar

2 cloves garlic, minced

½ cup thinly sliced green onions (white and light green parts)

½ cup golden raisins

1 medium red bell pepper, finely chopped

½ cup crumbled feta cheese (optional)

4 whole-wheat pita pocket breads, cut in half

Green-leaf or butter lettuce leaves

Preheat the oven to 300°F. In a medium saucepan, bring the water to a boil. Stir in the bulgur. Remove from the heat, cover, and let stand until tender but still a bit chewy, 10 to 15 minutes.

Transfer the bulgur to a large bowl. Add the curry powder, vinegar, garlic, green onions, raisins, and bell pepper, stirring well. Stir in the feta, if desired. Line the pita pockets with lettuce. Stuff the bulgur mixture into the pita pockets.

SERVES 4

SLOPPY JOES

For this recipe, you squeeze the tofu in your hand to remove the water. This will give it a texture similar to cottage cheese. This technique works great for making tofu fillings, scrambled tofu, and tofu salads.

Cut the tofu into small pieces (1 to 2 inches). Gently squeeze one piece at time over a sink until it resembles cottage cheese, then crumble it into a medium bowl.

In a large skillet over medium heat, warm the olive oil. Add the garlic, bell pepper, and onion and cook, stirring often, until softened, about 5 minutes. Add the crumbled tofu and tamari and cook, stirring often, until the tofu begins to brown, about 5 minutes.

Stir in the tomato sauce, chili powder, and cumin until well mixed. Cook, stirring occasionally, until heated through and the flavors are well blended, about 2 minutes. Spoon the mixture over the toasted buns and serve hot.

1   pound extra-firm tofu, drained

1   tablespoon olive oil

2   cloves garlic, minced

1   medium green bell pepper, chopped

½   cup chopped onion

2   tablespoons tamari or reduced-sodium soy sauce

1½ cups tomato sauce

1   tablespoon chili powder

½   teaspoon ground cumin

4   hamburger buns, split and toasted

VEGAN

PAN-GRILLED TOFU
WITH HORSERADISH MAYO

*In about 20 minutes you can go from looking at a package of tofu
in your refrigerator to sitting down to enjoy a savory sandwich.*

HORSERADISH MAYO

½   cup prepared horseradish

2   teaspoons fresh lemon juice

2   tablespoons Dijon mustard

6   tablespoons soy mayonnaise

    Salt and freshly ground
    black pepper

PAN-GRILLED TOFU

1   pound firm tofu, drained and
    sliced lengthwise into 4 pieces

½   cup tamari or reduced-sodium
    soy sauce

3   tablespoons vegetable oil

8   slices sourdough bread,
    lightly toasted

4   leaves green lettuce

4   slices tomato

5   ounces alfalfa sprouts

Make the mayo: In a small bowl, whisk together the horseradish, lemon juice, mustard, and mayonnaise. Season to taste with salt and pepper. Cover and refrigerate until ready to serve.

Make the tofu: Put the tofu on a plate and spoon the tamari over it. Turn the tofu until coated. In a large skillet over medium-high heat, warm the oil. Remove the tofu from the tamari mixture and cook until browned, 3 to 5 minutes on each side.

Spread a small amount of the horseradish mayo on the toasted bread slices. Place a lettuce leaf, some tofu, a tomato slice, and some sprouts on 4 slices of the bread. Close the sandwiches, cut in half, and serve.

SERVES 4

BARBECUED TOFU SANDWICH

SERVES 4

Draining tofu simply means pouring off the water that the tofu is packed in. Pressing means wrapping it in cloth or paper towels and letting it sit on toweling, weighted down, to force out the excess water within. There are several reasons for pressing the water out of tofu, including to make it firmer and chewier, to make room for it to absorb other liquids and seasonings, such as marinades and spice rubs, and to avoid diluting sauces and dressings.

To press the tofu, wrap the entire piece in an absorbent dish towel. Set on a cutting board and weight it down with something heavy, like a large can of tomatoes. Rest one end of the board on a plate so the board tilts toward the sink. The excess water will drain off and flow into the sink. Drain for about 30 minutes.

Cut the tofu into eight ½-inch-thick slices. Sprinkle with salt and pepper. Dredge the tofu slices in the flour, shaking off the excess. In a large, nonstick skillet over medium-high heat, warm the oil. Add the tofu, brush half of the barbecue sauce over it, and cook for 2 minutes. Turn the slices over, brush with the remaining barbecue sauce, and cook until the tofu is glazed, about 3 minutes. Place 2 tofu slices on the bottom half of each bun; cover with the tops of the buns and serve.

One 14-ounce package firm tofu, drained

Salt and freshly ground black pepper

⅓ cup unbleached all-purpose flour

1 teaspoon vegetable oil

1 cup prepared barbecue sauce

4 hamburger buns, split and toasted

VEGAN

ENGLISH MUFFIN MELTS

I refer to this sandwich as an updated version of grilled cheese. Nothing could be simpler to make for lunch or dinner. Add a simple green salad and the meal is complete.

4   English muffins, split

2   large beefsteak tomatoes, each cut into 4 slices, about ¾ inch thick, and seeded

Salt and freshly ground black pepper

2   cups coarsely grated Gruyère cheese

⅓   cup chopped fresh basil

¼   cup dried bread crumbs

2   cloves garlic, minced

Preheat the oven to 375°F. Place the muffin halves on a baking sheet and toast until golden. Put 1 slice of tomato on top of each muffin half and season to taste with salt and pepper. Bake for 17 to 20 minutes, until the tomatoes are softened.

In a medium bowl, mix the cheese, basil, bread crumbs, and garlic and season to taste with salt and pepper. Mound the cheese mixture on top of the tomatoes and continue baking until the cheese is melted, about 5 minutes. Serve immediately.

SERVES 4

NEW MEXICAN BEAN BURRITOS

Beans may be the best substitute for beef the world has ever known. They're economical, costing just pennies per serving. And just ½ cup of these "meaty" morsels provides around 15 percent of the protein you need each day, with very little saturated fat.

In a large, nonstick skillet over medium heat, warm the oil. Add the onion and bell pepper and cook, stirring occasionally, until the vegetables begin to soften, about 5 minutes. Add the garlic, chili powder, cumin, oregano, and coriander and cook, stirring, for 1 minute. Stir in the canned tomatoes, beans, and salt and pepper to taste. Reduce the heat to medium-low and simmer until most of the liquid has evaporated, stirring occasionally, for about 5 minutes. Remove from the heat.

Meanwhile, in a saucepan or skillet over medium-low heat, rewarm the rice if necessary.

In a large skillet over medium heat, warm each tortilla until soft and flexible, about 1 minute per side. Place each tortilla on a plate. Spoon some of the black bean mixture down the center of each. Top each with some rice, diced tomatoes, cheese, and red onion. Fold one end of each tortilla over the filling, then fold one side over the filling and roll each into a bundle. Serve immediately.

SERVES 4

1	tablespoon vegetable oil
1	medium onion, thinly sliced
½	medium green bell pepper, chopped
1	clove garlic, minced
1½	teaspoons chili powder
1	teaspoon ground cumin
1	teaspoon dried oregano
½	teaspoon ground coriander
1	cup canned crushed tomatoes in purée
One 16-ounce can black beans, drained and rinsed	
	Salt and freshly ground black pepper
2	cups cooked long-grain rice
4	flour tortillas, 9 to 10 inches in diameter
2	medium tomatoes, diced
1	cup grated cheddar or Monterey Jack cheese
¼	cup finely chopped red onion

SOUTHWESTERN TOFU BURRITOS

Tofu has a custard-like texture and is available in soft, firm, and extra-firm varieties; firm is preferable here. Serve these hearty burritos topped with purchased salsa and some plain nonfat yogurt.

4   flour tortillas, 7 to 8 inches in diameter

1   tablespoon olive oil

½   cup chopped onion

1½ teaspoons ground cumin

½   teaspoon ground turmeric

12 ounces firm tofu, crumbled (about 2 cups)

1   cup chopped red bell pepper

1½ tablespoons minced seeded jalapeño chile (wear rubber gloves)

1   clove garlic, minced

½   cup grated mozzarella cheese

    Salt and freshly ground black pepper

1   cup packed thinly sliced romaine lettuce

6   tablespoons chopped fresh cilantro

4   lime wedges

Preheat the oven to 350°F. Wrap the tortillas in foil. Place in the oven until heated through, about 15 minutes.

Meanwhile, heat the olive oil in a large, nonstick skillet over medium-high heat. Add the onion and sauté until golden, about 5 minutes. Add the cumin and turmeric and cook, stirring, for 30 seconds. Add the tofu, bell pepper, jalapeño, and garlic and sauté until heated through, about 3 minutes. Add the cheese and stir until melted, about 1 minute. Season to taste with salt and pepper.

Place each tortilla on a plate. Spoon some of the tofu mixture down the center of each tortilla, dividing it evenly. Top with the lettuce and cilantro. Squeeze the juice from the lime wedges over the filling. Fold one end of tortilla over the filling, then fold one side over the filling and roll each into a bundle. Serve immediately.

SERVES 4

CARAMELIZED ONION QUESADILLAS

Quesadillas are Mexico's answer to the American grilled cheese sandwich. Serve these with your favorite salsa or guacamole for dipping.

In a medium skillet over medium heat, melt 2 tablespoons of the butter. Add the onion, brown sugar, and vinegar and cook, stirring occasionally, until the onion is golden brown, about 25 minutes. Remove from the heat. Cool to room temperature.

Preheat the oven to 350°F. Place the tortillas on a work surface. Sprinkle cheese over half of each tortilla, dividing it evenly. Sprinkle the sautéed onion over the cheese. Season to taste with pepper. Fold the other half of each tortilla over the cheese mixture. Melt the remaining 2 tablespoons butter and brush the tortillas with some of it.

Brush a heavy, large skillet with some of the remaining melted butter. Place over medium-high heat. Working in batches, cook the quesadillas just until brown spots appear, brushing the skillet with butter between batches, about 2 minutes per side. Transfer the quesadillas to a heavy, large baking sheet. Bake for about 5 minutes, until the tortillas are golden and the cheese melts.

Transfer the quesadillas to a work surface. Cut each into 6 wedges. Arrange on a platter and serve hot.

4 tablespoons (½ stick) butter

1 large onion, thinly sliced

1 tablespoon light brown sugar

¼ teaspoon white wine vinegar

4 flour tortillas, 10 inches in diameter

1½ cups grated smoked Gouda cheese

Freshly ground black pepper

VEGETABLE PESTO WRAPS

Americans have gone wrap crazy, and with good reason. These portable packages provide a quick meal for those on the go, and the combinations of fillings—from healthy to decadent—are limitless. Prepare all of your sandwich ingredients before you warm the tortillas.

1½ cups part-skim ricotta cheese

3 tablespoons pesto (page 96)

½ cups chopped green or red bell pepper

3 radishes, finely diced

1 stalk celery, finely diced

2 tablespoons chopped fresh parsley

1½ tablespoons minced red onion

1½ teaspoons fresh lemon juice

Salt and freshly ground black pepper

4 flour tortillas, 9 to 10 inches in diameter

4 cups loosely packed mixed greens

2 medium tomatoes, thinly sliced

In a medium bowl, combine the ricotta, pesto, bell pepper, radishes, celery, parsley, onion, and lemon juice and mix well. Season to taste with salt and pepper. Cover and refrigerate for at least 2 hours or up to 24 hours.

In a large skillet over medium heat, warm each tortilla just until soft and flexible, about 1 minute per side. Place some greens down the center of each tortilla. Top with tomato slices, overlapping them slightly; season lightly with salt and pepper. Spoon the pesto-cheese mixture over the tomatoes, dividing it evenly. Fold one end of each tortilla over the filling, then fold one side over the filling and roll each into a bundle. Serve immediately.

SERVES 4

RADICAL REUBENS

Ever since New York City delicatessen owner Arthur Reuben layered a mountain of ham, Swiss cheese, and sauerkraut between two slices of rye bread in 1914 (reportedly for Annette Seelos, the star of a Charlie Chaplin film), the Reuben has satisfied hungry customers. And now, with this version that uses tempeh bacon strips, vegetarians can enjoy this famous sandwich as well. The tempeh strips have a smoky-nutty flavor that goes particularly well with tangy sauerkraut. Sauerkraut is naturally low in fat and calories—just be sure to drain it well to avoid a soggy sandwich.

Preheat the oven to 350°F. Lightly coat a baking sheet with vegetable oil spray. Add the tempeh strips in a single layer and bake for about 20 minutes, until crisp. Set aside.

Place 4 slices of the bread on a work surface. Spread each with a little mustard, then top each with 2 strips tempeh, 1 slice cheese, 2 tablespoons dressing, ⅓ cup sauerkraut. Top each with 2 more strips tempeh. Top with the remaining bread.

Heat a large, heavy skillet, preferably cast iron, over medium-high heat. Lightly brush both sides of each sandwich with olive oil. Add the sandwiches in batches to the skillet and cook until golden, 1 to 2 minutes per side. Serve hot.

16 tempeh bacon strips

8 slices rye bread

Dijon mustard for spreading on bread

4 thin slices Swiss cheese

½ cup Thousand Island or Russian dressing

1⅓ cups sauerkraut, drained

Olive oil for brushing

BROCCOLI AND CHEESE CALZONES

Turn these easy-to-make calzones into a great meal by serving a first course of grilled or roasted vegetables tossed with olive oil and arranged on a platter with olives and spicy peppers.

SERVES 2

One 10-ounce package frozen chopped broccoli, thawed, drained and squeezed dry

3 green onions (white and light green parts), chopped

½ cup part-skim ricotta cheese

½ cup crumbled Gorgonzola or other blue cheese

1 cup packed grated fontina cheese

Salt and freshly ground black pepper

Unbleached all-purpose flour for sprinkling

One 10-ounce tube refrigerated pizza dough

Preheat the oven to 425°F. In a medium bowl, mix the broccoli, green onions, ricotta, Gorgonzola, and fontina. Season to taste with salt and pepper.

Sprinkle a large baking sheet with flour. Unfold the dough on the prepared baking sheet. Gently stretch and/or roll the dough to an 11-inch square; cut the dough in half diagonally, forming 2 triangles. Place half of the filling in the center of each triangle. Fold one side of each triangle over the filling, forming 2 triangular calzones. Press the edges of the dough to seal. Cut 3 slits in the top of each to allow steam to escape.

Bake the calzones for about 15 minutes, until golden brown. Serve hot.

EGGPLANT AND ARUGULA SANDWICHES WITH HUMMUS

SERVES 2

This is one of my favorite ways to eat eggplant. The robust, earthy flavor of broiled eggplant is the perfect match for hummus and zesty arugula.

Preheat the broiler. On the rack of a broiler pan, arrange the eggplant slices in a layer, seasoning both sides with salt and pepper. Broil the eggplant about 4 inches from the heat, turning once, until golden, 3 to 5 minutes on each side.

In a blender or food processor, combine the chickpeas, parsley, garlic, salt, water, lemon juice, and pepper to taste. Process until smooth.

In a medium bowl, combine the arugula, olive oil, and vinegar. Toss to mix and season to taste with salt and pepper. Spread the hummus evenly on 2 of the bread slices and top each slice with half of the eggplant slices, half of the arugula mixture, and the remaining 2 bread slices. Serve immediately.

1   firm eggplant (12 ounces), sliced ½ inch thick

Salt and freshly ground black pepper

1   cup canned chickpeas, rinsed and drained

¼   cup fresh parsley leaves

1   clove garlic, minced

½   teaspoon salt

2   tablespoons water

1½ tablespoons fresh lemon juice

Freshly ground black pepper

2   cups fresh arugula, tough stems removed

1   teaspoon olive oil

1   teaspoon red wine vinegar

4   large slices country-style white bread, toasted lightly

VEGAN

GRILLED VEGETABLE HEROES WITH ROASTED RED PEPPER PESTO

Vegetables have no natural fat, so they must be marinated in an oil-based marinade or brushed with some oil before they go on the grill to keep them from sticking to the grill rack. To ensure even cooking, turn the vegetables often and regulate the heat. These sandwiches can be made ahead and wrapped in foil. Just before serving, warm them on the grill.

GRILLED VEGETABLES

½   cup olive oil

2   cloves garlic, minced

1   medium eggplant, peeled and sliced ½ inch thick

2   medium zucchini, cut in half crosswise, then sliced lengthwise ½ inch thick

1   medium sweet onion, such as Vidalia, sliced ½ inch thick

2   medium portobello mushrooms, sliced ½ inch thick

ROASTED RED PEPPER PESTO

¼   cup store-bought roasted red peppers, drained and chopped

2   tablespoons Pesto (page 96)

1   clove garlic, minced

¼   cup soy or low-fat regular mayonnaise

    Salt and freshly ground black pepper

6   crusty hero or grinder rolls

4   ounces provolone cheese, thickly sliced

2   large, ripe tomatoes, sliced

Prepare a medium-hot fire in a charcoal grill or preheat a gas grill to medium. In a small bowl, combine the olive oil and garlic. Brush over the eggplant, zucchini, onion, and mushrooms, reserving a little of the oil mixture for brushing the rolls. Grill the vegetables, turning occasionally, until well browned, 10 to 15 minutes. Remove from the grill as they are done.

Meanwhile, make the pesto: In a blender or food processor, combine the roasted peppers, pesto, garlic, and mayonnaise and process until well blended and smooth. Season to taste with salt and pepper. Scrape into a small bowl and set aside.

Slice the rolls in half horizontally. Remove some of the interior of the rolls to create a hollow space for the vegetables. Brush the inside of the rolls with the reserved oil and garlic, then spread with the pesto. Layer the provolone, grilled vegetables, and tomato slices over the bottom half of the rolls. Cover with the top half. Wrap each in foil.

Just before serving, place the wrapped rolls on a low-heat spot of the grill, away from direct heat. Cover and grill until the bread is lightly toasted and the cheese is melted, 5 to 10 minutes. Unwrap the sandwiches and serve hot.

SERVES 6

chapter **6**

DINNER
SPECIALS

THE

recipes in this chapter
(and in the entire book, for that matter)
are for everyone—vegetarian or not—who
wants to eat well and be well. Veteran vegetarians
will find some great new recipes to try, such as Asian
Primavera, Tuscan Quiche, and Tempeh Piccata. For
others who are just getting started on a plant-based diet,
recipes like Chipotle–Black Bean Chili, Vegetable Pot Pie,
and Linguine with Tempeh Bolognese Sauce are a great place
to begin. Enjoying vegetarian main dishes is about expanding the
scope of your diet and appreciating the variety and abund-
ance that comes with a meatless diet.
Keep in mind that planning meals in advance makes it
easier to eat a varied diet. It will also save you time
shopping because you won't have to run to the
store every day for this or that. And well-planned
meals make cooking easier during the week
because you don't have to worry
about what's for dinner.

PENNE WITH CAPONATA

Caponata is a Sicilian eggplant dish enjoyed throughout Italy. Its wonderfully complex flavor and texture make it perfect for serving over pasta.

12 ounces penne pasta

1 tablespoon olive oil

1 cup chopped celery

¾ cup chopped onion

1 medium eggplant, peeled and chopped

2 cloves garlic, minced

One 15-ounce can diced tomatoes, drained

½ cup pitted green olives, sliced

¼ cup drained capers

1 teaspoon dried oregano

2 teaspoons balsamic vinegar

1 teaspoon sugar

Salt and freshly ground black pepper

Bring a large pot of salted water to a boil. Add the pasta, stirring to prevent sticking. Cook until al dente, 8 to 10 minutes. Drain and return to the pot.

Meanwhile, in a large skillet over medium-high heat, warm the olive oil. Add celery and onion and cook, stirring often, until softened, about 5 minutes. Add the eggplant and cook, stirring to prevent sticking, until softened, 5 minutes. Add the garlic, tomatoes, olives, capers, oregano, vinegar, and sugar and stir well. Reduce the heat and simmer for 5 to 10 minutes. Season to taste with salt and pepper. Add the sauce to the pasta and toss to coat. Serve hot.

 SERVES 4

PENNE WITH ASPARAGUS PESTO

SERVES 4

Everyone thinks of basil first when they hear the word "pesto." But pesto can be made with a variety of ingredients, like asparagus. It makes a refreshing pasta topping, especially in the spring when asparagus is at its freshest.

Bring a large pot of salted water to a boil. Add the pasta, stirring to prevent sticking. Cook until al dente, 8 to 10 minutes. Reserve ⅓ cup of the pasta cooking water and drain the pasta in a colander. Return to the pot.

Meanwhile, in a saucepan fitted with a steamer basket, bring 1 inch of water to a boil. Place the asparagus stalks in the basket and steam, covered, for 4 minutes. Add the reserved asparagus tips, cover, and steam until just tender, about 1 minute. Transfer the asparagus to ice water to stop the cooking. Drain the asparagus well in a colander and pat dry.

In a food processor, combine the pine nuts, garlic, and basil and process until finely chopped. Add the asparagus, olive oil, and 2½ teaspoons salt and pulse until the asparagus is coarsely chopped. Transfer to a large bowl and stir in the Parmesan and reserved cooking water. Add the pasta, tossing to coat, and season to taste with salt and pepper. Serve hot.

1 pound penne or other tubular pasta

1 pound fresh asparagus, trimmed, stalks cut crosswise into 2-inch pieces, tips reserved

¼ cup pine nuts, toasted (see page 42)

2 cloves garlic, chopped

½ cup packed chopped fresh basil

½ cup extra-virgin olive oil

2½ teaspoons salt, plus more to taste

⅓ cup grated Parmesan cheese

Freshly ground black pepper

LINGUINE WITH TEMPEH BOLOGNESE SAUCE

This simple preparation is one of my favorite ways to enjoy tempeh. It's an excellent way to begin including this soy food in your diet. The sauce can also be used to make lasagna.

8 ounces tempeh

2 tablespoons olive oil

1 medium onion, finely chopped

2 cloves garlic, minced

1 cup water

1 tablespoon tamari or reduced-sodium soy sauce

One 28-ounce can crushed tomatoes in purée

1 cup canned tomato purée

2 tablespoons chopped fresh basil, or 2 teaspoons dried

2 tablespoons chopped fresh parsley

2 teaspoons dried oregano

1 small bay leaf

Salt and freshly ground black pepper

12 ounces linguine

Bring a large pot of salted water to a boil. Meanwhile, in a medium bowl, crumble the tempeh into fine pieces. Set aside.

In a large saucepan over medium heat, warm the olive oil. Add the onion and cook, stirring often, until softened, about 5 minutes. Add the garlic and cook, stirring often, for 1 minute. Stir in the tempeh, 1 cup water, and tamari and bring the mixture to a boil. Reduce the heat, cover, and simmer for 5 minutes. Uncover and cook until the liquid has evaporated. Add the tomatoes, purée, basil, parsley, oregano, and bay leaf, and stir well. Season to taste with salt and pepper. Cover and simmer for 10 minutes. Remove and discard the bay leaf.

Add the linguine to the boiling water, stirring to prevent sticking. Cook until al dente, 8 to 10 minutes. Drain. Transfer to a serving bowl. Ladle the sauce over the linguine and toss to coat. Serve hot.

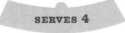

SERVES 4

BAKED ZITI WITH MUSHROOM SAUCE

In this popular Italian dish, ziti is combined with a ricotta-like tofu mixture and a tomato-mushroom sauce, then baked until browned and bubbly. It's comfort food at its best.

Preheat the oven to 400°F. Bring a large pot of salted water to a boil. Meanwhile, in a large saucepan over medium heat, warm 2 teaspoons of the oil. Add the mushrooms and cook, stirring often, until softened, about 10 minutes. Stir in the tomato sauce and bring to a simmer over medium-low heat. Cook, stirring occasionally, for 10 minutes. Remove from the heat and cover to keep warm.

In a blender or food processor, combine the tofu, basil, lemon juice, remaining 2 teaspoons olive oil, salt and pepper to taste and process until the consistency resembles ricotta cheese.

Add the ziti to the boiling water, stirring to prevent sticking. Cook until just tender, about 10 minutes. Drain.

Spread some of the tomato mixture over the bottom of a 13-by-9-inch baking dish.

In a large bowl, combine the drained pasta, tofu mixture, remaining tomato mixture, and parsley and fold gently to blend. Transfer to the baking dish and spread evenly. Bake, uncovered, for about 15 minutes, until heated through. Serve hot.

4   teaspoons olive oil

2   cups chopped cremini mushrooms

One 25-ounce jar tomato sauce

1   pound extra-firm tofu, drained

⅓   cup chopped fresh basil

2   tablespoons fresh lemon juice

    Salt and freshly ground black pepper

12 ounces ziti

½   cup chopped fresh flat-leaf parsley

VEGAN

SPINACH PASTA PIE

Even when the refrigerator seems bare, you can whip up this satisfying homemade alternative to take-out pizza with just a few staple ingredients.

SERVES 4 TO 6

5   tablespoons dried bread crumbs

3   teaspoons olive oil

½   cup chopped onion

1½ cups elbow macaroni (6 ounces)

4   large eggs

¾   cup low-fat milk

½   to 1 teaspoon hot pepper sauce

     Salt and freshly ground black pepper

1½ cups grated mozzarella cheese

One 10-ounce package frozen chopped spinach, thawed, drained, and sqeezed dry

Preheat the oven to 350°F. Bring a large pot of salted water to a boil. Meanwhile, grease a 9-inch deep-dish pie pan. Sprinkle with 2 tablespoons of the bread crumbs, tilting to coat evenly.

In a small bowl, mix the remaining 3 tablespoons bread crumbs with 1 teaspoon of the olive oil. Set aside. In a small skillet, heat the remaining 2 teaspoons olive oil over medium heat. Add the onion and cook, stirring often, until softened, 4 to 5 minutes.

Add the macaroni to the boiling water, stirring to prevent sticking. Cook until just tender, 4 to 5 minutes. Drain, rinse under cold running water, and drain again.

In a large bowl, whisk together the eggs, milk, hot pepper sauce, and salt and pepper to taste. Stir in the cheese, cooked onion, spinach, and macaroni. Pour into the prepared pan, spreading evenly. Sprinkle evenly with the reserved bread crumb mixture.

Bake the pie, uncovered, for about 45 minutes, until lightly golden and the tip of a knife comes out clean. Transfer to a wire rack and cool slightly. Cut into wedges and serve.

ASIAN NOODLES
WITH SPICY GINGER SAUCE

SERVES 4

Soba noodles, a specialty of Japan, are made from buckwheat flour and have an appealing nutty flavor and toothsome texture. They are a good source of protein, iron, and B vitamins. Soba noodles can be found frozen in well-stocked supermarkets, and dried or frozen in Asian groceries.

Bring a large pot of salted water to a boil. Add the noodles, stirring to prevent sticking, and cook according to the package directions. Drain and transfer to a serving bowl. Add the carrot, cucumber, green onions, and cilantro, tossing to mix

Meanwhile, in a small bowl, whisk together the vinegar, tamari, sesame oil, ginger, garlic, sugar, and chile oil. Pour the dressing over the noodle mixture and toss to coat. Serve warm or at room temperature.

VEGAN

12 ounces soba noodles

1 medium carrot, peeled and shredded

½ cucumber, peeled, seeded, and chopped

2 green onions (white and light green parts), thinly sliced

¼ cup chopped fresh cilantro

3 tablespoons rice vinegar

3 tablespoons tamari or reduced-sodium soy sauce

1 tablespoon dark (Asian) sesame oil

2 teaspoons minced peeled fresh ginger

2 cloves garlic, minced

1 teaspoon sugar

½ teaspoon chile oil

CLASSIC TOFU LASAGNA

**SERVES
10**

At first, I was skeptical of the no-boil (also called oven-ready) lasagna noodles that are now widely available in supermarkets. But after testing many different brands, I have to say that the noodles produce a great-tasting lasagna and are a real time-saver. Much like "instant rice," no-boil noodles are precooked at the factory. The extruded noodles are run through a water bath and then dehydrated mechanically. During baking, the moisture from the sauce softens, or rehydrates, the noodles, especially when the pan is covered as the lasagna bakes.

TOMATO SAUCE

2 tablespoons olive oil

1 cup chopped onion

2 cloves garlic, minced

⅓ cup tomato paste

Two 28-ounce cans plum tomatoes, chopped, undrained

½ cup chopped fresh basil, or 1 tablespoon dried

½ cup chopped fresh parsley

1½ teaspoons dried oregano

½ teaspoon red pepper flakes (optional)

Salt and freshly ground black pepper

2 pounds firm tofu, drained

2 cloves garlic, minced

¼ cup chopped fresh basil, or 1 tablespoon dried

Salt and freshly ground black pepper

1 pound no-boil lasagna noodles

Make the sauce: In a large, heavy saucepan over medium heat, warm the olive oil. Add the onion and garlic and cook, stirring frequently, until the onion is soft, about 5 minutes. Add the tomato paste and cook, stirring, for 1 minute. Add the tomatoes with their juice, basil, parsley, oregano, and red pepper flakes (if using). Reduce the heat, cover, and simmer, stirring occasionally, for 1 hour. Season to taste with salt and pepper.

Preheat the oven to 400°F. Crumble the tofu into a medium bowl. Add the garlic, basil, and salt and pepper to taste and stir until well blended.

To assemble: Spoon about 1 cup sauce over the bottom of a 13-by-9-inch baking dish. Add a layer of noodles and top with one-third of the tofu mixture. Spoon about 1½ cups sauce over the tofu on the dish and top with another layer of noodles. Cover with half of the remaining tofu mixture and top with 1½ cups of sauce and another layer of noodles. Top with the remaining tofu mixture and sauce. Cover with foil and bake for 30 minutes. Remove from the oven and let stand about for 15 minutes before cutting and serving.

VEGAN

EGGPLANT PARMIGIANA

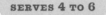

SERVES 4 TO 6

Many people complain that the eggplant in their eggplant parmigiana turns out soggy and oil soaked. The problem is that eggplant is packed with water and extremely porous, and therefore it soaks up oil like a sponge. I have found that the remedy for this is to salt the eggplant before cooking. Salt draws the water out of the eggplant, allowing it to cook up crisper and firmer. For the salt to do its job, the eggplant must macerate for at least 1 hour. It also helps to firmly press the eggplant between sheets of paper towel; this extrudes the juice and compacts the flesh.

1   large eggplant (about 2 pounds), peeled and sliced ½ inch thick

½   teaspoon salt, plus more for sprinkling

1   tablespoon olive oil

½   cup chopped onion

3   cloves garlic, minced

½   cup chopped green bell pepper

4   cups peeled, chopped tomatoes

¼   teaspoon freshly ground black pepper

1   tablespoon minced fresh basil, or 1 teaspoon dried

1   teaspoon minced fresh thyme, or ¼ teaspoon dried

1   tablespoon chopped fresh parsley

¼   to ⅓ cup Rich Vegetable Broth (page 109), canned broth, or water

½   to 1 cup dried whole-grain bread crumbs

¾   cup grated part-skim mozzarella cheese

¼   to ½ cup grated Parmesan cheese

Layer the eggplant slices in a colander, lightly sprinkling salt between the layers. Cover with a plate and set to a 2- to 3-pound weight, such as a can of food or a pot of water, on top. Let stand for 1 hour, then rinse and pat dry.

Meanwhile, in a large pot over medium heat, warm the oil. Add the onion and cook, stirring often, until it begins to soften, about 5 minutes. Add the garlic and bell pepper and cook, stirring often, until the vegetables are tender, about 5 minutes. Add the tomatoes, cover, and cook over low heat until tender, 5 to 10 minutes. Uncover the pot, stir in the ½ teaspoon salt and the pepper, and simmer gently until the sauce thickens, about 1 hour. Add the basil, thyme, and parsley and simmer for 1 to 2 minutes.

Preheat the oven to 350°F. Dip the eggplant slices in the broth and then in the bread crumbs to coat. Grease a large baking sheet and arrange the breaded slices on it. Bake for about 30 minutes, until the eggplant is tender and the crumbs are crisp.

Grease an 8-inch square baking dish. Spread a thin layer of the sauce on the bottom and arrange half of the eggplant slices on top of the sauce. Scatter about one-third of the mozzarella over the eggplant, spread on a thicker layer of sauce, and sprinkle with half of the Parmesan. Repeat the layers, beginning with eggplant and ending with Parmesan. You should have about one-third of the mozzarella left at this point.

Cover the dish with foil and bake until heated through, about 30 minutes. Uncover, scatter the remaining mozzarella over the top, and bake until the cheese is melted and bubbly, about 10 minutes more. Remove from the oven and let sit for 5 to 10 minutes before serving.

ASIAN PRIMAVERA

*Udon noodles are long, cylindrical wheat noodles sold fresh in the refrigerator sec-
tion of well-stocked supermarkets and Asian grocers. They are used extensively in
Japanese cooking. Linguine makes a good substitute if you cannot find udon.*

4   cups hot water

3   cups dried porcini mushrooms
    (about 2 ounces)

8   ounces udon noodles or linguine

2   tablespoons tamari or
    reduced-sodium soy sauce

2   tablespoons dark (Asian)
    sesame oil

1   cup cubed extra-firm tofu
    (about 4 ounces)

¼   cup chopped peeled fresh
    lemongrass

2   tablespoons minced peeled
    fresh ginger

2   cloves garlic, minced

2   cups julienne-cut zucchini
    (1 inch long)

1   cup sliced cremini mushrooms

1   cup sliced shiitake mushroom
    caps

8   cups thinly sliced bok choy leaves

¼   cup finely chopped fresh cilantro

In a small bowl, combine the hot water and dried mushrooms and
let stand for 20 minutes. Drain the mushrooms through a sieve over
a bowl, reserving the soaking liquid and mushrooms separately.

Bring a large pot of water to a boil. Add the noodles, stirring to prevent sticking. Cook for 3 minutes and drain. Return the noodles to the
pot. Add the reserved mushroom soaking liquid and tamari to the
noodles and bring to a boil. Reduce the heat and simmer until the
liquid is absorbed, about 8 minutes. Stir in the reserved porcini
mushrooms.

In a wok or large, nonstick skillet over medium-high heat, warm the
sesame oil. Add the tofu, lemongrass, ginger, and garlic and stir-fry
for 30 seconds. Add the zucchini, cremini and shiitake mushrooms,
and stir-fry for 2 minutes. Add the bok choy and stir-fry until wilted,
about 3 minutes.

Divide the noodle mixture among 4 shallow bowls, and top with the
tofu mixture. Sprinkle with the cilantro. Serve hot.

SERVES 4

VEGAN

PAD THAI

SERVES 4

Pad Thai is probably the most popular noodle dish on Thai restaurant menus. In Thailand, each street vendor sells a unique version of this wonderfully aromatic dish. It's a fascinating mix of flavors and an intriguing combination of textures—crunchy bean sprouts and nuts set off by soft noodles.

In a large bowl, soak the rice noodles in warm water to cover until limp and white, about 20 minutes.

In a small bowl, combine the lime juice, tamari, brown sugar, chile sauce, and 1 tablespoon water.

In a wok or large, deep skillet over high heat, heat the oil. Add the garlic and ginger and stir-fry for 30 seconds. Add the carrot and green onions and stir-fry for 1 minute. Stir in the lime juice–tamari mixture.

Drain the noodles and add to the wok, tossing with tongs until softened and curled, about 1 minute. Add the sprouts and toss to mix. Divide the mixture among 4 serving plates, sprinkle with peanuts, and garnish with cilantro and slices of lime, if desired.

VEGAN

8	ounces dried rice noodles
¼	cup fresh lime juice
2	tablespoons tamari or reduced-sodium soy sauce
2	tablespoons brown sugar
1	to 2 teaspoons hot chile sauce
1	tablespoon water
2	teaspoons peanut oil
3	cloves garlic, minced
1	to 2 teaspoon minced peeled fresh ginger
1	medium carrot, peeled and cut into narrow strips
8	to 10 green onions, halved lengthwise and then cut into 2-inch lengths
1	cup mung bean sprouts
2	tablespoons chopped dry-roasted peanuts
¼	cup chopped fresh cilantro (optional)
1	lime, sliced (optional)

CURRIED VEGETABLES

This curry-in-a-hurry is made with mushrooms, zucchini, and cauliflower. Keep in mind that whenever you buy cauliflower, the secret is to purchase it fresh, when its flavor is mild and delicate. Old cauliflower can have an assertive, cabbaggy flavor.

2 tablespoons vegetable oil

6 ounces cremini mushrooms, quartered

½ teaspoon ground cumin

1 tablespoon minced peeled fresh ginger

1 tablespoon ground coriander

1 teaspoon ground turmeric

¼ teaspoon ground cardamom

⅛ to ¼ teaspoon cayenne pepper

1 cup thinly sliced onion

1 head cauliflower, cut into bite-size pieces (5 to 6 cups)

1 cup Rich Vegetable Broth (page 109) or canned broth

1½ teaspoons salt

2 small zucchini, quartered lengthwise and cut into ¾-inch slices (2½ cups)

¼ cup chopped fresh cilantro

In a large Dutch oven over medium-high heat, heat 1 tablespoon of the oil. Add the mushrooms and cook, stirring occasionally, until browned, about 5 minutes. Transfer to a plate. Add the remaining 1 tablespoon oil to the pan and heat over medium heat. Add the cumin and cook, stirring constantly, for 30 seconds. Add the ginger, coriander, turmeric, cardamom, and cayenne and cook, stirring, for 30 seconds more. Stir in the onion and cook, stirring often, until softened, about 4 minutes. Add the cauliflower, broth, and salt. Cover, reduce the heat, and simmer until the cauliflower is barely tender, about 12 minutes.

Add the zucchini and reserved mushrooms to the cauliflower mixture. Cover and cook for 4 to 5 minutes. Stir in the cilantro. Serve hot.

SERVES 4 TO 6

POTATO RAGOUT WITH FENNEL AND TOFU

Versatile and well loved by the Italians, fennel is prized for its crisp, juicy texture and almost sweet flavor, reminiscent of licorice. It's high in vitamin A and is an excellent source of potassium and calcium. To prepare fennel for this recipe, peel off any outer stalks that are discolored, bruised, or dry. Cut the stalks off flat across the top of the bulbous part, then cut that part in half to rinse. Trim the root end and then chop the bulb. The feathery fronds at the top can be chopped fine for garnishes and flavorings.

1	tablespoon olive oil
½	cup chopped onion
1	fennel bulb, cored and chopped (8 cups)
1	large leek (white and light green parts), chopped (2½ cups)
¼	cup chopped fresh parsley
2	tablespoons finely chopped fresh rosemary
2	teaspoons fennel seed
2	tablespoons balsamic vinegar
2½	cups chopped canned tomatoes
2	pounds extra-firm tofu, drained and cubed
2	cups cooked or canned cannellini beans, drained and rinsed if canned
	Large pinch of saffron threads
2	cups Rich Vegetable Broth (page 109) or canned broth
1	pound tiny red-skinned potatoes, quartered if necessary
	Salt and freshly ground black pepper

In a large Dutch oven over medium-high heat, warm the olive oil. Add the onion, fennel, leek, parsley, rosemary, and fennel seed. Reduce the heat to medium and cook, stirring often, until the vegetables are very tender, about 10 minutes. Add the vinegar and cook, stirring, until it is almost evaporated, about 2 minutes.

Stir in the tomatoes. Cook, stirring occasionally, until thickened slightly, about 7 minutes. Stir in the tofu and beans.

Dissolve the saffron in the broth and add to the tofu mixture. Add the potatoes, stirring gently to avoid breaking the tofu. Bring to a boil. Reduce the heat, cover, and simmer, stirring occasionally, until the ragout is thickened and the potatoes are tender, about 45 minutes. Season to taste with salt and pepper and serve hot.

VEGAN

CREAMY BUTTERNUT SQUASH RISOTTO

SERVES 4 TO 6

4 cups Rich Vegetable Broth (page 109) or canned broth

2 cups water

2 tablespoons butter

1 tablespoon olive oil

½ cup finely chopped onion

1 clove garlic, minced

2 cups Arborio rice

¼ cup dry white wine

2½ cups peeled, diced butternut squash (1-inch dice)

2 tablespoons finely chopped fresh rosemary, or ½ teaspoon dried

Salt and freshly ground black pepper

¼ cup grated Parmesan cheese (optional)

Making a good risotto is like making good soup. It involves no special tricks, just careful observation. While frequent stirring is necessary to produce the characteristic creaminess of a good risotto, constant stirring is not. Walking over to the pan every minute or two and stirring the rice for about 10 seconds with a wooden spoon is sufficient. The rice does require attention, but it is not all-consuming. Between stirs you can be preparing other items for the recipe or menu.

However, the type of rice you use is critical. Italian medium-grain rices, such as Arborio or Carnaroli, are the best choices. Other medium-grain or long-grain rices are not suitable because they have a different ratio of starches and will not yield slightly chewy grains surrounded by a creamy sauce.

In a medium saucepan over medium heat, bring the broth and water just to a simmer. In a medium, heavy saucepan over medium heat, melt the butter with the olive oil. Add the onion and garlic and cook, stirring often, until the onion is softened, 4 to 5 minutes. Add the rice and cook, stirring, for 1 minute to completely the coat the grains. Add the wine and stir until almost completely absorbed, about 1 minute.

Add ½ cup of the hot broth mixture to the rice and cook, stirring constantly, until the liquid is almost completely absorbed. Repeat with another ½ cup broth. Stir in the squash and continue adding the broth ½ cup at a time, making sure that most of the liquid is absorbed before adding more. Remove the pan of broth from the heat when about ½ cup broth mixture remains. Start checking for doneness by biting into a grain of rice—it should be firm but tender. (The timing from the first to last addition of broth is 25 to 30 minutes.) Stir in the rosemary, salt and pepper to taste, and Parmesan, if using. Serve hot.

JAMBALAYA

This recipe requires that you freeze the tofu ahead of time. Freezing tofu completely changes its texture. The whey, which crystallizes into ice when frozen, melts away, leaving a spongy, solid mass of creamy beige tofu. Tofu that has been frozen and then thawed has a chewy, meatlike texture that absorbs marinades and flavorings and is great for using crumbled in this vegetarian jambalaya.

1   pound firm tofu, drained

One 14½-ounce can diced tomatoes

1   tablespoon vegetable oil

1   large onion, coarsely chopped

3   cloves garlic, minced

2   medium green bell peppers, diced

2   stalks celery, thinly sliced

⅔   cup chopped fresh parsley

2   bay leaves

1   teaspoon liquid smoke

2   teaspoons dried thyme

2   teaspoons salt, plus more to taste

¼   teaspoon cayenne pepper

1½ cups long-grain brown rice

    Freshly ground black pepper

    Hot pepper sauce for serving (optional)

Cut the tofu into 1-inch-thick slices, arrange in a single layer on a baking sheet, and freeze until firm. (Once frozen, the slices can be stored in a plastic freezer bag.) Freeze the tofu for 1 to 2 days. Thaw at room temperature for about 4 hours. Drain and squeeze out the excess moisture with your hands. Cut into ½-inch cubes; set aside.

Drain the tomatoes, reserving the juice. In a large glass measure, combine the reserved juice with enough water to equal 2½ cups. Set aside.

In a large pot over medium-high heat, warm the oil. Add the onion and garlic and cook, stirring often, until lightly browned, about 3 minutes. Add the tomatoes and juice mixture, bell peppers, celery, parsley, bay leaves, liquid smoke, thyme, salt, and cayenne and stir well. Bring to a boil. Stir in the tofu cubes and rice. Cover, reduce the heat to low, and simmer until the rice is tender, about 45 minutes.

Remove from the heat and let stand, covered, for 10 minutes. Discard the bay leaves. Season to taste with salt and pepper. Serve with hot pepper sauce, if desired.

SERVES 6

STEWED BROCCOLI RABE, WHITE BEANS, AND POTATOES

In this hearty, quick stew, the slightly bitter taste of the broccoli rabe is offset by the mild flavor of the white beans and potatoes. Serve it in large, shallow soup bowls with hard-crusted Italian bread to soak up the delicious sauce.

In a medium saucepan, combine the potatoes and lightly salted water to cover and bring to a boil over high heat. Reduce the heat to medium-low, cover, and cook until fork-tender, about 5 minutes. Drain well and set aside.

Meanwhile, in a large pot over medium heat, warm the olive oil. Add the garlic and red pepper flakes and cook, stirring occasionally, for 2 minutes. Stir in the broccoli rabe, salt, pepper, and ¼ cup water. Cover and cook, stirring occasionally, until the broccoli rabe is tender, 5 to 8 minutes.

Add the cooked potatoes, beans, and broth and mix well. Bring to a boil over medium-high heat. Reduce the heat and simmer, uncovered, stirring occasionally, until heated through, about 5 minutes. Serve hot.

3   medium Yukon gold potatoes, peeled, quartered, and sliced

2   tablespoons olive oil

3   cloves garlic, minced

1   teaspoon red pepper flakes

2   bunches fresh broccoli rabe, tough stems trimmed and the remainder cut in half crosswise

½   teaspoon salt

¼   teaspoon freshly ground black pepper

¼   cup water

2   cups cooked or canned Great Northern beans, drained and rinsed if canned

1¾ cups Rich Vegetable Broth (page 109) or canned broth

VEGAN

MIDDLE EASTERN CHICKPEA STEW

Hearty, nutritious, and easy to make describes this humble dish. The chickpea's ability to hold its shape even after long cooking makes it an ideal choice for a stew.

1½ tablespoons olive oil

1   small onion, finely chopped

1   medium red bell pepper, chopped

3   cloves garlic, minced

½   teaspoon ground cumin

½   teaspoon dried oregano

2   medium tomatoes, seeded and chopped

3   tablespoons chopped fresh cilantro

3   tablespoons chopped fresh parsley

3   tablespoons tomato paste

2   cups Rich Vegetable Broth (page 109) or canned broth

2   medium russet potatoes, peeled and cut into 1-inch pieces

Two 15-ounce cans chickpeas, rinsed and drained

Salt and freshly ground black pepper

In a large, nonstick skillet over medium-high heat, warm the olive oil. Add the onion, bell pepper, garlic, cumin, and oregano. Cook, stirring often, until the vegetables are soft but not brown, 5 to 6 minutes. Add the chopped tomatoes, cilantro, and parsley. Cook, stirring occasionally, until most of the liquid has evaporated and the mixture has thickened, 5 minutes.

Stir in the tomato paste and cook for 1 minute. Stir in the broth and bring to a boil over high heat. Stir in the potatoes. Reduce the heat and simmer for 6 minutes. Stir in the chickpeas and simmer until the potatoes are tender and the sauce has thickened, about 10 minutes. Season to taste with salt and pepper. Serve hot.

SERVES
6

ASIAN VEGETABLE AND TOFU STEW

The taste and texture of this stew is delicious and satisfying, especially when served over hot rice. Daikon is a long, white Japanese radish. It has a mild flavor and crisp bite. Look for it in large supermarkets or Asian groceries.

In a Dutch oven over medium heat, warm the oil. Add the onion and cook, stirring often, until beginning to soften, 5 minutes. Add the tofu and cook, stirring often, until golden brown, about 5 minutes.

Add 6 cups of the water and the daikon, parsnip, rutabaga, carrot, tamari, rice wine, and mushrooms. Bring to a boil. Cover, reduce the heat, and simmer for 35 minutes.

In a small bowl, mix the remaining ⅓ cup water with the cornstarch until blended. Stir into the stew and bring to a boil. Cook, stirring constantly, for 2 minutes. Just before serving, stir in the salt and sesame oil and sprinkle with the green onions.

SERVES 4 TO 6

1 tablespoon vegetable oil

2 cups chopped onion

2 pounds extra-firm tofu, drained and cut into 1-inch cubes

6⅓ cups water

1 cup cubed peeled daikon radish (1-inch cubes)

1 cup sliced peeled parsnip (1-inch-thick slices)

1 cup cubed peeled rutabaga (1-inch cubes)

1 cup sliced peeled carrot (1-inch-thick slices)

¼ cup tamari or reduced-sodium soy sauce

2 tablespoons rice wine (mirin)

1 cup chopped fresh shiitake mushrooms caps

¼ cup cornstarch

¼ teaspoon salt

2 teaspoons dark (Asian) sesame oil

¼ cup chopped green onion (white and light green parts)

VEGAN

INDIAN LENTIL STEW

Garam masala is a distinctive blend of dry-roasted Indian spices that usually includes cinnamon, cloves, coriander, cumin, cardamom, fennel, and dried chiles. Look for it in well-stocked supermarket spice or ethnic sections, and at Indian groceries.

1   tablespoon olive oil

1   cup chopped onion

1½ teaspoons garam masala

1   cup chopped plum tomatoes

1   teaspoon ground turmeric

1   teaspoon minced peeled fresh ginger

2   cloves garlic, minced

1   medium eggplant (1 pound), peeled and chopped

1   cup dried lentils, sorted and rinsed

2   cups Rich Vegetable Broth (page 109) or canned broth

2   cups water

1½ teaspoons salt

2   bay leaves

2   cups chopped fresh portobello mushroom caps

    Salt and freshly ground black pepper

In a Dutch oven over medium-high heat, warm the olive oil. Add the onion and cook, stirring often, until softened, about 6 minutes. Add the garam masala and cook, stirring, for 1 minute. Stir in the tomatoes, turmeric, ginger, garlic, and eggplant and cook, stirring occasionally, until the eggplant is tender, about 10 minutes.

Add the lentils, broth, water, salt, and bay leaves to the pan and bring to a boil. Cover, reduce the heat and simmer for 15 minutes. Stir in the mushrooms and bring to a boil. Reduce the heat to a simmer and cook until the mushrooms are tender, about 10 minutes. Discard the bay leaves. Season to taste with salt and pepper. Serve hot.

SERVES 6

GRILLED POLENTA WITH PUTTANESCA SAUCE

Classically Italian, a puttanesca sauce is a basic tomato sauce with olives, capers, and garlic. It makes a wonderful sauce for grilled polenta and is also good over pasta.

Prepare a medium-hot fire in a charcoal grill or preheat a gas grill to medium.

Make the sauce: In a large skillet over medium-high heat, warm the olive oil. Add the onion and garlic and cook, stirring often, until beginning to soften, about 5 minutes. Stir in the wine, sugar, basil, tomato paste, and tomatoes and bring to a boil. Reduce the heat to medium and cook, uncovered, for about 15 minutes. Stir in the olives, parsley, capers, and red pepper flakes and cook, stirring occasionally, until thoroughly heated. Season to taste with salt and pepper. Remove from the heat.

Arrange the polenta slices on a baking sheet. Brush the slices on both sides with the olive oil and season to taste with salt and pepper. Lightly oil the grill rack, and grill the polenta until nicely caramelized, 3 to 5 minutes on each side. Divide among 4 plates. Top with the sauce, garnish with basil sprigs, and serve hot.

SERVES 4

PUTTANCESCA SAUCE

1 tablespoon olive oil

1 cup chopped onion

4 cloves garlic, minced

½ cup dry red wine, or 2 tablespoons balsamic vinegar

1 tablespoon sugar

1 tablespoon chopped fresh basil, or 2 teaspoons dried basil

2 tablespoons tomato paste

Two 14½-ounce cans diced tomatoes, undrained

¼ cup chopped pitted green olives

2 tablespoons chopped fresh parsley

1 tablespoon capers, drained

¼ to ½ teaspoon red pepper flakes

Salt and freshly ground black pepper

One 18-ounce package prepared polenta, sliced ½ inch thick

2 teaspoons extra-virgin olive oil

Salt and freshly ground pepper

Fresh basil sprigs for garnish

VEGAN

EGGPLANT AND POLENTA LASAGNA

This recipe is incredibly simple to prepare. It's a great dish to whip up on a busy weeknight. I like to serve it with a spinach and mushroom salad.

1   large eggplant (1½ pounds), cut lengthwise into 8 slices

3   cups prepared marinara sauce

2   cups grated part-skim mozzarella cheese

¼   cup grated Parmesan cheese

One 18-ounce package prepared polenta, cut into 20 slices

Preheat the oven to 450°F. Coat the eggplant slices with vegetable oil spray, place on a large baking sheet, and bake for about 20 minutes, until tender. Reduce the oven temperature to 375°F.

Place 4 of the eggplant slices in the bottom of a 13-by-9-inch baking dish. Spread with 1 cup of the sauce; sprinkle with ⅔ cup of the mozzarella and 1 tablespoon of the Parmesan cheese. Repeat the layers once. Top with the polenta slices and the remaining sauce and cheese. Bake, uncovered, for about 20 minutes, until bubbly and the cheese melts. Serve hot.

SERVES 6

STIR-FRIED TOFU WITH ASPARAGUS

SERVES 6

In Thai cooking, you often see chile peppers and fresh basil used as a flavoring together. Here, these ingredients combine with tofu and asparagus for a satisfying and flavorful one-dish meal.

Heat a wok or large, deep skillet over high heat. Add the oil and, when hot, add the garlic, asparagus, and chile peppers and stir-fry for 2 to 3 minutes. Add the tofu and stir-fry for 2 minutes.

Add the tamari and sugar and cook, stirring often, for 1 to 2 minutes. Stir in the basil and serve right away.

1 tablespoon vegetable oil

4 cloves garlic, minced

8 ounces thin asparagus, cut into ½-inch pieces

2 small fresh red or green chile peppers, seeded and minced (wear rubber gloves)

1 pound extra-firm tofu, well drained and cut into 1-inch cubes

1 tablespoon tamari or reduced-sodium soy sauce

1 teaspoon sugar

½ cup chopped fresh basil

VEGAN

RATATOUILLE WITH PARMESAN POLENTA

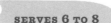

SERVES 6 TO 8

Long before I ever visited Provence, I had simmered many batches of the region's most famous vegetable dish, ratatouille. I had learned to make it by following recipes in French cookbooks. Over the years I have simplified the method, but the end result still closely resembles the ratatouilles I savored almost every day while traveling in Provence. If time is short, you can skip the polenta and serve the dish with rice or couscous.

RATATOUILLE

2½ tablespoons olive oil

1 large onion, quartered and thinly sliced

1 large eggplant (1½ pounds), peeled and cut into ¾-inch cubes

1 teaspoon salt

1 large green bell pepper, thinly sliced

2 cloves garlic, minced

2 cups canned crushed tomatoes

1 medium zucchinl, cut into ½-inch dice

2 tablespoons chopped fresh parsley

1 tablespoon tomato paste

2 teaspoons red wine vinegar

1 tablespoon chopped fresh basil, or 1 teaspoon dried

Freshly ground black pepper

PARMESAN POLENTA

1 cup yellow cornmeal

2½ cups water

1½ cups Rich Vegetable Broth (page 109) or canned broth

⅓ cup grated Parmesan cheese

1 to 2 teaspoons butter

¼ teaspoon salt

Make the ratatouille: In a large Dutch oven over medium-high heat, warm 1 tablespoon of the olive oil. Add the onion and cook, stirring often, until softened, about 6 minutes. Add the remaining 1½ tablespoons olive oil, the eggplant, and ½ teaspoon of the salt and cook, stirring often, for 3 minutes. Add the bell pepper and garlic and cook, stirring often, until the eggplant begins to soften, 6 to 7 minutes. Stir in the tomatoes and zucchini. Reduce the heat, cover partially, and simmer, stirring often, for 10 minutes.

Stir in the parsley, tomato paste, vinegar, basil, remaining ½ teaspoon salt, and pepper to taste. Simmer, uncovered, for 3 minutes. Remove from the heat, cover, and keep warm.

Make the polenta: In a small bowl, mix the cornmeal and 1½ cups of the water. In a medium saucepan, combine the broth and the remaining 1 cup water; bring to a boil. Slowly add the cornmeal mixture, stirring until blended. Bring to a simmer, reduce the heat to low, and simmer, partially covered, stirring occasionally, until the polenta has thickened, 10 to 12 minutes. Remove from the heat. Stir in the Parmesan cheese, butter, and salt and stir until the butter is melted. Serve warm with the ratatouille.

SHEPHERD'S PIE WITH POTATO TOPPING

Although this dish is called a "pie," there isn't any pastry involved. It is simply a mix of ground soy crumbles and vegetables in a sauce with a topping of mashed potatoes. The dish is browned in the oven for a delicious example of British comfort food. For a pretty effect, pipe the topping over the filling, using a pastry bag fitted with a star tip.

VEGAN

POTATO TOPPING

3½ pounds russet potatoes, peeled and cut into 2-inch pieces

1 cup Rich Vegetable Broth (page 109) or canned broth

2 teaspoons Dijon mustard

¾ teaspoon salt

Freshly ground black pepper

3 medium carrots, peeled and diced

1 medium onion, chopped

3 cloves garlic, chopped

1½ pounds ground fat-free soy "meat"

1 cup thawed frozen peas

¾ cup fresh or thawed frozen corn kernels

One 14½-ounce can diced tomatoes, drained

1 tablespoon tomato paste

Freshly ground black pepper

Make the potato topping: In a large saucepan, combine the potatoes with enough cold water to cover by 1 inch. Bring to a boil and cook until tender, about 15 minutes. Drain well. In a large bowl, combine the potatoes, broth, mustard, salt, and pepper to taste. Using an electric mixer, beat on high speed until smooth. Set aside.

Preheat the oven to 350°F. Bring a small saucepan of lightly salted water to a boil. Add the carrots and cook for 2 minutes to blanch. Drain and set aside.

Spray a large skillet with vegetable oil spray and set over low heat. Add the onion and cook, stirring, until softened, about 2 minutes. Add the garlic and cook for 15 seconds. Stir in the soy "meat," breaking it up with a fork. Add the blanched carrots, peas, corn, tomatoes, and tomato paste. Mix well. Cook, stirring often, until the flavors have blended, about 10 minutes. Season with pepper to taste.

Spray a 3-quart gratin dish or shallow casserole with vegetable oil spray. Spoon the vegetable-soy mixture into the prepared dish. Top with dollops of the mashed potatoes. Bake for 30 to 45 minutes, until heated through. Serve hot.

BASMATI RICE–STUFFED ROASTED PEPPERS

SERVES 6

Slightly different than classic stuffed peppers, the bell peppers in this recipe are first roasted, imparting a rich, sweet flavor to the filling. Serve these peppers with cannellini or white beans and a mixed green salad.

Preheat the broiler. Cook the rice according to the package directions.

Meanwhile, in a shallow baking pan, place the bell peppers cut sides down and coat with vegetable oil spray. Broil for 5 minutes on each side, or until lightly charred. Remove the pan from the oven and reduce the oven temperature to 375°F.

In a large, nonstick skillet, heat the olive oil over medium heat. Add the onion and cook, stirring often, until softened, for 2 to 3 minutes. Add the garlic and cook for 1 minute more, stirring often. Add the zucchini and carrot and cook, stirring occasionally, just until tender, about 5 minutes more. Stir in the cooked rice, tomato sauce, basil, Asiago, and 2 tablespoons of the Parmesan cheese. Fill the roasted pepper halves with the vegetable mixture.

Loosely cover the pan with foil and bake for 25 minutes. Remove the foil, sprinkle with the remaining 2 tablespoons Parmesan cheese, and bake for 5 minutes more. Serve right away.

1 cup basmati or long-grain white rice

4 medium bell peppers (red, green, and/or yellow), halved and seeded

1 tablespoon olive oil

½ cup finely chopped onion

2 cloves garlic, minced

1 large zucchini or yellow squash, shredded (about 1½ cups)

1 large carrot, peeled and shredded (about 1 cup)

¾ cup tomato sauce

2 tablespoons chopped fresh basil

½ cup grated Asiago or fontina cheese

4 tablespoons grated Parmesan cheese

STUFFED CABBAGE ROLLS

Plump cabbage-wrapped packets of rice and vegetables are steamy and delicious. Try to find a good-size cabbage so you will end up with large leaves that hold plenty of filling.

SERVES
6

1   tablespoon olive oil

1   cup chopped onion

½   cup diced celery

½   cup diced red or green
     bell pepper

3   cups sliced mushrooms

2   cloves garlic, minced

3   cups Rich Vegetable Broth
     (page 109) canned broth
     or water

1½ cups uncooked basmati rice

½   teaspoon salt

¼   teaspoon freshly ground
     black pepper

2   tablespoons chopped fresh
     parsley

1   large green cabbage
     (about 4 pounds)

2½ cups tomato sauce

In a large saucepan over medium heat, warm the olive oil. Add the onion, celery, and bell pepper and cook, stirring often, for 5 minutes. Stir in the mushrooms and garlic, cover, and cook for 5 minutes.

Add the broth, rice, salt, and pepper. Stir and raise the heat to bring to a boil, then cover tightly, reduce the heat to medium-low, and cook for 15 minutes. Remove from the heat and fluff the rice with a fork. Stir in the parsley. Set aside.

Cut out the core from the cabbage and carefully separate 8 outer leaves. (Reserve the remaining cabbage for another use.) Cut away a V-shaped piece from the thickest part at the base of each leaf. Place the leaves loosely in a large skillet. Add just enough water to cover the bottom of the pan. Cover and cook just until the leaves are wilted, 2 to 3 minutes. Remove from the pan and drain.

Preheat the oven to 375°F. Pour 1½ cups of the tomato sauce into the bottom of a 13-by-9-inch baking dish. Lay the cabbage leaves on a work surface with the edges curling up. Spoon about ¾ cup of the rice mixture into the center of each leaf. Fold in the sides of the leaves and roll up loosely. Place the stuffed leaves, seam sides down, in the dish. Spoon the remaining 1 cup tomato sauce over the cabbage rolls. Cover with foil and bake for about 45 minutes, until bubbly and heated through. Uncover and bake 10 to 15 minutes more. Serve hot.

VEGAN

CHILES RELLEÑOS

SERVES 6

These stuffed chile peppers are a Mexican specialty. Here they feature the flavor of grilled corn, with only a minimal amount of cheese. Fresh tomato salsa makes a nice accompaniment.

Preheat the broiler. Coat the corn with vegetable oil spray and season with salt and pepper. Broil the corn 4 inches from the heat source, turning occasionally, until the kernels are well browned, about 12 minutes. Transfer to a cutting board and let cool. When cool enough to handle, cut the kernels from the cobs and place in a medium bowl (you should have about 1½ cups).

Broil the chiles until nicely charred, about 3 minutes on each side. Transfer to a paper bag and seal closed. Let stand for 15 minutes to loosen the skins. Scrape off and discard the skin (wear rubber gloves). Set 6 of the roasted chiles aside.

Seed and chop the remaining 2 chiles. Add to the bowl with the corn kernels. Stir in the cheese, green onions, garlic, and cilantro. Season to taste with salt and pepper.

Carefully make a 2-inch-long lengthwise cut in each of the 6 reserved chiles. Using a spoon, scrape out the core and seeds, leaving the stems intact. Stuff each chile with the corn mixture.

Preheat the oven to 400°F. Lightly grease a baking sheet. Put the flour in a shallow bowl and the egg whites in a second bowl. Stir together the bread crumbs and cornmeal in a third bowl. Dip each chile first in the flour, shaking off the excess, then in the egg, then in the crumb mixture. Place on the baking sheet. Generously coat the tops of the chiles with vegetable oil spray. Bake for about 20 minutes, until the chiles are golden brown and the filling is heated through. Serve hot.

2 large or 3 medium ears corn, shucked

Salt and freshly ground black pepper

8 fresh poblano chiles

½ cup grated cheddar cheese

3 green onions (white and light green parts), finely chopped

1 clove garlic, minced

¼ cup finely chopped fresh cilantro

1 cup unbleached all-purpose flour

3 large egg whites, lightly beaten

¾ cup unseasoned dried bread crumbs

¼ cup stone-ground yellow or blue cornmeal

GRAIN-STUFFED ACORN SQUASH

Stuffed vegetables offer the cook, especially the vegetarian cook, many creative options for meals. In this recipe, round acorn squash make a stunning container for a stuffing of wild rice and quinoa. Be sure to use small squash for this dish.

6   small acorn squash, halved and seeded

6½   cups water

1   cup wild rice, rinsed

½   teaspoon salt, plus more to taste

1   cup quinoa, rinsed

1   tablespoon olive oil

½   cup chopped red onion

½   cup chopped celery

½   cup dried cranberries

⅓   cup chopped pecans or walnuts

1   teaspoon dried sage

½   to ¾ cup fresh orange juice
     Freshly ground black pepper

SERVES 6

Preheat the oven to 350°F. Arrange the squash halves, cut sides down, in a baking dish. Pour ½ cup of the water into the dish. Cover and bake until tender, 25 to 30 minutes.

Meanwhile, in a large saucepan, bring 4 cups of the remaining water to a boil. Add the wild rice and ½ teaspoon salt. Reduce the heat, cover, and simmer until the rice is tender, about 40 minutes. Drain if necessary. In a medium saucepan, bring the remaining 2 cups water to a boil. Add the quinoa. Reduce the heat, cover, and simmer until the water is absorbed and the quinoa is tender, about 12 minutes.

In a large, deep skillet over medium heat, warm the oil. Add the onion and celery and cook, stirring often, until the vegetables begin to soften, about 3 minutes. Add the cranberries, pecans, and sage and cook, stirring often, until heated through. Using a fork, fluff the quinoa and wild rice, then add both to the skillet. Add the orange juice and mix until heated through. Season to taste with salt and pepper.

Remove the squash from the oven and arrange, cut sides up, on a serving platter. Spoon some of the filling into each squash cavity and place 2 halves on each serving plate.

VEGAN

THAI TOFU CURRY

SERVES 6

This Thai curry is made with coconut milk, which gives the dish a rich, complex flavor and sweet heat. Serve the curry over rice, quinoa, or couscous.

In a medium saucepan, combine the coconut milk, broth, tofu, green onions, 1 tablespoon of the ginger, half of the garlic, the salt, and red pepper flakes. Bring to a boil, reduce the heat to low, and simmer for 20 minutes. Remove from the heat.

In a large saucepan, combine the remaining garlic, remaining 1 tablespoon ginger, mushrooms, carrots, and squash. Add 1½ cups of the coconut mixture. Bring to a simmer. Reduce the heat, cover, and simmer until the vegetables are tender but still firm, about 8 minutes.

Add the cabbage to the saucepan with the vegetables and stir just until it begins to wilt, about 1 minute. Pour the remaining coconut mixture over the vegetables and stir gently to combine. Stir in the cilantro and cook just until heated through. Serve hot.

One 14-ounce can light coconut milk

1 cup Rich Vegetable Broth (page 109) or canned broth

1 pound extra-firm tofu, well drained and diced (1-inch cubes)

4 green onions (white part only), sliced

2 tablespoons minced peeled fresh ginger

4 cloves garlic, minced

1½ teaspoons salt

¼ teaspoon red pepper flakes

2 cups chopped shiitake mushroom caps

1 cup peeled and thinly sliced carrots

1 cup peeled and diced butternut squash (1-inch cubes)

4 cups shredded Chinese cabbage (bok choy)

¼ cup finely chopped fresh cilantro

VEGAN

NO-MEAT FAJITAS

Here is a simple Southwestern combination of flavorful vegetables wrapped into soft, warm tortillas. The recipe calls for toppings of salsa and guacamole, but other accompaniments you might want to include are grated cheese, shredded lettuce, and chopped tomato and onion.

VEGAN

8   flour tortillas, 9 to 10 inches in diameter

2   cups thinly sliced onions

2   medium red, yellow, and/or green bell peppers, cut into thin strips

1   mild fresh chile, such as poblano or Anaheim, cut into thin strips

2   medium zucchini, cut into thin strips

1   tablespoon fresh lime juice

Salt and freshly ground black pepper

2   tablespoons olive oil, plus more if necessary

Fresh Tomato and Corn Salsa for serving (page 64)

Great Guacamole for serving (page 56)

Preheat the oven to 350°F. Wrap the tortillas in foil and heat in the oven for 15 minutes.

In a large bowl, combine the onions, bell peppers, chile, zucchini, lime juice, and salt and pepper to taste and toss to coat. In a large skillet over medium-high heat, warm the olive oil. Cook the vegetables in batches, stirring often and adding more oil to the skillet if necessary, until tender, about 12 minutes.

Serve the warmed tortillas and cooked vegetables at the table, with salsa and guacamole for topping.

SERVES 4

SWEET POTATO AND BLACK BEAN HASH

Hash makes the perfect weeknight fare: everyone loves it and it takes only minutes to prepare in one pan. Using a cast-iron skillet will give the hash a crusty brown exterior. This Southwestern-inspired dish is good served with Chili Cornbreads (page 264).

In a large cast-iron skillet over medium-high heat, warm the oil. Add the onions and bell pepper and cook, stirring often, until beginning to brown, about 4 minutes. Add the sweet potato and cook, stirring often, until beginning to brown, about 5 minutes. Add the garlic, cumin, chili powder, and salt and cook, stirring, for 30 seconds. Add the broth and cook until almost absorbed, about 5 minutes. Stir in the corn and black beans and cook, stirring occasionally, until heated through. Stir in the cilantro and season to taste with pepper. Serve hot.

1   tablespoon canola oil

2   medium onions, chopped

1   small green bell pepper, chopped

1   medium sweet potato, peeled and diced (1-inch cubes)

2   cloves garlic, minced

1½ teaspoons ground cumin

1   teaspoon chili powder

½   teaspoon salt

¾   cup Rich Vegetable Broth (page 109), canned broth, or water

¾   cup frozen corn kernels (no need to defrost)

One 15-ounce can black beans, rinsed and drained

2   tablespoons chopped fresh cilantro

Freshly ground black pepper

VEGAN

CHIPOTLE–BLACK BEAN CHILI

There are probably as many different vegetarian chili recipes as there are vegetarian cooks. This simple version gets a kick of flavor from ground chipotle chiles. Chipotle chiles are smoked jalapeño peppers. They come packed in adobo sauce or dried and ground into a powder.

1 tablespoon vegetable oil

1 medium onion, chopped

1 medium green bell pepper, diced

2 jalapeño chiles, seeded and minced (wear rubber gloves)

2 cloves garlic, minced

1 tablespoon chili powder

1 teaspoon ground cumin

1 teaspoon dried oregano

½ teaspoon ground chipotle

⅛ teaspoon cayenne pepper

One 14-ounce can Mexican-style diced or stewed tomatoes

Two 16-ounce cans black beans, rinsed and drained

1 cup fresh or frozen corn kernels (no need to defrost if frozen)

⅓ cup chopped fresh cilantro

In a large pot over medium heat, warm the oil. Add the onion, bell pepper, jalapeño, and garlic and cook, stirring often, until the vegetables begin to soften, about 5 minutes. Add the spices, tomatoes, and beans and simmer for 15 minutes. Stir in the corn and cook for 1 minute. Stir in the cilantro and serve.

SERVES 4 TO 6

MOO SHU VEGETABLES

Chinese cuisine has contributed many great dishes to vegetarian meals. One of the most popular is this vegetable stir-fry flavored with rice vinegar, tamari, and hoisin sauce. The vegetables are traditionally served with Chinese Pancakes to roll them in; to save time, you can substitute flour tortillas.

In a small bowl, combine the mushrooms and boiling water. Cover and let stand for 30 minutes, or until soft. Drain and cut the mushrooms into thin strips.

In a wok or large, deep skillet over medium-high heat, warm the sesame and vegetable oils. Add the eggs and stir-fry for 2 minutes. Remove from the pan. Add the ginger and garlic and stir-fry for 1 minute. Add the mushrooms, cabbage, bell pepper, and yellow onion and stir-fry for 2 minutes. Add the green onion, vinegar, tamari, and hoisin sauce and stir-fry for 1 minute. Stir in the reserved eggs. Serve with Chinese Pancakes, if desired.

One ½-ounce package dried wood ear mushrooms

2 cups boiling water

1 teaspoon dark (Asian) sesame oil

1 teaspoon vegetable oil

3 large eggs, lightly beaten

1 tablespoon minced peeled fresh ginger

2 cloves garlic, minced

4 cups thinly sliced green cabbage

1 cup thinly sliced red bell pepper

½ cup thinly sliced yellow onion

½ cup diagonally sliced green onion

3 tablespoons rice vinegar

3 tablespoons tamari or reduced-sodium soy sauce

2 tablespoons hoisin sauce

Chinese Pancakes for serving (page 200; optional)

CHINESE PANCAKES

Although these pancakes are traditionally served with moo shu dishes, they are so full of flavor that you can also eat them without a topping. Five-spice powder is a Chinese spice blend that may include such flavorings as star anise, cinnamon, cloves, peppercorns, and fennel seed. Look for it in the spice or ethnic section of well-stocked supermarkets and Asian groceries.

1¼ cups unbleached all-purpose flour

1½ cups low-fat milk

1 tablespoon butter, melted

1 large egg

¼ teaspoon Chinese five-spice powder

1 tablespoon minced green onion (optional)

Put the flour in a medium bowl. In a small bowl, whisk together the milk, butter, and egg. Add the milk mixture to the flour, whisking until blended. Stir in the five-spice powder and green onion (if using). Cover and chill for 1 hour.

Place an 8-inch crêpe pan or nonstick skillet coated with vegetable oil spray over medium-high heat until hot. Pour a scant ¼ cup batter into the pan; quickly tilt the pan in all directions so the batter covers the bottom of the pan. Cook for about 1 minute.

Carefully lift the edge of the pancake with a spatula to test for doneness. The pancake will be ready to turn when it can be shaken loose from the pan and the underside is lightly browned. Turn the pancake over and cook for 30 seconds on the other side.

Place the pancake on a towel and let cool. Repeat with the remaining batter. Stack the pancakes between single layers of wax paper or paper towels to prevent the pancakes from sticking.

MAKES 12 PANCAKES

ITALIAN RICE AND VEGETABLE CASSEROLE

SERVES 6

This casserole is hearty and full of flavor. Serve it with a salad of mixed greens and some good bread.

Preheat the oven to 350°F. Lightly grease a 3-quart baking dish. In a large skillet over medium-high heat, warm the olive oil. Add the onion, carrot, and celery and cook, stirring often, until softened, about 10 minutes. Add the mushrooms, garlic, and thyme and cook, stirring often, for 2 minutes. Stir in the brown sugar, paprika, salt, and rice and cook, stirring often, for 1 minute. Stir in the tomatoes, broth, pine nuts, and basil and bring to a simmer.

Transfer the mixture to the prepared baking dish. Cover and bake until the rice is tender, about 1½ hours. Serve warm.

2 tablespoons olive oil

1 medium onion, chopped

1 large carrot, peeled, quartered lengthwise, and chopped

2 stalks celery, chopped

2 medium portobello mushroom caps, cut into 1-inch pieces

3 cloves garlic, minced

½ teaspoon dried thyme

1 teaspoon brown sugar

1½ teaspoons paprika

½ teaspoon salt

1 cup long-grain brown rice

1½ cups diced plum tomatoes

1 cup Rich Vegetable Broth (page 109), canned broth, or water

½ cup toasted pine nuts (see page 42)

¼ cup chopped fresh basil

VEGAN

TUSCAN QUICHE

SERVES 8

The trick to an excellent vegan pastry crust is to keep all the ingredients cold. Even after you have rolled it out, keep the pastry-lined tart pan in the refrigerator until you are ready to bake it. For this recipe, both the prebaked tart shell and the filling can be made one day in advance and then assembled and baked just before serving.

CRUST

¾ cup unbleached all-purpose flour

¾ cup whole-wheat pastry flour

½ teaspoon baking powder

½ teaspoon salt

¼ cup cold canola oil

⅓ cup ice water

1½ pounds firm tofu, well drained

3 tablespoons olive oil

2 teaspoons balsamic vinegar

2 teaspoons white miso

1½ teaspoons salt

⅓ cup water

½ cup finely chopped onion

½ cup chopped red bell pepper

2 cloves garlic, minced

1½ teaspoons chopped fresh thyme, or ½ teaspoon dried

1½ teaspoons chopped fresh oregano, or ½ teaspoon dried

¾ cup sliced cremini mushrooms

½ cup chopped kalamata olives

Make the crust: In a medium bowl, whisk together the flours, baking powder, and salt. Add the oil and ice water. Working the dough as little as possible, mix and roll it into a ball. Wrap the dough in wax paper and chill for 20 to 30 minutes. On a lightly floured surface, roll the dough into a 10-inch circle and fit it into a greased 9-inch pie pan. Cover and chill for 20 minutes.

Preheat the oven to 350°F. Uncover and bake the crust for 15 minutes, or until set. Set on a wire rack to cool.

In a food processor, combine the tofu, 2 tablespoons of the olive oil, the vinegar, miso, salt, and water and process until smooth and creamy. Transfer to a medium bowl.

In a large skillet over medium-high heat, warm the remaining 1 tablespoon oil. Add the onion, bell pepper, and garlic and cook, stirring often, until the vegetables begin to soften, about 3 minutes. Stir in the thyme, oregano, mushrooms, and olives. Cook, stirring often, until the vegetables are tender, about 5 minutes more. Add to the tofu mixture, stirring until blended.

Pour the filling into the prebaked crust. Bake for about 40 minutes, until the top is lightly browned. Serve warm.

VEGAN

TOMATO-BASIL GALETTE

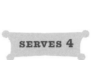

SERVES 4

This savory pie occupies a place somewhere between a pizza and a tart. The free-form crust makes it a rustic, casual meal that can be served warm or at room temperature.

PASTRY

1 cup unbleached all-purpose flour

¾ cup whole-wheat pastry flour

1 teaspoon sugar

½ teaspoon salt

5 tablespoons canola oil

5 tablespoons plain soymilk, chilled

1 tablespoon extra-virgin olive oil

1 large onion, thinly sliced (3 cups)

Salt and freshly ground black pepper

1 tablespoon finely chopped fresh basil

3 ripe medium tomatoes, sliced ¼ inch thick

Make the pastry: In a large bowl, mix the all-purpose and whole-wheat flours, sugar, and salt. Slowly add the oil and stir with a fork until blended. The mixture will look like pea-sized crumbs. Add the soymilk, a little at a time, and stir until the mixture comes together.

Turn the pastry out onto a lightly floured work surface and gently knead 2 or 3 times into a ball. Place the dough on a large sheet of plastic wrap and flatten it into a round disk about ¾ inch thick. Wrap the disk in plastic wrap and refrigerate for 30 to 60 minutes.

Preheat the oven to 375°F. In a medium skillet over medium-high heat, warm the olive oil. Add the onion and cook, stirring often, until softened and golden brown, 8 to 10 minutes. Season to taste with salt and pepper. Remove from the heat.

Between 2 sheets of lightly floured wax paper, roll the pastry out into a 13-inch circle. Remove and discard the top sheet of wax paper. Slide your hand under the bottom sheet of wax paper and carefully invert onto a baking sheet. Remove and discard the wax paper.

Distribute the onion mixture evenly on top of the pastry, leaving a 1-inch border all around. Sprinkle with the basil and salt and pepper to taste. Starting from the outer edge of onion, arrange the tomato slices on top, overlapping them lightly. Fold the edge of the pastry over the topping, pleating it every inch or two.

Bake for about 20 minutes, until the crust is golden. Transfer the galette to a wire rack to cool slightly. Cut into wedges and serve.

VEGAN

ROASTED VEGETABLE TART

SERVES 6 TO 8

Roasted vegetables are always a treat. The natural sugars in the vegetables caramelize during roasting and create an incredible sweet-savory flavor. This is a very adaptable tart, so you can experiment with different vegetables, such as eggplant, bell peppers, and zucchini, and other cheeses, like grated fontina or Jarlsberg.

3 medium carrots, peeled and cut into matchsticks

3 medium parsnips, peeled and cut into matchsticks

1½ cups cubed peeled rutabaga (1-inch cubes)

1½ cups cubed peeled butternut squash (1-inch cubes)

1 medium beet, peeled and cut into 1-inch cubes (1 cup)

2 tablespoons olive oil

1 teaspoon chopped fresh rosemary, or ¼ teaspoon dried

¼ teaspoon salt

⅛ teaspoon freshly ground black pepper

PASTRY

2¼ cups unbleached all-purpose flour

2 teaspoons baking powder

½ teaspoon salt

¾ cup water

3 tablespoons olive oil

½ cup finely chopped kalamata olives

3 ounces goat cheese (optional)

Preheat the oven to 400°F. Line a large, rimmed baking sheet with foil. In a large bowl, combine the carrots, parsnips, rutabaga, squash, and beet. Add the olive oil, rosemary, salt, and pepper and toss to coat. Roast, stirring every 10 minutes, until the vegetables are tender and beginning to brown, about 25 minutes total.

Meanwhile, make the pastry: In a food processor, combine the flour, baking powder, and salt; pulse several times to mix. Add the water and olive oil and process just until blended. Add the olives and pulse to mix. (Alternatively, combine the flour, baking powder, and salt in a large bowl. Make a well in the center of the mixture. Add the water and oil to the flour mixture, stirring until well blended. Stir in the olives.)

Turn the dough out onto a lightly floured surface (knead 4 to 5 times if mixed by hand). Divide in half. Press each dough half gently into a 4-inch circle on heavy-duty plastic wrap; cover with additional plastic wrap. Place one dough half in the refrigerator until ready to use. Roll the remaining dough half, still covered, into an 11-inch circle. Remove the top layer of plastic wrap. Invert into a 10-inch tart pan with a removable bottom. Remove the remaining plastic wrap and press the dough into the pan. Bake for 10 minutes; let cool slightly.

Crumble the cheese (if using) over the bottom of the tart. Arrange the roasted vegetables over the cheese.

Roll out the remaining dough between 2 pieces of plastic wrap into an 11-inch circle. Remove the top layer of plastic wrap. Cut into ½-inch-wide strips. Arrange the strips over the tart in a lattice pattern.

Bake the tart for 20 to 25 minutes, until the crust is lightly golden. Let cool slightly on a wire rack. Serve warm.

VEGAN

VEGETABLE POT PIE

SERVES 6

This recipe lends itself to creativity, as it can be prepared with almost any vegetables you like. The biscuit crust is a low-fat version of a traditional pot pie topping. Soymilk can be substituted for the buttermilk and maple syrup for the honey to make it vegan; however, the topping may be a bit heavier as a result. This recipe can also be made into individual pot pies, in which case reduce the baking time to 15 to 18 minutes.

1	tablespoon butter
1	tablespoon canola oil
1	cup chopped onion
1	cup thinly sliced celery
1½	cups small broccoli florets
1	cup diced red bell pepper
1	cup frozen green beans, thawed
⅓	cup unbleached all-purpose flour
1	cup milk or plain soymilk
2	cups Rich Vegetable Broth (page 109) or canned broth
2	tablespoons chopped fresh parsley
1	teaspoon tamari or reduced-sodium soy sauce
½	teaspoon dried thyme
¼	teaspoon dried sage
	Salt and freshly ground black pepper

BISCUIT TOPPING

1¾	cups whole-wheat pastry flour
½	teaspoon salt
2	teaspoons baking powder
½	teaspoon baking soda
2	tablespoons butter
¾	cup buttermilk or plain soymilk
2	teaspoons honey

Preheat the oven to 400°F. In a medium skillet over medium-high heat, melt the butter with the oil. Add the onion and cook, stirring often, until soft, about 5 minutes. Add the celery, broccoli, bell pepper, and green beans and cook, stirring often, until the vegetables are tender, about 10 minutes. Reduce the heat to low. Sprinkle the flour over the vegetable mixture. Cook, stirring constantly, for 2 minutes.

In glass measuring cup, combine the milk and broth. Slowly add to the vegetable mixture while whisking constantly. The sauce will start to thicken. Add the parsley, tamari, thyme, and sage. Season to taste with salt and pepper. Cook, stirring constantly, until thickened. Remove from the heat, transfer to a 2-quart casserole, and set aside.

Make the topping: In a large bowl, mix the flour, salt, baking powder, and baking soda. Using a pastry blender or fork, cut the butter into the flour mixture until it resembles coarse meal. In a measuring cup, combine the buttermilk and honey. Add to the flour mixture, stirring with a fork to form a stiff dough. Add more buttermilk if the dough is too dry. Knead lightly in the bowl for 3 to 5 minutes, until the dough is no longer sticky. Turn the dough out onto a lightly floured surface. Roll out into a shape to cover the casserole dish.

Lay the biscuit topping lightly over the filling. Do not seal the edges. Bake for 20 to 30 minutes, until the crust is golden brown and the filling is bubbling.

MISO MARINATED AND BAKED TOFU

For thousands of years, dedicated Japanese craftsmen have transformed soybeans and grains into a salty, fermented paste called miso, one of Japan's most celebrated culinary staples. There is no Western counterpart for this rich condiment. It is thick and spreadable, with the consistency of peanut butter. The color, texture, and flavor of miso are affected by the length of time the paste is aged. Misos have a lovely array of earth colors. They range from golden tans and ambers through rusts and russets to a rich, dark chocolate brown. The color of the miso is determined by how long it has been aged. Light-colored misos are milder in flavor and aroma and have a taste that is sweeter than the full-flavored, well-aged dark misos.

1   large carrot, peeled and coarsely chopped

1   small onion, coarsely chopped

1   tablespoon maple syrup

1   tablespoon tamari or reduced-sodium soy sauce

½   cup brown miso

¼   cup rice vinegar

¾   cup water

½   cup vegetable oil

2   pounds firm tofu, drained

In a food processor, finely chop the carrot and onion. With the motor running, add the maple syrup, tamari, miso, vinegar, water, and oil through the feed tube and process until well blended.

Cut each slab of tofu lengthwise into 3 slices. Cover the bottom of a 13-by-9-inch dish with about ½ cup of the miso marinade. Arrange half of the tofu slices over it. Spoon another ½ cup of marinade over the tofu, then repeat with the remaining tofu and marinade. Cover tightly and marinate for 2 days in the refrigerator.

Preheat the oven to 450°F. Uncover the dish and bake the tofu for 10 to 15 minutes, until heated through. Serve warm.

SERVES 8

CRISPY SESAME TOFU CUTLETS

This basic recipe should be part of every vegetarian cook's repertoire. It can be varied with sauces and toppings of your choice.

Preheat the oven to 200°F. In a shallow bowl, mix the flour, sesame seeds, and salt. In another shallow bowl, mix the water and liquid smoke. Put the bread crumbs on a sheet of wax paper. Carefully dip the tofu into the water mixture, then into the flour mixture, coating it evenly. Quickly dip the coated tofu into the water mixture again, then into the bread crumbs, coating it evenly. Place the coated tofu cutlets on a plate.

In a large skillet over medium heat, warm 2 tablespoons of the oil. Cook the tofu cutlets in batches until lightly browned, about 3 minutes on each side. Transfer to a baking sheet and keep warm in the oven until ready to serve. Repeat with the remaining cutlets, adding more oil to the skillet, if necessary. Serve hot.

½ cup unbleached all-purpose flour

1 tablespoon sesame seeds

½ teaspoon salt

1 cup cold water

1 teaspoon liquid smoke

1 cup dried whole-grain bread crumbs

2 pounds extra-firm tofu, well drained and each block cut crosswise into 4 slices

2 to 3 tablespoons vegetable oil

VEGAN

TEMPEH PICCATA

Good served all year-round, this dish has a fresh, clean flavor. The lemon accent comes through loud and clear and highlights the tempeh and other flavors.

VEGAN

1½ cups unbleached all-purpose flour

½ cup yellow cornmeal

1 teaspoon dried thyme

1 teaspoon dried oregano

½ teaspoon paprika

1 cup plain soymilk

One 8-ounce package marinated tempeh

4 teaspoons vegetable oil

2 cloves garlic, minced

½ cup fresh lemon juice

1 cup dry white wine

1 cup Rich Vegetable Broth (page 109) or canned broth

1 tablespoon drained capers

1 tablespoon cornstarch

3 tablespoons water

Salt and freshly ground black pepper

Preheat the oven to 200°F. In a shallow bowl, mix the flour, cornmeal, thyme, oregano, and paprika. Pour the soymilk into another shallow bowl. Dredge the tempeh slices in the flour mixture, shaking off the excess. Dip in the soymilk and dredge in the flour mixture again.

In a large, nonstick skillet over medium-high heat, warm 2 teaspoons of the oil. Cook the tempeh slices, in batches if necessary, until lightly browned, 2 to 3 minutes on each side. Transfer to a baking sheet and keep warm in the oven.

Wipe out the pan, place over medium heat, and warm the remaining 2 teaspoons oil. Add the garlic and cook, stirring often, until fragrant, about 30 seconds. Add the lemon juice, wine, broth, and capers. Bring to a boil. Reduce the heat and simmer until reduced by half, about 5 minutes. In a small bowl, mix the cornstarch and water until well blended. Stir into the pan and cook, stirring often, until thickened. Season to taste with salt and pepper. Transfer the tempeh slices to a serving platter and spoon the sauce over them. Serve hot.

SERVES 4

TOFU CACCIATORE

SERVES 4

Tofu provides a tasty foundation for an Italian-style sauce of mushrooms, peppers, and tomatoes.

Preheat the oven to 375°F. Put the tofu into an ungreased pie plate and bake until slightly firm and the liquid is released, about 20 minutes. Pour off any remaining liquid. Set the tofu aside.

In a Dutch oven over medium-high heat, warm the olive oil. Add the onions and cook, stirring often, until beginning to soften, about 5 minutes. Add the bell peppers, mushrooms, garlic, parsley, basil, and thyme and cook, stirring often, for 2 minutes. Reduce the heat to medium and cook, stirring occasionally, until the vegetables are tender, about 6 minutes. Stir in the wine, tomatoes, tomato paste, olives, and salt and pepper to taste and cook, stirring occasionally, until the sauce has thickened, about 5 minutes.

Gently ease the tofu into the vegetable mixture. Cover and simmer until heated through, about 5 minutes. Serve hot.

1 pound firm tofu, well drained and sliced 1½ inches thick

1 tablespoon olive oil

2 medium onions, thinly sliced

3 medium bell peppers, preferably 1 red, 1 yellow, and 1 green, thinly sliced (3 to 4 cups)

1 cup thinly sliced cremini mushrooms

1 clove garlic, minced

¼ cup finely chopped fresh parsley

1 tablespoon chopped fresh basil, or 1 teaspoon dried

1 teaspoon chopped fresh thyme, or ½ teaspoon dried

½ cup dry white wine

1 cup chopped plum tomatoes

1 tablespoon tomato paste

½ cup chopped kalamata olives

Salt and freshly ground black pepper

VEGAN

TEMPEH WITH BRAISED RED CABBAGE AND APPLES

SERVES 4 TO 6

I came up with this dish to celebrate Oktoberfest with some friends one brisk October weekend. To carry through the German theme, you could serve the tempeh with spaetzle and an apple strudel for dessert. And of course, for a true Oktoberfest celebration, don't forget to include a sampling of German beers.

¼ cup tamari or reduced-sodium soy sauce

1 tablespoon dark (Asian) sesame oil

2 tablespoons water

Two 8-ounce packages tempeh, cut into 1-inch cubes

2 tablespoons vegetable oil

1 small head red cabbage, halved lengthwise, cored, and shredded

1½ cups thinly sliced red onion

1 cup apple juice

2 teaspoons cider vinegar

1 teaspoon fennel seed

1 teaspoon mustard seed, crushed

½ teaspoon salt

1 medium tart apple, peeled and thinly sliced

In a small bowl, mix the tamari, sesame oil, and water. Add the tempeh, tossing to coat. Let stand for 5 minutes, then drain and reserve the liquid. (Do not let it stand any longer than 5 minutes or the tempeh will become too salty.)

In a large skillet over medium-high heat, warm the oil. Add the tempeh and cook, stirring often, until golden, about 5 minutes. Transfer to a plate.

In a large saucepan, combine the cabbage, onion, apple juice, vinegar, fennel seed, mustard seed, and salt. Bring to a simmer. Cover and cook, stirring occasionally, for 15 minutes. Reduce the heat, add the apple, cover, and cook, stirring occasionally, for 15 minutes. Stir in the tempeh and reserved marinade and cook just until heated through. Serve hot.

BAKED TOFU SHANGHAI

For this recipe, the tofu is marinated for 2 hours and then baked. It is topped with a simple Asian sauce made from peanut butter, garlic, and coconut milk.

1 clove garlic, minced

2 tablespoons tamari or reduced-sodium soy sauce

2 tablespoons sweet sherry

1 tablespoon rice vinegar

One 10-ounce package firm tofu, drained and cut into 1½-inch cubes

SAUCE

2 tablespoons smooth peanut butter

½ cup water

2 cloves garlic, minced

2 tablespoons coconut milk

Salt

In a shallow bowl, mix the garlic, tamari, sherry, and vinegar. Add the tofu and toss gently to coat. Cover and marinate for 2 hours.

Preheat the oven to 200°F. Drain the tofu, reserving the marinade. Arrange the tofu on a greased baking sheet and bake for 25 to 30 minutes, until browned.

Meanwhile, make the sauce: In a small saucepan, combine the peanut butter, reserved marinade, water, and garlic. Cook over medium heat, stirring often, until smooth and heated through. Stir in the coconut milk and season to taste with salt.

Transfer the tofu to a serving platter and spoon the sauce over it. Serve hot.

SERVES 4

STIR-FRIED TEMPEH WITH ZUCCHINI

SERVES 4 TO 6

Stir-frying begins with a wok or stir-fry pan that has deep, sloping sides. This design allows food at the bottom to cook rapidly over intense heat, while other ingredients along the sloped sides can cook more slowly or be kept warm. If you do not have a wok, the next best thing is a heavy, large skillet. This dish is quick and easy to prepare, great for a busy weeknight. Serve it with rice or noodles.

In a wok or heavy, large skillet over medium-high heat, warm 1 tablespoon of the olive oil. Add the tempeh and stir-fry for 2 minutes. Add the oregano and basil and stir-fry for 1 minute. Add ½ cup of the broth and simmer for 2 minutes. Transfer to a large bowl and set aside. Wipe the wok clean.

Set the wok over medium-high heat and add the remaining 1 tablespoon olive oil. Add the onion and garlic and stir-fry for 2 minutes. Add the zucchini and stir-fry for 2 minutes. Add the tomatoes, reserved tempeh mixture, remaining ½ cup broth, and parsley and stir-fry for 2 minutes. Season to taste with salt and pepper and serve right away.

2   tablespoons olive oil

8   ounces tempeh, crumbled (2 cups)

½   teaspoon dried oregano

½   teaspoon dried basil

1   cup Rich Vegetable Broth (page 109) or canned broth

1   large onion, thinly sliced

3   cloves garlic, minced

2   medium zucchini, halved lengthwise and then thinly sliced on the diagonal

2   cups chopped plum tomatoes

¼   cup finely chopped fresh flat-leaf parsley

    Salt and freshly ground black pepper

VEGAN

chapter 7

ON THE SIDE

THE

main dish does not always
have to be the main event. Inventive
side dishes like Curried Couscous,
Edamame Succotash, Mushroom-Barley
Pilaf, Mashed Sweet Potatoes with Apples,
and a host of other recipes found in this
chapter can turn vegetarian mealtime
standbys into real standouts.

Most of the following recipes are
quick and easy, too—desirable
qualities for busy
home cooks.

MASHED POTATOES

If you're serving mashed potatoes with sauce or gravy, this is the recipe you want. It delivers spectacularly smooth, fluffy potatoes, not too rich and not too assertively flavored. Consider one of the variations when the mashed potatoes will stand alone. Be careful not to overcook the potatoes you plan to mash, because the starch cells will break down and create a sticky mash. Cook them just until a thin-bladed knife meets a bit of resistance. It is also important to drain the potatoes well after cooking to prevent gumminess.

2   pounds russet or Yukon gold potatoes, peeled and cut into 2-inch chunks

¾   teaspoon salt

¼   cup butter or soy butter, at room temperature

1   cup whole milk or plain soymilk, warmed

Freshly ground black pepper

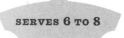

SERVES 6 TO 8

Put the potatoes in a large saucepan and add enough cold water to cover and ½ teaspoon of the salt. Bring to a boil and cook over medium heat until the potatoes are tender when pierced with a knife, 15 to 20 minutes.

Drain the potatoes well and return the pan to low heat. Rice or strain the potatoes into the pan and then, with a whisk or wooden spoon, blend in the butter (or soy butter for vegan mashed potatoes) and then the warm milk. (Alternatively, return the potatoes to the saucepan and mash over low heat with a potato masher, adding the butter as you mash. Stir in the warm milk or soymilk.) Season with the remaining ¼ teaspoon salt and pepper to taste. Serve hot.

VARIATIONS

Garlic Mashed Potatoes: Add 2 large peeled cloves of garlic and 2 bay leaves to the cooking water. Remove the bay leaves when you drain the potatoes, and mash the garlic with the potatoes. Decrease the butter to 2 tablespoons and stir in ¼ cup extra-virgin olive oil with the butter.

Parmesan Mashed Potatoes: Stir 2 tablespoons grated lemon zest and 1 cup grated Parmesan cheese into the finished potatoes.

TWICE-BAKED POTATOES

These twice-baked potatoes are a perfect winter lunch or brunch treat. The potatoes can be made up to one day ahead. Cover them tightly with plastic wrap and refrigerate. Bring to room temperature before baking.

Preheat the oven to 350°F. Pierce the skin of each potato several times with a fork. Bake until tender, about 1½ hours. Let cool slightly.

Cut the potatoes in half lengthwise and, using a spoon, scoop the flesh out into a medium bowl, leaving a ¼-inch-thick shell. Using a fork, mash the potatoes in the bowl. Add the yogurt and olive oil and stir until blended. Season to taste with salt and pepper.

Spoon the mixture into the potato shells, mounding it slightly. Put the filled potatoes on a baking sheet and sprinkle the grated Parmesan cheese over each. Bake until the tops are golden and the potatoes are heated through, about 25 minutes. Serve hot.

4   large russet potatoes, scrubbed

½   cup plain low-fat yogurt

2   tablespoons olive oil

    Salt and freshly ground black pepper

¼   cup grated Parmesan cheese

POTATOES GRATIN

The traditional method of cooking potatoes gratin-style is also one of the simplest. Contrary to popular belief, cheese is not necessarily part of the equation; the dish is defined by the browning on the top. But cheese in a potato gratin does taste wonderful, so I've included it in this recipe. For a nice variation, you can also add some sliced and sautéed mushrooms to the potato layer.

2 pounds boiling potatoes, peeled and sliced ⅛ inch thick

2 tablespoons butter

1 medium onion, chopped

1 clove garlic, minced

½ teaspoon dried thyme

½ teaspoon salt

½ teaspoon freshly ground black pepper

3 tablespoons unbleached all-purpose flour

1½ cups milk

½ cup grated Jarlsberg cheese

Preheat the oven to 350°F. Coat a 13-by-9-inch baking dish with vegetable oil spray. Arrange the potato slices, slightly overlapping, in a single layer in the dish.

In a medium saucepan over medium-low heat, melt the butter. Add the onion, garlic, thyme, salt, and pepper and cook, stirring often, until the onion is softened, 4 to 5 minutes. Stir in the flour and cook until frothy. Let the mixture bubble for about 2 minutes, stirring often to prevent browning. Gradually stir in the milk until well blended. Increase the heat to medium and simmer until the sauce is thick, stirring constantly. Spread the sauce over the potatoes.

Cover the dish with foil and bake for 45 minutes, or until the potatoes are tender when pierced with a fork. Sprinkle the cheese over the top. Bake, uncovered, for 10 minutes more, or until the cheese is melted and the sauce is bubbly. Let stand for 5 minutes before serving.

SERVES 8

OVEN FRIES

SERVES 4

Better than any fast-food fries, this healthier homemade version is baked instead of fried. Oven baking results in a crispy, golden exterior and tender, moist interior that's irresistible. As a welcome bonus, you can leave the skins on the potatoes for extra crispness. This technique also works well with other tubers or root vegetables like carrots, sweet potatoes, and parsnips.

Preheat the oven to 425°F. Using a sharp knife, cut the potatoes lengthwise into ¼-inch-thick slices, then cut the slices into thin strips.

Pour the olive oil into a medium bowl. Add the potato sticks and toss to coat. Spread on a baking sheet. Bake for 20 minutes, then turn the potatoes and bake for about 30 minutes more, until crisp. While still warm, season to taste with salt and pepper. Serve right away.

2 medium russet potatoes, scrubbed (leave peels on if preferred)

2 tablespoons olive oil

Salt and freshly ground black pepper

VEGAN

VARIATIONS
Sweet Potato Oven Fries: Substitute sweet potatoes for the baking potatoes.

Spicy Oven Fries: Stir ¼ teaspoon each cayenne pepper and chili powder into the oil before tossing it with the potatoes.

MASHED SWEET POTATOES WITH APPLES

The sweet, dense flesh of sweet potatoes is enhanced by tart apples, cinnamon, and nutmeg in this recipe.

2 pounds sweet potatoes, scrubbed

1½ tablespoons butter

½ cup chopped onion

2 large Granny Smith apples, peeled, cored, and coarsely chopped (2½ cups)

2½ tablespoons water

¼ teaspoon salt

¼ teaspoon freshly ground black pepper

½ teaspoon ground cinnamon

¼ teaspoon ground nutmeg

Bring a large pot of water to a boil. Add the sweet potatoes and boil gently for 30 to 35 minutes, or until tender. Drain and let cool slightly.

Meanwhile, in a large skillet over medium heat, melt 1 tablespoon of the butter. Add the onion and cook, stirring occasionally, until golden and tender, 6 to 8 minutes. Add the apples and water. Cover and cook over medium-low heat, stirring occasionally, until tender, 10 to 15 minutes.

Peel the sweet potatoes, cut into chunks, and put into a large bowl. Add the remaining ½ tablespoon butter, the salt, pepper, cinnamon, nutmeg, and apple mixture. Mash until smooth, then spoon into a serving dish. Serve hot.

SERVES 6

CURRIED COUSCOUS

SERVES 4

Most people think of couscous as a whole grain, but it is a type of pasta. It's very quick to prepare and is great to keep on hand as a pantry staple.

In a medium saucepan over medium heat, warm the olive oil. Add the curry powder and allspice and cook, stirring constantly, for 1 minute. Add the broth and bring to a boil. Stir in the couscous. Remove from the heat, cover, and let stand for 5 minutes. Fluff with a fork and serve.

2   teaspoons olive oil

½   teaspoon curry powder

¼   teaspoon ground allspice

1¼ cups Rich Vegetable Broth
     (page 109) or canned broth

¾   cup couscous

VEGAN

LEMON RICE PILAF

Pilaf is one of the Middle East's and India's great contributions to the world of cooking. Cooks in those parts of the world are masters at the technique of sautéing rice before adding liquid to create rice dishes that are full-flavored and light in texture.

¼ cup sesame seeds

2 teaspoons olive oil

1 cup chopped onion

1 cup basmati or long-grain rice

1³⁄4 cups Rich Vegetable Broth (page 109) or canned broth

¼ cup chopped fresh parsley

2 teaspoons grated lemon zest

1 tablespoon fresh lemon juice

Salt and freshly ground black pepper

In a small, nonstick skillet, toast the sesame seeds over low heat for 5 minutes, stirring constantly. Remove from the heat.

In a medium saucepan over medium heat, warm the olive oil. Add the onion and cook, stirring often, until softened, about 5 minutes. Add the rice and cook, stirring constantly, for 1 minute.

Stir in the broth and bring to a boil. Reduce the heat, cover, and simmer until the rice is tender and the liquid is absorbed, about 20 minutes. Remove from the heat; fluff with a fork. Stir in the sesame seeds, parsley, lemon zest, and lemon juice. Season to taste with salt and pepper. Serve hot.

SERVES 6

THREE-GRAIN PILAF

SERVES 6

In this pilaf, quinoa, basmati rice, and millet combine for a flavorful dish. Quinoa and millet are nutritional giants in the family of grains. Both have impressive amounts of protein and B vitamins, as well as iron and potassium. Sautéing the grains before cooking gives them a delicious nutty flavor.

In a large skillet over medium heat, warm the olive oil. Add the onion and carrot and cook, stirring often, for 5 minutes. Add the rice, quinoa, and millet and cook, stirring often, for 3 minutes.

Stir in the broth and salt. Bring to a boil. Cover, reduce the heat, and simmer until the liquid is absorbed and the grains are tender, about 25 minutes. Stir in the cilantro and serve hot.

2   tablespoons olive oil

½   cup finely chopped onion

½   cup finely chopped peeled carrot

1   cup basmati rice

½   cup quinoa

½   cup millet

3   cups Rich Vegetable Broth (page 109) or canned broth

¼   teaspoon salt

⅓   cup chopped fresh cilantro or parsley

VEGAN

FAVORITE FRIED RICE

Great as a side dish, this fried rice, if topped with diced steamed sweet potato or winter squash, can also make a satisfying meal.

3 tablespoons Rich Vegetable Broth (page 109) or canned broth

1 tablespoon tamari or reduced-sodium soy sauce

1½ teaspoons dark (Asian) sesame oil

5 cups cooked white or brown long-grain rice

2 tablespoons vegetable oil

2½ cups chopped green onion (2 to 3 bunches; white and light green parts)

3 tablespoons minced peeled fresh ginger

2½ cups fresh bean sprouts

⅓ cup rice wine (mirin)

Salt and freshly ground black pepper

In a small bowl, mix the broth, tamari, and sesame oil. In a shallow baking pan, spread the rice and separate the grains with a fork.

In a deep skillet or wok over medium-high heat, warm the oil until hot but not smoking. Add the green onion and ginger and stir-fry until fragrant, about 20 seconds. Add the bean sprouts and rice wine and stir-fry until the sprouts begin to soften, about 1 minute. Add the rice and cook, stirring frequently, until heated through, 2 to 3 minutes. Add the broth mixture to the pan, tossing to coat evenly. Season to taste with salt and pepper. Serve hot.

 SERVES 6

VEGAN

MEDITERRANEAN QUINOA

Quinoa (pronounced KEEN-wah) is an ancient grain, cultivated 5,000 years ago by the Incas. It grows in places where other grains won't—poor soil and dry climates. It has a soft but crunchy texture and nutty flavor, and is high in protein, calcium, and phosphorus.

In a medium saucepan over medium heat, warm the olive oil. Add the onion, celery, carrot, and fennel and cook, stirring occasionally, until the onion is softened, 5 to 6 minutes. Add the quinoa and cook, stirring constantly, until lightly toasted, 2 to 3 minutes.

Add the water and bring to a boil. Cover, reduce the heat, and simmer over medium-low heat until the quinoa is tender and the liquid is absorbed, 12 to 15 minutes. Fluff with a fork. Stir in the olives, season to taste with salt and pepper, and serve hot.

1	tablespoon olive oil
½	cup finely chopped onion
½	cup finely chopped celery
½	cup finely chopped peeled carrot
1	cup finely chopped fennel bulb
1	cup quinoa, rinsed
1½	cups water
½	cup finely chopped black olives
	Salt and freshly ground black pepper

VEGAN

WILD AND BROWN RICE PILAF

Wild rice is not really rice, but the seed of an aquatic grass native to states in the Great Lakes region. Soaking the wild rice ahead of time reduces the cooking time and produces tender grains.

½   cup wild rice, rinsed

1½ ounces dried porcini mushrooms

1   cup hot water

1¾ cups cold water

1   cup long-grain brown rice

2   tablespoons olive oil

1   cup chopped onion

½   cup chopped fresh parsley

Salt and freshly ground black pepper

In a small bowl, combine the wild rice with enough warm water to cover. Let stand for 30 minutes. In another small bowl, combine the porcini and hot water and let soak for 30 minutes. Strain the porcini through a fine sieve set over a measuring cup, reserving ¾ cup of the soaking liquid. Rinse the porcini under cold water to remove any grit. Chop them and set aside.

In a large saucepan, bring the cold water and reserved porcini soaking liquid to a boil. Add the wild rice and brown rice. Cover, reduce the heat, and simmer until the liquid is absorbed and the rice is tender, about 40 minutes.

Meanwhile, in a large skillet over medium heat, warm the olive oil. Add the onion and cook, stirring occasionally, until softened, about 5 minutes. Stir in the reserved mushrooms. Add the cooked rice mixture to the skillet with the parsley and salt and pepper to taste; mix well. Serve hot.

SERVES 6

MUSHROOM-BARLEY PILAF

SERVES 6

Barley comes in many forms—unhulled, hulled, pearl, black, and white. In the pearl form—the most common variety—the grains have been polished. This substantial grain dish uses cremini and fresh shiitake mushrooms, but other varieties, like button and portobello, can be substituted.

In a medium saucepan, combine the barley and broth. Bring to a boil, reduce the heat to medium-low, cover, and simmer until the barley is tender and the liquid is absorbed, about 1 hour.

In a large saucepan over medium heat, warm the oil. Add the onion and cook, stirring often, until golden, about 7 minutes, adding a little water to prevent sticking, if needed. Add the garlic and all of the mushrooms and cook, stirring often, for 5 minutes.

Stir in the barley and spinach cook, stirring occasionally, until the barley is heated through, 3 to 5 minutes. Stir in the tamari and sesame oil and serve hot.

1   cup pearl barley

3   cups Rich Vegetable Broth (page 109) or canned broth

1   tablespoon vegetable oil

1   large onion, diced

2   medium cloves garlic, minced

8   ounces cremini mushrooms, thinly sliced

4   ounces fresh shiitake mushrooms, stemmed and thinly sliced

4   cups loosely packed spinach leaves

2   tablespoons tamari or reduced-sodium soy sauce

2   teaspoons dark (Asian) sesame oil

VEGAN

CRISPY PAN-FRIED NOODLES

The trick to this recipe is knowing how to flip the noodle cake in the pan.
I have found that the best way to do this is to slip the noodles onto a plate,
cover them with another plate, invert them, and slide the noodle cake back
into the skillet to finish cooking.

1 pound fresh Chinese egg noodles

½ cup finely chopped green onion (white and light green parts)

2 tablespoons tamari or reduced-sodium soy sauce

3 tablespoons vegetable oil

Bring a large pot of water to a boil. Add the noodles and cook until tender, about 2 minutes or according to the package directions. Drain and transfer to a large bowl. Add the green onion, tamari, and 1 tablespoon of the oil and toss to mix.

In a large, nonstick skillet over medium-high heat, warm the remaining 2 tablespoons oil. Add the noodle mixture, spreading it evenly in the pan and pressing it down. Cook for 2 minutes, reduce the heat to medium-low, and cook until nicely browned on the bottom, about 10 minutes. Carefully turn the noodles and cook until the underside is browned, about 10 minutes longer. Cut into wedges and serve.

SERVES 4 TO 6

ASPARAGUS WITH GARLIC AÏOLI

*Fresh spring-green asparagus is an elegant vegetable, but it's often
paired with calorie-packed sauces. Try serving it with a healthier soy
mayonnaise flavored with garlic, and be sure not to overcook the
asparagus. The cooking time will depend on the thickness of the spears.
Asparagus is a great source of folic acid, which is known to help
lower the risk of heart disease.*

Make the aïoli: In a medium bowl, mix the mayonnaise, herbs,
lemon juice, garlic, and salt and pepper to taste. Cover and chill
for at least 1 hour or up to 2 days. Whisk well before serving.

In a large pot, bring 1 inch of water to a boil. Put the asparagus in
a steamer basket and carefully place the basket in the pot. Cover
and steam over medium-high heat until the asparagus spears
bend slightly when picked up, 4 to 5 minutes for asparagus under
½ inch in diameter, 5 to 6 minutes for thicker spears.

Arrange the steamed asparagus on plates and serve hot, with the
aïoli spooned on the side.

GARLIC AÏOLI

1   cup soy mayonnaise

½   cup chopped fresh herbs, such
    as basil, tarragon, or chervil

1   tablespoon fresh lemon juice

2   cloves garlic, minced

    Salt and freshly ground
    black pepper

1   to 1½ pounds asparagus,
    trimmed

VEGAN

SAUTÉED MEDITERRANEAN VEGETABLES

This sauté is great served over couscous, quinoa, or rice.

1 tablespoon olive oil

2 cloves garlic, minced

1 cup coarsely chopped onion

1 small fennel bulb, cut into ½-inch strips (about 2½ cups)

1 large red bell pepper, thinly sliced

1 large carrot, peeled and cut into ½-inch slices

4 ounces cremini mushrooms, halved

1½ cups coarsely chopped plum tomatoes

⅓ cup pitted oil-cured black olives

1½ teaspoons dried basil

1½ teaspoons dried oregano

½ teaspoon salt

¼ teaspoon ground cinnamon

⅛ teaspoon freshly ground black pepper

2 tablespoons balsamic vinegar

In a large skillet over medium heat, warm the olive oil. Add the garlic and onion and cook, stirring often, until just browned, about 5 minutes. Add the fennel bulb, bell pepper, carrot, mushrooms, tomatoes, olives, basil, oregano, salt, cinnamon, and pepper. Reduce the heat, cover, and simmer until the vegetables are tender, about 4 minutes. Add the vinegar, stir well, and cook for 1 minute. Serve hot.

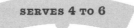

SERVES 4 TO 6

VEGAN

ROASTED BEETS WITH DILL

SERVES 6

This simple side dish is even quicker to prepare if you roast the beets the day before you plan to serve them.

Preheat the oven to 400°F. Place the beets in a small roasting pan with the water. Cover the pan tightly with foil. Bake until the beets are tender when pierced with a knife, about 1 hour. Cool slightly. Peel the beets. Cut into ¼-inch-thick slices.

In a large bowl, whisk together the vinegar, lemon juice, olive oil, and salt. Add the beets and toss gently to coat. Stir in the dill and serve.

2   pounds beets (about 6 medium), trimmed but unpeeled

¼   cup water

1   tablespoon red wine vinegar

1   teaspoon fresh lemon juice

¼   cup extra-virgin olive oil

1   teaspoon salt

¼   cup chopped fresh dill

VEGAN

STIR-FRIED SESAME VEGETABLES

When it comes to fast food, stir-fries might well be the first kind that was invented. Developed by the Chinese centuries ago, stir-frying involves cooking bite-sized pieces of food quickly over high heat in a small amount of oil. The food is cooked by both the heat of the pan and the heat of the oil. It's an ideal way to preserve the colors, flavors, textures, and nutrients in foods.

1½ tablespoons vegetable oil

1 clove garlic, minced

1 teaspoon minced peeled fresh ginger

4 ounces green beans, cut into 2-inch pieces (about 1¼ cups)

4 small carrots, peeled and cut into thin strips

1 medium red bell pepper, cut into thin strips

2 teaspoon dark (Asian) sesame oil

Salt and freshly ground black pepper

In a wok or large skillet over medium-high heat, warm the oil. Add the garlic and ginger and stir-fry for 20 seconds. Add the vegetables and stir-fry until crisp-tender, about 8 minutes. Stir in the sesame oil and season to taste with salt and pepper. Serve hot.

SERVES 6

BRAISED ROOT VEGETABLES

SERVES 4

Although braising is a technique that has long been associated with turning economical cuts of meats into fork-tender morsels, this method of cooking also works well with vegetables. Slow cooking in just a small amount of liquid imparts a delicious, melting tenderness and a caramel glaze to vegetables.

In a large, heavy saucepan over medium-low heat, melt the butter with the wine. Add the celery root, carrots, shallots, salt, and pepper to taste, stirring to coat the vegetables, Cover and cook, stirring occasionally, for 20 minutes.

Add the beans to the vegetables, stirring to coat. Cover and cook, stirring once or twice, until all of the vegetables are tender, about 10 minutes. Serve hot.

1 tablespoon butter

3 tablespoons dry white wine or Rich Vegetable Broth (page 109) or canned broth

1 pound celery root (sometimes called celeriac), peeled and cut into 1½-inch pieces

4 large carrots, peeled and sliced diagonally 1 inch thick

8 large shallots, quartered

¾ teaspoon salt

Freshly ground black pepper

8 ounces green beans, trimmed

STUFFED BABY EGGPLANT

Stuffed eggplant is a popular dish in Italy. It takes a fair amount of time to prepare, but the results are worth it. Theses eggplants can be made ahead and kept, covered, in the refrigerator. To serve, reheat in microwave.

SERVES 8

8   baby eggplants (6 ounces each), halved lengthwise

2   teaspoons olive oil

2   cloves garlic, minced

2   medium bell peppers (1 orange and 1 yellow), chopped

4   ripe plum tomatoes, chopped

    One 5- to 6-ounce bag fresh baby spinach

2   tablespoons freshly grated lemon zest

½   teaspoon salt

2   teaspoons fresh lemon juice

3   tablespoons grated Parmesan cheese

Preheat the oven to 425°F. Lightly coat 2 large, rimmed baking sheets with vegetable oil spray. Scoop out the eggplant flesh with a spoon and reserve, leaving ¾-inch-thick shells. Chop the removed eggplant (you should have 3 to 4 cups). Place the shells, cut side up, on the prepared baking sheets. Lightly coat the shells with vegetable oil spray.

Bake for 20 to 25 minutes, or until the eggplants are almost tender. Turn the shells cut side down, and bake for 10 to 15 minutes more, or until very tender.

Meanwhile, in a large, nonstick skillet over medium heat, warm the olive oil. Add the garlic and chopped eggplant and cook, stirring often, for 3 minutes. Add the bell peppers and cook, stirring often, until crisp-tender, about 6 minutes. Add the tomatoes and cook, stirring often, until the vegetables are tender, about 2 minutes. Add the spinach, cover, and cook until just wilted but still bright green, about 1 minute (if the spinach doesn't all fit, let some cook down and then add the rest). Remove from the heat. Stir in the lemon zest and ¼ teaspoon of the salt.

Remove the sheet with the eggplant shells from the oven. Reduce the oven temperature to 350°F. Turn the shells over, sprinkle with the remaining ¼ teaspoon salt and the lemon juice. Fill each shell with the vegetable mixture. Sprinkle the filled eggplants with the Parmesan cheese. Return the stuffed eggplants to the baking sheets and bake for about 20 minutes, or just until heated through.

GRILLED EGGPLANT WITH YOGURT-MINT SAUCE

This is a simple yet delicious way to serve eggplant. Its earthy flavor goes well with the warm Indian flavors in the sauce.

In a medium bowl, mix the yogurt, mint, lemon juice, and curry powder. Season to taste with salt and pepper.

Prepare a medium-hot fire in a charcoal grill or preheat a gas grill to medium. Rub the eggplant slices on both sides with sesame oil, then sprinkle with coriander, salt, and pepper. Grill until slightly charred, about 6 minutes on each side. Arrange the eggplant slices on a serving platter. Serve hot with the yogurt-mint sauce.

1 cup plain yogurt

3 tablespoons chopped fresh mint

2 tablespoons fresh lemon juice

1 teaspoon curry powder

Salt and freshly ground black pepper

2 eggplants (each about 1 pound) cut crosswise into 1-inch-thick slices

¼ cup dark (Asian) sesame oil

2 tablespoons coriander seed, crushed

GREEN BEANS WITH CARAMELIZED ONIONS

Besides its wonderful flavor, this dish is prized because it can be made ahead. To prepare the beans, trim the stem ends, leaving the pointed ends intact, if desired. Most fresh beans today do not require stringing, as the fibrous string has been bred out of them.

5   cups water

1   pound green beans, trimmed

1   tablespoon olive oil

3   medium red onions (about 1¾ pounds), each cut into 16 wedges

½   cup Rich Vegetable Broth (page 109), or canned broth

1   tablespoon balsamic vinegar

2   teaspoons light brown sugar

¼   teaspoon salt

¼   teaspoon freshly ground black pepper

In a large saucepan, bring the water to a boil. Add the beans and cook until crisp-tender, about 6 minutes. Drain and keep warm.

In a large skillet over medium-high heat, warm the olive oil. Add the onions and cook until golden, about 10 minutes. Add the broth and cook for 5 minutes, stirring occasionally. Stir in the vinegar, brown sugar, salt, and pepper. Stir in the beans, cover, and cook for 2 minutes. Serve warm.

SERVES 6

EDAMAME SUCCOTASH

SERVES 6

This dish includes edamame (fresh soybeans), which are often associated with Asian cuisine. The edible beans come two inside a fuzzy pod and have a sweet, nutty flavor. They are easy to digest and are exceptionally high in protein (¹/₂ cup contains 16 grams). Look for edamame in natural food stores or large supermarkets.

In a large saucepan, combine the potatoes with enough cold salted water to cover by 1 inch. Bring to a boil, reduce the heat, and simmer until the potatoes are just tender, about 20 minutes. Drain and cool, then cut into bite-size pieces.

In a large skillet over medium-high heat, warm 1 tablespoon of the oil and 1 tablespoon of the butter. Add the potatoes, with salt and pepper to taste, and cook, turning once or twice, until nicely crusted, 8 to 10 minutes. Transfer to a serving bowl.

Heat the remaining tablespoon of oil and butter in the skillet. Add the corn and zucchini and cook, stirring often, until crisp-tender, about 5 minutes. Stir in the edamame and cook, stirring often, until heated through. Season with salt and pepper and add to the potatoes along with the onion and chives, stirring to combine. Serve warm or at room temperature.

1 pound small potatoes, such as Yukon gold

2 tablespoons vegetable oil

2 tablespoons butter

Salt and freshly ground black pepper

2 cups fresh corn kernels (cut from 4 medium ears)

1 medium zucchini, cut in half lengthwise and then sliced ½ inch thick

8 ounces frozen shelled edamame (fresh soybeans) or baby lima beans (1½ cups), cooked according to the package directions and cooled

¼ cup finely chopped red onion

¼ cup finely chopped fresh green onion

BROCCOLI WITH PINE NUTS

This easy-to-prepare broccoli dish, tossed with sun-dried tomatoes, pine nuts, and vinaigrette, is served at room temperature. When storing fresh broccoli, be sure it has plenty of air circulation. Putting it in a plastic bag will cause humidity to build up, and the broccoli will decay quickly. Wrap the broccoli in a damp kitchen towel or place it in a perforated plastic bag and refrigerate for up to 3 days.

SERVES 4

1 large head broccoli (about 1 pound)

¼ cup sun-dried tomato bits

¼ cup boiling water

¼ cup pine nuts

2 tablespoons olive oil

2 tablespoons red wine vinegar or cider vinegar

1 small clove garlic, minced

Salt and freshly ground black pepper

Cut the broccoli into florets. Peel the stems and cut in half lengthwise, and then cut crosswise into ½-inch-thick slices. Bring a large saucepan of water to a boil over high heat. In a medium bowl, combine the dried tomato bits with the ¼ cup boiling water and set aside.

Toast the pine nuts in a large, preferably nonstick skillet over medium heat for 7 to 8 minutes, stirring often. Scrape into a small bowl.

Add the broccoli stems to the pan of boiling water and boil for 2 minutes. Add the florets and boil until bright green and crisp-tender, 2 to 3 minutes more. Drain well.

Add the olive oil, vinegar, and garlic to the dried tomatoes and water. Whisk until well blended. Add the broccoli and pine nuts, tossing to coat. Season to taste with salt and pepper. Serve warm or at room temperature.

VEGAN

SWISS CHARD WITH RAISINS

*Swiss chard has large, curly leaves and white stems.
The leaves have a mild taste with a touch of bitterness.
The fresher the chard, the milder its flavor will be.*

In large, deep skillet, combine the chard and water (if the greens don't all fit, let some cook down then add the rest). Cover and cook, stirring and turning occasionally with 2 spoons, until the leaves are just wilted and most of the liquid is evaporated, 4 to 5 minutes.

Stir in the apple juice and raisins. Cook, uncovered, stirring often, until the apple juice is almost evaporated, 2 to 3 minutes. Serve hot.

2 pounds fresh Swiss chard, rinsed, stems removed, and leaves chopped (20 cups)

½ cup water

½ cup apple juice

¼ cup golden raisins

VEGAN

SQUASH AND POTATO PANCAKES

MAKES 20 PANCAKES

2　cups peeled, grated uncooked butternut squash

2　cups peeled, grated russet potatoes (2 medium)

½　cup grated red onion

2　teaspoons salt

2　cloves garlic, minced

1　teaspoon dried sage

¼　teaspoon ground nutmeg

1　large egg, beaten

3　tablespoons unbleached all-purpose flour

　Freshly ground black pepper

　Vegetable oil for frying

Potato pancakes are given a new dimension with the addition of winter squash. The results are light, crisp, and flavorful. These crisp little pancakes are great with a dollop of sour cream, applesauce, or even salsa. To speed up the preparation, you can grate the vegetables using the shredding disk of a food processor.

In a colander set over a sink, combine the squash, potatoes, and onion. Add the salt and toss to blend. Let stand for 15 minutes, pressing the vegetables several times to extract as much liquid as possible.

Preheat the oven to 200°F. Transfer the squash mixture to a medium bowl. Stir in the garlic, sage, nutmeg, and egg until well combined. Add the flour and pepper to taste and mix well.

In a large skillet over medium-high heat, warm about ⅛ inch oil until hot but not smoking. Using a large tablespoon, drop the mixture into the oil in large spoonfuls, flattening with a spatula to ensure even cooking. Cook until well browned, turning once, 1 to 3 minutes on each side. Drain on paper towels.

Transfer the pancakes to an ovenproof plate and keep warm in the oven. Cook the remaining pancakes, adding more oil to the skillet as needed. Serve hot.

HERBED APPLE STUFFING

The apples for this recipe are roasted, which brings out their sweetness and gives the stuffing a depth of flavor. The nuts add a great crunchy texture. The stuffing is wonderful served with the Portobello Gravy (facing page).

1   tablespoon olive oil

4   cups sliced peeled tart apples (about 3½ pounds)

1   cup chopped onion

1   cup chopped peeled celery root (celeriac)

3   cloves garlic, minced

½   cup brandy

5   cups cubed dense white bread, about 8 ounces, (½-inch cubes)

1   cup Rich Vegetable Broth (page 109) or canned broth

½   cup chopped pecans, toasted (see page 114)

2   teaspoons chopped fresh thyme, or ½ teaspoon dried thyme

½   teaspoon salt

¼   teaspoon freshly ground black pepper

2   large eggs, lightly beaten

Preheat the oven to 350°F. In a large skillet over medium-high heat, warm the olive oil. Add the apples and cook, without stirring, until golden brown, about 2 minutes. Carefully turn the apple slices and cook until golden brown on the other side, about 2 minutes more. Add the onion, celery root, and garlic and cook, stirring occasionally, until lightly browned, about 3 minutes. Add the brandy and cook until the liquid almost evaporates. Remove from the heat and let cool.

In a large bowl, combine the apple mixture, bread, broth, pecans, thyme, salt, pepper, and eggs, tossing gently. Spoon into a 2-quart casserole. Cover and bake for about 45 minutes, until thoroughly heated.

SERVES 6 TO 8

PORTOBELLO GRAVY

MAKES 3 CUPS

Portobello mushrooms give this gravy a rich, earthy taste. You can also substitute fresh shiitake mushrooms in this recipe.

In a medium saucepan over medium heat, warm the olive oil. Add the onion and garlic and cook, stirring often, until the onion is soft, about 5 minutes. Add the mushrooms and cook, stirring often, until they begin to release their juices, about 10 minutes.

Add the broth, tamari, thyme, and sage and simmer for 10 minutes. In a small bowl, dissolve the cornstarch in the water. Stir into the saucepan and simmer, stirring occasionally, until thickened slightly, about 10 minutes more. Season with salt and pepper.

Pour the gravy through a fine sieve into a clean saucepan, discarding the mushrooms and onions, or leave it unstrained for a chunky-style gravy.

2   tablespoons olive oil

1   medium onion, finely chopped

2   cloves garlic, minced

1½ cups cleaned, chopped portobello mushrooms (about 2 medium mushrooms)

2¼ cups Rich Vegetable Broth (page 109) or canned broth

3   tablespoons tamari or low-sodium soy sauce

¼   teaspoon dried thyme

⅛   teaspoon dried sage

1   tablespoon cornstarch

¼   cup water

¼   teaspoon salt

⅛   teaspoon freshly ground black pepper

VEGAN

BREAD WINNERS

WHEN

it comes to vegetarian meal planning, the
breads in this chapter offer a tempting variety
of options. Homemade pizza is always a favorite,
and making it at home allows you to create just the
kind you or your family likes best. Warm batches of flaky
biscuits or fragrant muffins are a delightful addition with a
minimum of effort to almost any meal, while whole-grain
quick breads can be interpreted as making a good
thing even better. And nothing compares to the
aroma of home-baked yeast loaves. The range
of recipes offered in this chapter demon-
strates the diverse role of bread
in meals and in between.

WHOLE-WHEAT PIZZA DOUGH

1¼ cups warm water (105° to 115°F)

1 envelope or 1 scant tablespoon active dry yeast

1 teaspoon sugar

3 cups unbleached all-purpose flour, or as needed

2 cups whole-wheat pastry flour

2 large eggs

2 teaspoons salt

Once you begin making your own pizza, you will never want to stop. The dough is easy and keeps well in the freezer. This recipe can be made in a food processor with a capacity of at least 8 cups, or it can be halved for a smaller machine. To bake the pizzas, you'll need a 12-inch round pizza pan or a large cookie sheet. Dark, heavy pans are best because they absorb heat quickly and evenly for a crisp, browned crust.

You can make the dough up to 2 days ahead. Wrap flattened balls of dough in plastic wrap and refrigerate (the dough may rise a bit). Use directly from the refrigerator. To freeze, wrap flattened balls of dough in plastic wrap, then put them into a zipper-lock food storage bag and freeze for up to 3 months. Thaw at room temperature for 1½ hours, or until workable.

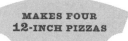

MAKES FOUR
12-INCH PIZZAS

In a small bowl, mix the water, yeast, and sugar and let stand for about 10 minutes, or until foamy.

In a food processor, combine the all-purpose and whole-wheat flours, eggs, and salt. Pulse to mix. With the motor running, pour the yeast mixture through the feed tube in a steady stream. Process until the dough cleans the sides of the bowl, then process for 45 seconds longer (this takes the place of kneading), or until the dough is smooth and elastic.

Put the dough into a large, oiled bowl, turning to coat. Cover loosely with plastic wrap and let rise in a warm, draft-free place for about 1 hour, or until doubled in volume.

Punch down the dough and divide into 4 equal pieces. Shape the pieces into balls. Lightly cover the dough with a kitchen towel and let rest for 30 minutes so it will be easier to handle. (The dough will rise but not double in volume.)

For each pizza: Brush a 12-inch round pizza pan or large baking sheet with 1 teaspoon olive oil, or spray with olive oil spray. Place one piece of the dough on a lightly floured surface. With floured hands, pat into a 6-inch round. Stretch or roll out the dough with a rolling pin into an 11-inch circle. Lift onto the prepared pan and press the dough to the edges of the pan or press into a 12-inch circle on the baking sheet. Add the topping of your choice (some topping recipes follow) and bake on the lowest oven rack. Cut into wedges with a pizza wheel or knife and serve warm.

PESTO PRIMAVERA PIZZA

It's worth tucking away a container or two of frozen pesto during the season of fresh basil so that later you can make this great-tasting pizza.

2 tablespoons Pesto (page 96)

1 piece Whole-Wheat Pizza Dough (page 250), shaped into a crust

1 cup grated mozzarella or provolone cheese

12 thin slices yellow squash

12 thin slices plum tomatoes

1 cup very small broccoli florets, blanched

Preheat the oven to 500°F. Leaving a 1-inch edge, spread the pesto on the circle of pizza dough. Sprinkle with ½ cup of the mozzarella. Top with the squash, tomatoes, and broccoli. Sprinkle with the remaining ½ cup mozzarella. Bake for 10 to 15 minutes, or until the edge of the crust is browned and crisp.

MAKES ONE
12-INCH PIZZA

WILD MUSHROOM AND SPINACH PIZZA

For those who enjoy pizza that isn't traditionally Italian, here is a vegetable version that is abundantly hearty.

Preheat the oven to 500°F. In a large, nonstick skillet over medium-high heat, warm the oil. Add the mushrooms and cook, stirring often, until lightly golden and the liquid from the mushrooms has evaporated, about 6 minutes. Leaving a 1-inch edge, spread the creamed spinach over the pizza dough. Top with the mushrooms and fontina cheese. Sprinkle with the Parmesan cheese. Bake for 10 to 15 minutes, or until the edge of the crust is browned and crisp.

2 teaspoons of olive oil

5 cups sliced fresh wild mushrooms, such as portobello, shiitake, or chanterelle

One 9-ounce package frozen creamed spinach, thawed

1 piece Whole-Wheat Pizza Dough (page 250), shaped into a crust

1 cup grated fontina or mozzarella cheese

3 tablespoons grated Parmesan cheese

PROVENÇALE PIZZA

Pizza is as omnipresent in Southern France as it is in Italy.
This version is typical of the way it is served in Provence.

½ cup chopped kalamata olives

1 tablespoon chopped fresh
   rosemary, or 1 teaspoon dried

1 piece Whole-Wheat Pizza
   Dough (page 250)

3½ teaspoons olive oil

2 cups thinly sliced onion

½ cup grated mozzarella cheese

Preheat the oven to 500°F. Knead the olives and rosemary into the pizza dough. Shape the dough into a 12-inch crust as directed on page 251.

In a large, nonstick skillet over medium-high heat, warm 2 teaspoons of the olive oil. Add the onion and cook, stirring often, until lightly browned and tender, about 10 minutes. Brush the pizza dough with the remaining 1½ teaspoons olive oil. Leaving a 1-inch edge, sprinkle with the mozzarella cheese and then cover with the onions. Bake for 10 to 15 minutes, or until the edge of the crust is browned and crisp.

**MAKES ONE
12-INCH PIZZA**

OATMEAL PEASANT BREAD

These plump, round loaves have a richness that makes them a satisfying part of a soup or salad supper.

In a small bowl, sprinkle the yeast over the warm water and stir. Let stand for 5 minutes, until foamy.

In a large bowl, combine the boiling water, oats, molasses, butter, and salt. Mix well and let cool to room temperature. Stir in 2 cups of the flour, the yeast mixture, and the eggs until well blended. Add enough of the remaining flour, 1 cup at a time, to make a soft dough; you may not need all 4¾ remaining cups.

Turn the dough out onto a lightly floured surface. With floured hands, knead the dough for 5 minutes, or until smooth and elastic. Put the dough into a large, oiled bowl, turning to coat. Cover with greased plastic wrap and let rise in a warm, draft-free place for 1½ to 2 hours, or until doubled in volume.

Lightly grease a baking sheet. Punch down the dough and divide it in half. Shape each half into a round loaf. Place the loaves 5 inches apart on the prepared baking sheet. Cover loosely with greased plastic wrap or a kitchen towel and let rise in a warm place for no more than 1 hour, or just until doubled in volume. Meanwhile, preheat the oven to 375°F.

Uncover the dough. In a small bowl, beat the egg white with 2 teaspoons water to make an egg wash. Brush gently over the loaves. Sprinkle each loaf with oats. Bake for 35 to 45 minutes, until the tops are golden brown and the loaves sound hollow when tapped on the bottom. Transfer to a wire rack and let cool completely.

2   envelopes or a scant 2 tablespoons active dry yeast

½   cup warm water (105° to 110°F)

1¼ cups boiling water

1   cup old-fashioned rolled oats, plus more for sprinkling

½   cup molasses

6   tablespoons (¾ stick) butter, at room temperature

1   tablespoon salt

6   to 6 ¾ cups unbleached all-purpose flour

2   large eggs

1   large egg white

2   teaspoons water

MAKES 2 ROUND LOAVES
(24 SLICES)

ROSEMARY FOCACCIA

**MAKES 1 FLATBREAD
(12 SLICES)**

1   medium russet potato (about 9 ounces), peeled and quartered

1½ teaspoons rapid-rise yeast

3½ cups unbleached all-purpose flour

1   cup warm water (105° to 115°F)

4   tablespoons extra-virgin olive oil

1¼ teaspoons salt

2   tablespoons chopped fresh rosemary

¾   teaspoon coarse sea salt, or 1¼ teaspoons kosher salt

Rapid-rise yeast reduces the preparation time by more than an hour. If you use an equal amount of regular active dry yeast instead, let the sponge develop for 30 minutes rather than 20, and increase the first and second rises to 1½ hours each. The focaccia can be kept at room temperature for several hours and reheated just before serving. Or wrap the cooled focaccia in plastic and then in foil and freeze for up to 1 month; unwrap and defrost in a 325°F oven for about 15 minutes.

In a saucepan, bring 4 cups water to a boil. Add the potato and simmer until tender, about 25 minutes. Drain well and let cool until the potato can be handled comfortably. Grate it through the large holes on a box grater. Measure 1⅓ cups lightly packed potato; discard any extra or reserve for another use.

Meanwhile, in a large bowl with an electric mixer or in a food processor, mix or process the yeast, ½ cup of the flour, and ½ cup of the warm water until combined. Cover tightly with plastic wrap (or put the work-bowl lid on) and set aside until bubbly, about 20 minutes. Add the remaining 3 cups flour, ½ cup warm water, 2 tablespoons of the olive oil, the salt, and the grated potato. If using a mixer, fit it with the paddle attachment and mix on low speed until dough comes together. Switch to the dough hook attachment, increase the speed to medium, and continue kneading until the dough is smooth and elastic, about 5 minutes. For a food processor, process until the dough is smooth and elastic, about 40 seconds.

Transfer the dough to a lightly oiled bowl, turn to coat with oil, and cover loosely with plastic wrap. Let rise in a warm, draft-free area until puffy and doubled in volume, about 1 hour.

With wet hands (to prevent sticking), press the dough flat into a generously oiled 15½-by-10½-inch jelly-roll pan, or halve and flatten each piece of dough into an 8-inch round on a large (at least 18 inches long), generously oiled baking sheet. Cover loosely with lightly greased or oil-sprayed plastic wrap and let rise in a warm, draft-free area until puffy and doubled in volume, 45 minutes to 1 hour.

Meanwhile, preheat the oven to 425°F. With 2 wet fingers, dimple the risen dough at regular intervals. Drizzle the dough with the remaining 2 tablespoons olive oil and sprinkle evenly with the rosemary and coarse salt, landing some in the pools of oil.

Bake for about 25 minutes, until golden brown and crisp on the bottom. Transfer to a wire rack to cool slightly. Cut a rectangular focaccia into squares, or cut round focaccia into wedges; serve warm.

VARIATIONS

Sage Focaccia: Add 1 tablespoon chopped fresh sage leaves when mixing the dough, and substitute 24 whole fresh sage leaves (one per oil-filled dimple) for the rosemary.

Parmesan Focaccia: Substitute ⅔ cup grated Parmesan cheese for the rosemary and coarse sea salt.

VEGAN

CARAMELIZED ONION FLATBREAD

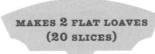

**MAKES 2 FLAT LOAVES
(20 SLICES)**

The best types of onions for caramelizing are the sweet varieties, such as Vidalia, Maui, and Walla Walla. If none of these are available, use yellow onions. This bread requires advance planning and preparation. Letting the yeast mixture or sponge sit overnight enhances the bread's wheat flavor.

SPONGE

1   cup warm water (105° to 110°F)

½   teaspoon active dry yeast

1   cup bread flour

2   tablespoons olive oil

2   teaspoons brown sugar

2   medium onions, sliced into ¼-inch rings

1   cup warm water (105°F to 110°F)

1   envelope or 1 scant tablespoon active dry yeast

2¼ cups bread flour

½   cup whole-wheat flour

2¼ teaspoons salt

½   teaspoon freshly ground black pepper

Make the sponge: Place the water in a medium bowl. Sprinkle the yeast over the water and stir. Let sit for 2 minutes. Mix in the bread flour. Cover the bowl with plastic wrap and let sit overnight, or for 14 to 16 hours.

In a heavy-bottomed saucepan over medium heat, heat the olive oil and brown sugar for 1 minute. Add the onions, stir well, and cook, stirring occasionally, until browned and caramelized, about 12 minutes. Remove from the heat and set aside.

Place the warm water in the bowl of an electric mixer or in a mixing bowl. Sprinkle the yeast over the water and stir. Let sit for 2 minutes. Add the sponge, bread and whole-wheat flours, salt, and pepper. Beat with the dough hook until the ingredients are combined, about 2 minutes, or beat vigorously with a wooden spoon for 8 to 10 minutes. Let rest for 15 minutes. Add the caramelized onions and mix until the dough is silky and elastic and pulls away from the sides of the bowl. The dough should be very wet and sticky but still elastic.

Transfer the dough to a lightly oiled bowl and cover loosely with plastic wrap. Let rise in a warm place until doubled in size, about 1½ hours. Turn over a baking sheet and sprinkle the underside with cornmeal or flour. Place the dough on a well-floured work surface, handling it gently to preserve as much volume as possible; cut into 2 equal pieces.

Gently pull and stretch each piece of dough into a flat round about 1¼ inches thick. Transfer to the prepared baking sheet. Cover loosely with plastic wrap and let rise in a warm place for 45 minutes to an hour.

Place a baking stone on the middle rack in the oven and preheat to 450°F. Using a spray bottle, spritz the oven walls with water. Work quickly so the oven does not lose heat. Slide the loaves onto the hot stone. Bake for 16 to 18 minutes, until brown. Transfer to a wire rack to cool.

VEGAN

BROCCOLI AND MUSHROOM BREAD

MAKES 1 RING-SHAPED LOAF (16 SLICES)

Many home bakers add too much flour to their bread dough, which can result in dry loaves. To tell if bread dough has enough flour before adding more, squeeze the dough gently with your hand. If your hand pulls away clean, there is already enough flour.

DOUGH

About 2 cups warm water (105° to 115°F)

1   envelope or 1 scant tablespoon active dry yeast

3½ cups unbleached all-purpose flour

1½ teaspoons salt

3   tablespoons olive oil

FILLING

2   teaspoons butter

½   cup chopped onion

1   clove garlic, minced

1   cup frozen chopped broccoli, thawed, drained, and squeezed dry

1   cup chopped portobello or cremini mushrooms

1   tablespoon finely chopped fresh basil, or 1 teaspoon dried

1   teaspoon finely chopped fresh rosemary, or ¼ teaspoon dried

    Salt and freshly ground black pepper

½   cup grated plain or smoked mozzarella cheese

    Olive oil for brushing

    Rosemary leaves for sprinkling

    Freshly ground black pepper

Make the dough: In a small bowl, combine 1 cup of the warm water and the yeast and let stand until foamy, about 5 minutes.

In a large bowl, mix the flour and salt. Make a well in the center and pour in the yeast mixture and the olive oil. Mix in flour from the sides of the well. Stir in the remaining 1 cup warm water just as needed to form a soft, sticky dough. Turn out onto a lightly floured work surface. Knead until smooth, silky, and elastic, about 10 minutes.

Put the dough into a greased bowl and turn to coat. Cover with a towel or greased plastic wrap and let rise until doubled in volume, 1½ to 2 hours.

Meanwhile, make the filling: In a large skillet over medium heat, melt the butter. Add the onion and garlic and cook, stirring often, until softened, about 5 minutes. Add the broccoli and mushrooms and cook, stirring often, until the broccoli is tender and the mushrooms release their juices, about 7 minutes. Stir in the basil, rosemary and salt and pepper to taste. Remove from the heat and let cool.

Preheat the oven to 400°F. Grease a 9- to 10-inch ring pan; set aside. Punch down the dough, turn out onto a lightly floured surface, and let rest for 5 minutes. Roll into a 14-by-10-inch rectangle. Stir the cheese into the filling, then spoon over the dough, leaving a narrow border on all sides. Roll the dough up from one long side and seal the edges well. Coil into a circle and seal the ends together. Fit into the prepared pan. Cover loosely with greased plastic wrap and let rise until the dough is just below the top of the pan. Remove the plastic wrap, brush with olive oil, then sprinkle with rosemary leaves and pepper.

Bake for about 50 minutes, until golden. Remove from the pan and set on a wire rack to cool.

HONEY WHOLE-WHEAT BREAD

**MAKES 1 LOAF
(12 SLICES)**

⅓ cup flax seed

1¾ cups warm water
(105° to 115°F)

2 tablespoons honey

1 envelope or 1 scant
tablespoon active dry yeast

1 cup bread flour

¼ cup toasted wheat germ

1½ teaspoons salt

2 cups whole-wheat flour

¼ cup plain soymilk

Many whole-wheat loaves of bread are short on flavor and less than satisfying in texture. I find that the addition of wheat germ and flax seed gives the bread a wonderful nutty flavor and a slightly more complex texture.

In a blender or mini food processor, grind the flax seed into a coarse meal. Set 2 teaspoons aside.

In a large bowl, combine the warm water and honey, stirring until the honey is dissolved. Sprinkle the yeast over this mixture and stir to dissolve. Let stand for 5 minutes, until foamy. Add the bread flour, wheat germ, salt, and remaining ground flax seed. Stir vigorously until smooth. Gradually stir in the whole-wheat flour.

Turn the dough out onto a lightly floured surface. With floured hands, knead for 10 minutes, or until smooth and elastic. Put the dough into a large, oiled bowl, turning to coat. Cover loosely with greased plastic wrap and let rise in a warm, draft-free place for 1½ to 2 hours, or until doubled in volume.

Lightly oil a 9-by-5-inch loaf pan. Punch down the dough. Flatten into a disk and roll tightly into a log. Place, seam side down, in the prepared pan. Cover loosely with plastic wrap and let rise in a warm place until the dough domes over the top of the pan, about 45 minutes.

Preheat the oven to 400°F. Lightly brush the top of the loaf with the soymilk and sprinkle with the reserved 2 teaspoons ground flax seed. Bake for 15 minutes. Reduce the oven temperature to 350°F and bake for 20 to 25 minutes more, until the bread pulls away from the sides of the pan. Turn out onto a wire rack and cool completely before slicing.

CHILI CORNBREADS

Warm from the oven, these savory cornbread muffins are the perfect accompaniment for chili. The trick to turning out light and tender muffins lies in not working the batter too hard. Mix the ingredients until they are just blended—too much stirring will make them tough.

½ cup yellow cornmeal

¾ cup unbleached all-purpose flour

1 teaspoon baking powder

¾ teaspoon baking soda

½ teaspoon salt

¾ cup plain soy yogurt

⅓ cup plain soymilk or rice milk

¼ cup egg substitute

One 4-ounce can chopped green chiles

Preheat the oven to 350°F. Lightly grease a 12-cup muffin pan. In a medium bowl, whisk together the cornmeal, flour, baking powder, baking soda, and salt. In a medium bowl, mix the yogurt, soymilk, egg substitute, and chiles. Make a well in the dry ingredients. Add the yogurt mixture and stir until just blended.

Divide the batter among the prepared muffin cups. Bake for 15 to 20 minutes, until the tops spring back when lightly pressed. Let cool in the pan for 5 minutes, then loosen the edges, turn out onto a wire rack, and let cool completely.

MAKES 12 MUFFINS

DATE-NUT BREAD

Resist the urge to cut into this bread while it is still hot; the texture improves as it cools, making it easier to slice.

Preheat the oven to 350°F. In a large bowl, whisk together the all-purpose and whole-wheat flours, cocoa powder, baking soda, and baking powder. Stir in the dates, nuts, and ½ cup of the oats.

In a medium bowl, whisk together the butter, oil, brown sugar, eggs, milk, molasses, and vanilla. Stir the dry ingredients into the milk mixture with a wooden spoon just until combined.

Lightly grease two 8-by-4-inch loaf pans, then dust lightly with flour. Divide the batter evenly between the loaf pans. Sprinkle the remaining ¼ cup oats over the loaves. Bake for 45 to 50 minutes, until a toothpick or paring knife comes out the clean when inserted in the center. Let cool in the pans for 5 minutes. Turn the loaves out onto a wire rack and let cool completely.

2¼ cups unbleached all-purpose flour

1 cup whole-wheat flour

2 tablespoons unsweetened cocoa powder

2 teaspoons baking soda

1 teaspoon baking powder

2 cups chopped pitted dates

1½ cups chopped walnuts or pecans, toasted (see page 114)

¾ cup old-fashioned rolled oats

1 cup (2 sticks) butter, melted

¼ cup canola oil

1 cup packed light brown sugar

3 large eggs, beaten

1½ cups milk

½ cup dark molasses

1 teaspoon vanilla extract

SWEET POTATO BREAD

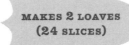

**MAKES 2 LOAVES
(24 SLICES)**

2	medium sweet potatoes, scrubbed
¾	cup warm water (105° to 115°F)
2	tablespoons olive oil
1	envelope or 1 scant tablespoon active dry yeast
2	cups bread flour
1	cup whole-wheat flour
2	teaspoons salt
2	teaspoons maple syrup
1	cup chopped pecans, toasted (see page 114)

Many cooks are leery of baking bread that uses yeast. But yeast is very easy to use if you remember a few things, such as warm water (about 110°F) is necessary to activate dry yeast. Very warm water (hotter than 130°F) will kill the yeast, and cool water will not activate the yeast enough to provide for a good rise. An instant-read thermometer is a fail-safe method for checking the water temperature. Lukewarm water should be comfortable to the touch, not too hot, but not too cool. Another method is to mix two-thirds cold tap water with one third boiling water. Adding a small amount of honey or sugar will also allow the yeast to grow faster and better because it will have enough food (sugar) to feed on.

Preheat the oven to 375°F. Bake the sweet potatoes for 30 minutes. Remove from the oven and let cool. (Alternatively, poke several holes in the potatoes with a fork and microwave on high power for 10 to 12 minutes.) Let cool slightly. Peel the sweet potatoes and cut into 1-inch pieces.

In a large bowl, combine the warm water and olive oil. Sprinkle the yeast over the mixture and stir. Let stand for 5 minutes, until foamy. Add the sweet potato, bread and whole-wheat flours, salt, and maple syrup. Using the dough hook of an electric mixer or kneading by hand, mix until the dough is smooth and elastic, about 5 minutes.

Add the pecans and mix or knead for 2 minutes. Transfer the dough to a lightly oiled bowl, cover loosely with plastic wrap, and let rise in a warm, draft-free place until doubled in volume, about 1 hour.

Lightly oil two 8-by-4-inch loaf pans. Punch the dough down and turn out onto a lightly floured work surface. Cut into 2 equal pieces. Flatten each into a disk and roll tightly into a log. Place, seam sides down, in the prepared pans. Cover loosely with greased plastic wrap and let rise in a warm place until the dough domes over the top of the pans, about 30 minutes.

Preheat the oven to 400°F. Bake for 15 minutes. Reduce the oven temperature to 350°F and bake for 20 to 25 minutes more, until the bread pulls away from the sides of the pans. Turn out onto a wire rack and cool completely before slicing.

VEGAN

IRISH SODA BREAD

Soda bread is associated with Irish cooking, and it is often served with a cup of tea. This classic bread is leavened with baking soda, hence the name. Before it is baked, a cross is cut in the top of the dough. Tradition has it that this cross was meant to keep the devil away. Soda bread, similar in texture to a biscuit, makes an inviting breakfast when spread with jam or marmalade. It also goes nicely with stew or a main-dish soup.

2 cups unbleached all-purpose flour

1 cup, plus 1 tablespoon quick-cooking oats

1½ teaspoons baking soda

½ teaspoon salt

1 cup, plus 1 tablespoon buttermilk

2 tablespoons honey

1 tablespoon butter, melted

**MAKES 1 ROUND LOAF
(12 SLICES)**

Preheat the oven to 375°F. Lightly grease a baking sheet. In a medium bowl, mix the flour, 1 cup of the oats, the baking soda, and salt. In a small bowl, whisk together 1 cup of the buttermilk, the honey, and butter until well blended. Add to the dry ingredients, stirring until just combined.

Turn the dough out onto a lightly floured surface and knead gently 5 or 6 times, then shape it into a ball. Place on the prepared baking sheet and pat into an 8-inch round. Brush the top of the loaf with the remaining 1 tablespoon buttermilk and sprinkle with the remaining 1 tablespoon oats. With a sharp knife, score a cross in the top of the dough.

Bake for 35 to 40 minutes, until golden brown and the loaf sounds hollow when tapped on the bottom. Transfer to a wire rack to cool. Serve warm or at room temperature.

MAPLE-BLUE CORN STICKS

A trademark way of baking cornbread in the South is in a molded cast-iron pan with 6 or 7 compartments that yield individual breads shaped like ears of corn about 5 inches long and 1 inch wide. These pans are available in kitchen supply shops. The cast-iron pan gives the cornbread a crisp crust. This recipe can also be made in a small (8-inch) cast-iron skillet.

Preheat the oven to 375°F. In a medium bowl, mix the maple syrup, butter, milk, brown sugar, and eggs. In another bowl, mix the flour, cornmeal, baking powder, and salt. Stir in the pine nuts, if using. Add the dry ingredients to the milk mixture and mix thoroughly.

Coat 2 or 3 cast-iron corn stick pans with vegetable oil or butter and heat in the oven for about 8 minutes. Remove the hot pans from the oven and pour the batter into them, filling each mold to within ⅛ inch of the top.

Bake for 11 to 14 minutes, until lightly browned and a toothpick inserted into the center comes out clean. Let cool in the pans until slightly warm. Turn out of the pans and serve warm.

6 tablespoons maple syrup

6 tablespoons (¾ stick) butter, melted

½ cup milk

¼ cup packed light or dark brown sugar

2 medium eggs, beaten

1 cup all-purpose flour

6 tablespoons blue cornmeal

1½ teaspoons baking powder

½ teaspoon salt

¼ cup pine nuts (optional)

ORANGE-WHEAT BISCUITS

Whole-wheat flour gives these light and fluffy biscuits a slightly nutty flavor. The biscuits are made into squares, so they are easier to cut than the traditional round ones and there's no re-rolling of scraps.

1 cup unbleached all-purpose flour

1 cup whole-wheat pastry flour

4 tablespoons sugar

1 tablespoon baking powder

¼ teaspoon baking soda

½ teaspoon ground cinnamon

6 tablespoons (¾ stick) chilled butter or soy margarine, cut into small pieces

1 cup, plus 1 tablespoon plain low-fat yogurt

1 tablespoon grated orange zest

Preheat the oven to 375°F. In a large bowl, mix the all-purpose and whole-wheat flours, 3 tablespoons of the sugar, the baking powder, baking soda, and cinnamon until blended. Cut in the butter with a pastry blender until the mixture resembles coarse crumbs. Add 1 cup of the yogurt and the orange zest and stir just until blended.

Transfer the dough to a well-floured surface and knead 4 or 5 times. Roll out with a floured rolling pin or pat out with your fingers into a 7-inch square. With a lightly floured sharp knife, cut the dough into 12 rectangles. Place the biscuits on an ungreased baking sheet, setting them close together for biscuits with soft sides or 2 inches apart for biscuits with crisper sides. Brush the tops with the remaining 1 tablespoon yogurt and sprinkle with the remaining 1 tablespoon sugar.

Bake for 18 to 20 minutes, until the tops begin to turn golden brown. Serve warm or at room temperature.

MAKES 12 BISCUITS

CRANBERRY BISCUITS

The combination of cranberries, cornmeal, and orange zest gives these biscuits an addictive quality, so be prepared. They are not heavy, which is why they work well for a Thanksgiving feast.

In a food processor, combine the flour, cornmeal, baking powder, salt, and orange zest; pulse several times to mix. Add the shortening and process until blended, about 10 seconds.

In a small bowl, dissolve the sugar and yeast in the warm buttermilk and water; let stand for 5 minutes. With the motor running, slowly add the yeast mixture through the feed tube of the food processor and process until the dough leaves the sides of the bowl and forms a ball.

Lightly grease a baking sheet. Turn the dough out onto a lightly floured surface and knead in the cranberries. Roll out to a thickness of ½ inch. Cut with a 1½-inch biscuit cutter into 24 biscuits. Arrange the biscuits about 1 inch apart on the prepared baking sheet. Let rise, uncovered, in a warm, draft-free place for about 20 minutes, or until puffy. Meanwhile, preheat the oven to 425°F. Bake the biscuits for about 8 minutes, until golden. Serve warm.

1½ cups unbleached all-purpose flour

½ cup cornmeal

1 teaspoon baking powder

¼ teaspoon salt

1 tablespoon grated orange zest

2 tablespoons vegetable shortening

3 tablespoons sugar

1 envelope or 1 scant tablespoon active dry yeast

⅔ cup warm buttermilk (105° to 115°F)

2 tablespoons warm water (105° to 115°F)

½ cup dried cranberries

chapter

9 HAPPY ENDINGS

DESSERTS

can be an essential part of a meal's satisfaction and nutritional value. Try making a bread or rice pudding from a previous day's leftovers. Or have a baked apple (take out the core and fill it with raisins and a drizzle of maple syrup). Dried fruit can be stewed into an iron-rich compote, and fresh fruit can be enjoyed in a myriad of ways. Of course, there's always the decadent route: cookies, cakes, pies, and the like. These too can make a respectable contribution to a meal, particularly if you make them with whole-grain flour, natural sweeteners, and a minimum of fat.

CHOCOLATE MAJESTY CAKE

1   cup firm silken tofu, drained and puréed

1   cup maple syrup

½   cup brewed strong coffee or espresso, chilled

1   teaspoon vanilla extract

½   cup ice water

1¼ cups whole-wheat pastry flour

1   cup unsweetened cocoa powder

1   teaspoon baking powder

1   teaspoon baking soda

SYRUP

¼   cup maple syrup

¼   cup brewed strong coffee or espresso

2   teaspoons vanilla extract

CHOCOLATE FROSTING

One 10½-ounce package extra-firm silken tofu, drained

1   teaspoon vanilla extract

6   ounces semisweet chocolate, melted

This chocolate layer cake is perfect to serve for a celebration or special occasion. The texture is soft and tender, and the flavor is intensely chocolaty yet pleasantly sweet. The coffee-flavored frosting balances the rich chocolate flavor.

Preheat the oven to 350°F. Grease and flour two 8-inch round cake pans. In a large bowl, mix the tofu, maple syrup, coffee, vanilla, and ice water until smooth. In a medium bowl, whisk together the flour, cocoa powder, baking powder, and baking soda. Add the to the wet ingredients and stir until smooth. Pour the batter into cake pans, dividing it evenly. Bake for about 25 minutes, until the cakes are springy to the touch. Set the pans on a wire rack and let cool for 10 minutes. Turn the cakes out onto wire racks and cool completely.

Make the syrup: In a small saucepan, combine the maple syrup, coffee, and vanilla and bring to a simmer over medium heat, stirring often. Using a pastry brush, brush the mixture over the top of the cooled cake layers.

Make the frosting: In a blender or food processor, combine the tofu, vanilla, and melted chocolate and process until smooth. Place one cake layer on a serving plate. Spread with ½ cup frosting. Top with the second layer. Spread the remaining frosting over the top and sides.

SERVES 8 TO 10

ALMOND TOFU CHEESECAKE

SERVES 10

The flavor and texture of this cheesecake are best if the cake is allowed to stand at room temperature for 30 minutes before serving. When cutting the cake, have a pitcher of hot tap water nearby; dipping the blade of the knife into the water and wiping it clean with a kitchen towel after each cut helps make neat slices.

Make the crust: Preheat the oven to 325°F. Lightly grease a 9-inch springform pan. Wrap the outside of the pan with a double thickness of aluminum foil.

In a food processor, combine the graham cracker crumbs, apricots, and almonds and process until finely ground. Press the mixture evenly over the bottom of the prepared pan.

Wipe out the bowl of the food processor and the blade. Add the tofu, cream cheese, sour cream, sugar, egg substitute, liqueur, and salt. Process until smooth, stopping to scrape down the sides of the bowl. Pour the mixture over the crust.

Place the cheesecake in a shallow roasting pan and pour in enough hot water to come ½ inch up the sides of the springform pan. Bake for about 50 minutes, until the edges are set but the center still jiggles when the pan is tapped.

Put the cheesecake on a wire rack and run a knife around the inside edge of the pan. Remove the foil and let cool at room temperature for about 2 hours. Refrigerate until firm, up to 2 days. Serve chilled.

CRUST

- ½ cup graham cracker crumbs
- ½ cup packed dried apricots
- 2 tablespoons chopped almonds

- 2 cups firm silken tofu, drained
- 8 ounces soy cream cheese
- ¼ cup soy sour cream
- ⅔ cup sugar
- ½ cup egg substitute
- ¼ cup almond-flavored liqueur, such as amaretto
- ¼ teaspoon salt

VEGAN

CORNMEAL SHORTCAKES WITH LEMON-BLUEBERRY COMPOTE

SERVES 8

While some cooks like to spoon berries over pound cake, sponge cake, and even angel food cake, my idea of a shortcake definitely involves a biscuit, with juicy fruit to ladle over it.

LEMON-BLUEBERRY COMPOTE

4   cups fresh or thawed frozen blueberries

½   cup water

⅓   cup sugar

2   teaspoons grated lemon zest

1   teaspoon vanilla extract

SHORTCAKES

1   cup unbleached all-purpose flour

1   cup yellow cornmeal

¼   cup, plus 1 tablespoon sugar

2   teaspoons baking powder

1   teaspoon baking soda

½   teaspoon salt

¼   cup reduced-fat cream cheese

¾   cup, plus 2 tablespoons buttermilk

1   tablespoon canola oil

1   teaspoon vanilla extract

2   tablespoons chopped pecans

Make the compote: In a medium saucepan, combine 2 cups of the blueberries, the water, and sugar. Bring to a simmer over medium heat. Cook, stirring often, until the berries soften into a sauce, 3 to 5 minutes. Remove from the heat. Stir in the remaining 2 cups berries, lemon zest, and vanilla. Set aside.

Make the shortcake: Preheat the oven to 425°F. Lightly grease a baking sheet. In a medium bowl, whisk together the flour, cornmeal, ¼ cup of the sugar, the baking powder, baking soda, and salt. Using a pastry blender or your fingers, cut the cream cheese into the dry ingredients until the mixture resembles coarse crumbs.

In a small bowl, combine ¾ cup of the buttermilk, the oil, and vanilla. Make a well in the dry ingredients. Add the buttermilk mixture and stir with a fork just until combined. Turn the dough out onto a lightly floured surface. Gently pat into a ¾-inch-thick disk. With a floured knife, cut the dough into 8 wedges. Arrange on the prepared baking sheet.

In a small bowl, combine the pecans and the remaining 1 tablespoon sugar. Brush the tops of the shortcakes with the remaining 2 tablespoons of buttermilk and sprinkle with the pecan mixture.

Bake for 10 to 12 minutes, until golden. To serve, split the warm shortcakes in half with a serrated knife. Set the bottom halves on dessert plates. Spoon the blueberry compote over them. Set the tops at an angle over the compote and serve right away.

PEACH UPSIDE-DOWN CAKE

In the 1930s, the rage among most home bakers was the pineapple upside-down cake. This not-too-sweet version uses sugar-glazed peaches instead of pineapple.

SERVES 8

6   tablespoons (¾ stick) butter

1½ cups packed brown sugar

2   tablespoons thawed apple juice concentrate

¼   cup sliced almonds, toasted (see page 114)

3   cups sliced peeled peaches (about 2 pounds)

1   large egg

1   teaspoon vanilla extract

1½ cups unbleached all-purpose flour

1½ teaspoons baking powder

½   teaspoon baking soda

½   teaspoon ground cinnamon

¼   teaspoon salt

¾   cup buttermilk

Preheat the oven to 350°F. In a 10-inch ovenproof skillet over medium-low heat, melt 3 tablespoons of the butter. Add ¾ cup of the brown sugar and the apple juice and cook, stirring constantly, until the sugar melts, about 2 minutes. Remove from the heat.

Sprinkle the sliced almonds over the brown sugar mixture. Arrange the peach slices in a spoke pattern on top of the almonds, working from the center of the skillet to the edge.

In a large bowl, combine the remaining 3 tablespoons butter and ¾ cup brown sugar. Beat with an electric mixer on medium speed until creamed, about 4 minutes. Add the egg and vanilla and beat well. In a medium bowl, whisk together the flour, baking powder, baking soda, cinnamon, and salt. Add the flour mixture to the creamed butter mixture alternately with the buttermilk, beginning and ending with the flour mixture; mix well after each addition.

Spoon the batter evenly over the peaches. Bake for about 45 minutes, until a wooden toothpick inserted in the center comes out clean. Let cool in the pan for 5 minutes, and then invert onto a serving plate.

APPLE CRUMBLE

You can make this crumble with almost any fruit, using similar quantities and adjusting the sweetness. Serve it warm in shallow bowls.

Preheat the oven to 350°F. Lightly grease a 13-by-9-inch baking pan. In a large bowl, mix the apples, maple syrup, vanilla, cinnamon, and nutmeg. Pour into the prepared baking pan, spreading it evenly.

Make the topping: In a small bowl, combine the flour, wheat germ, almonds, soy margarine, brown sugar, and cinnamon and mix well. Sprinkle evenly over the fruit mixture. Bake for 40 to 45 minutes, until the fruit is tender and the topping is golden. Let cool until just warm, and serve.

6   medium Granny Smith apples, peeled and thinly sliced

¼   cup maple syrup

1   teaspoon vanilla extract

½   teaspoon ground cinnamon

¼   teaspoon ground nutmeg

TOPPING

½   cup whole-wheat pastry flour

½   cup wheat germ

⅓   cup finely chopped almonds

2   tablespoons soy margarine, at room temperature

2   tablespoons light brown sugar

¼   teaspoon ground cinnamon

VEGAN

APPLE-CRANBERRY CRUMB TART

CRUST

1½ cups unbleached all-purpose flour

⅛ teaspoon salt

1½ tablespoons brown sugar

6 tablespoons chilled soy margarine, cut into small pieces

3 tablespoons cold water

FILLING

4 medium apples, peeled and sliced ¼ inch thick

¾ cup fresh cranberries, rinsed

3 tablespoons unbleached all-purpose flour

⅔ cup granulated sugar

½ teaspoon ground cinnamon

TOPPING

½ cup old-fashioned rolled oats

6 tablespoons unbleached all-purpose flour

⅓ cup packed light brown sugar

3 tablespoons soy margarine, at room temperature

The addition of fresh cranberries makes this tart a great dessert for Thanksgiving or the winter holidays.

Make the crust: In a food processor, combine the flour, salt, and brown sugar and process for 30 seconds. With the machine running, add the soy margarine through the feed tube, then add the cold water, processing until the dough forms a ball, about 20 seconds. Wrap the dough in plastic and chill for at least 30 minutes.

Preheat the oven to 375°F. Press the dough into the bottom and sides of a 10-inch tart pan with a removable bottom. Cover and refrigerate until ready to use.

Make the filling: In a large bowl, combine the apples, cranberries, and flour and toss to coat. Stir in the granulated sugar and cinnamon. Spoon the filling into the pastry shell.

Make the topping: In a medium bowl, combine the oats, flour, and brown sugar. Add the soy margarine and crumble with your fingers until the mixture resembles coarse crumbs. Spoon the topping mixture over the apples.

Bake for about 40 minutes, until the topping is golden and the apples are tender. Transfer to a wire rack to cool. Remove the sides of the pan and serve.

SERVES 8 TO 10

VEGAN

MAPLE-PECAN PIE

I have found that most pecan pies I try are overwhelmingly sweet, with no real pecan flavor. Then I came upon a recipe from Eric Tucker of the Millennium restaurant in San Francisco that produced a pecan pie with a silky smooth texture and a rich but no-too-sweet pralinelike flavor. This recipe is a variation of the one served at his restaurant.

Preheat the oven to 375°F. Between 2 sheets of lightly floured wax paper, roll the pastry into a 12½-inch circle. Remove and discard the top sheet of wax paper. Invert and center a pie pan over the dough. Slide your hand under the bottom sheet of wax paper and carefully invert the paper, dough, and pie pan in one motion. Remove and discard the wax paper and press the dough into the edges of the pan. Trim the excess dough to within ¼ inch of the rim, and flute as desired. Bake for about 10 minutes, until light golden brown. Set the pie pan on a wire rack. Reduce the oven temperature to 350°F.

In a medium saucepan, combine the maple syrup, rice syrup, vanilla, ginger, and salt. Bring to a simmer over medium heat and simmer for 5 minutes, stirring occasionally. Remove from the heat and let cool.

In a blender, process the flax seed until finely ground. Add the arrowroot and soymilk and process until blended. Add the maple syrup mixture to the blender and process until blended. Pour into a large bowl and stir in the pecans. Pour the filling into the pie shell. Bake for about 30 minutes, until the filling is set. Set on a wire rack to cool.

Whole-Wheat Pie Crust (page 282)

- ¾ cup maple syrup
- ⅓ cup brown rice syrup
- 2 teaspoons vanilla extract
- 2 teaspoons minced peeled fresh ginger
- ¼ teaspoon salt
- 3 tablespoons flax seed
- 1½ teaspoons arrowroot
- ⅓ cup plain soymilk
- 1½ cups chopped, pecans, toasted (see page 114)

SERVES 8

PUMPKIN PIE

SERVES 8

Fresh pumpkin is so complicated to use that few modern cooks go down this road. Canned pumpkin is surprisingly good and, given a little special treatment, can be as tasty as fresh. One problem with canned pumpkin is its fibrous nature, which is easily corrected by puréeing it in a food processor. You can freshen the taste of canned pumpkin by cooking it with the sugar and spices before combining it with the custard ingredients.

WHOLE-WHEAT PIE CRUST

1　cup unbleached all-purpose flour

¾　cup whole-wheat pastry flour

2　tablespoons sugar (optional)

½　teaspoon salt

5　tablespoons canola oil

5　tablespoons cold plain soymilk

PUMPKIN FILLING

2　cups canned solid-pack pumpkin

1　cup plain soymilk or rice milk

½　cup maple syrup

¼　cup cornstarch

1　tablespoon dark molasses

1　teaspoon vanilla extract

½　teaspoon salt

1　teaspoon ground cinnamon

½　teaspoon ground ginger

¼　teaspoon grated nutmeg

¼　teaspoon ground allspice

Make the pie crust: In a large bowl, mix the all-purpose and whole-wheat flours, sugar (if using), and salt. Slowly add the oil and stir with a fork until blended. The mixture will look like coarse crumbs. Add the soymilk, a little at a time, and stir until the mixture comes together.

Turn the pastry out onto a lightly floured work surface and gently knead 2 or 3 times into a ball. Place on a large sheet of plastic wrap and flatten into a round disk about ¾ inch thick. Wrap in the plastic and refrigerate for 30 to 60 minutes.

Meanwhile, make the filling. Preheat the oven to 425°F. Lightly grease a 9-inch deep-dish pie pan. In a large bowl, mix the pumpkin, soymilk, maple syrup, cornstarch, molasses, vanilla, salt, and spices until smooth and blended. Set aside.

Between 2 sheets of lightly floured wax paper, roll the pastry out into a 12½-inch circle. Remove and discard the top sheet of wax paper. Invert and center the pie pan over the dough. Slide your hand under the bottom sheet of wax paper and carefully invert the paper, dough, and pie pan in one motion. Remove and discard the wax paper and press the dough into the edges of the pan. Trim the excess dough to within ¼ inch of the rim, and flute as desired.

Pour the pumpkin mixture into the prepared pie crust and smooth the top. Bake for 10 minutes. Reduce the oven temperature to 350°F and bake about 50 minutes, until the filling is set. Set on a wire rack to cool, then refrigerate until the filling is firm, 6 to 8 hours. Serve chilled.

VEGAN

OLD-FASHIONED BERRY BUCKLE

You can make this traditional crumb-topped cake with any type of berries. It is called a buckle because the cake is said to buckle as it bakes.

TOPPING

⅓ cup old-fashioned rolled oats

⅓ cup unbleached all-purpose flour

⅓ cup packed light brown sugar

1 tablespoon canola oil

1 tablespoon apple juice

¼ teaspoon ground cinnamon

1½ cups unbleached all-purpose flour

½ cup granulated sugar

1 tablespoon baking powder

½ teaspoon salt

1 large egg

1 cup buttermilk

3 tablespoons canola oil

2 teaspoons grated lemon zest

1 teaspoon vanilla extract

2 cups fresh or thawed frozen berries (blueberries, raspberries, or blackberries)

Preheat the oven to 350°F. Make the topping: In a small bowl, combine the oats, ⅓ cup flour, brown sugar, oil, apple juice, and cinnamon. Stir with a fork until evenly moistened. Set aside.

Lightly grease a 9-inch springform pan. In a large bowl, whisk together the 1½ cups flour, granulated sugar, baking powder, and salt. In a medium bowl, mix the egg, buttermilk, oil, lemon zest, and vanilla. Add the egg mixture to the dry ingredients and stir just until blended. Spread the batter into the prepared pan. Sprinkle the berries over the top, then sprinkle with the topping.

Bake for 40 to 45 minutes, until the top feels firm when lightly pressed. Remove the side of the pan and let cool on a wire rack. Serve warm or at room temperature.

SERVES 8 TO 10

ARBORIO RICE PUDDING WITH FRESH CHERRIES

The flavor of this deceptively simple dessert says comfort right down to last the spoonful. Using a short-grain rice, such as Arborio, gives the dish an extra-creamy quality. If cherries are not in season, use dried cherries that have been soaked in orange juice to make them plump and soft. The pudding will keep, tightly covered, in the refrigerator for up to 5 days.

In a medium saucepan over medium-low heat, warm the milk. Stir in the rice. In a small bowl, whisk together the egg, sugar, vanilla, and cinnamon. Stir the egg mixture into the milk and rice until well blended.

Bring to a simmer and cook, stirring almost constantly, until the mixture thickens, about 30 minutes. Stir in the cherries. Remove from the heat and let cool. Spoon the mixture into 6 custard cups and cool completely. Serve at room temperature or chilled.

4   cups milk

⅓   cup Arborio rice

1   large egg

⅓   cup sugar

1   teaspoon vanilla extract

½   teaspoon ground cinnamon

1   pound fresh cherries, stemmed and pitted

SERVES 6

BANANA BREAD PUDDING

SERVES 8 TO 10

A firm, white American-style bakery loaf gives the best texture to this pudding. Avoid chewy, crusty European-style breads because they do not soften properly in the custard. For an extra-creamy bread pudding with a sauce beneath a crisp top layer, remove about 1 cup of the soaked bread and 1 cup of the soaking liquid to a food processor or blender and purée until smooth, about 10 seconds. Add the purée back to the rest of the mixture and stir to combine before transferring it to the baking dish. If you're a chocolate lover, add 1 cup of mini chocolate chips to the batter before baking.

4   large eggs

1   large egg yolk

¾   cup, plus 2 tablespoons sugar

½   cup mashed banana (1 medium)

2½ cups whole milk

2½ cups heavy cream

1   tablespoon vanilla extract

1   teaspoon ground cinnamon

¼   teaspoon grated nutmeg

¼   teaspoon salt

8   cups cubed good-quality white bread, 12 ounces (1½-inch cubes)

1   tablespoon butter, melted

Preheat the oven to 325°F. Grease a 13-by-9-inch baking dish. In a large bowl, whisk together the whole eggs, egg yolk, ¾ cup of the sugar, and the banana until well blended. Whisk in the milk, cream, vanilla, ½ teaspoon of the cinnamon, the nutmeg, and salt. Stir in 6 cups of the bread cubes and mix thoroughly to moisten. Let stand for 20 minutes.

Pour into the prepared baking dish. Scatter the remaining 2 cups bread pieces on top, pushing them down gently to partially submerge them. Brush the exposed bread with the melted butter. In a small bowl, mix the remaining 2 tablespoons sugar and ½ teaspoon cinnamon and sprinkle over the pudding.

Bake for about 45 to 50 minutes, until the pudding is deep golden brown, is beginning to rise up the sides of the baking dish, and jiggles very slightly at the center when shaken. A knife inserted into the custard should not come out clean but be partially coated with half-set custard. Let the pudding cool until set but still warm, about 45 minutes.

CHOCOLATE TOFU PUDDING

This recipe is creamy smooth, chocolaty, and incredibly simple to make.
It also makes a great filling for a tart or pie.

1   pound firm silken tofu, drained

3   ounces unsweetened chocolate, melted

2   tablespoons honey

2   tablespoons vanilla soymilk

1   tablespoon vanilla extract

In a blender or food processor, combine all of the ingredients and process until the mixture is smooth. Pour into 4 individual serving dishes, cover with plastic wrap, and refrigerate for at least 30 minutes before serving.

**SERVES
4**

FUDGY BROWNIES

MAKES 12 BROWNIES

These vegan brownies have a moist, velvety texture, a hint of chew, and a deep chocolate flavor. The secret lies in the balance of ingredients, two different types of chocolate, and the addition of flax seed, which acts as an emulsifier.

Preheat the oven to 350°F. Grease a 9-inch square baking pan and coat with flour, shaking out the excess.

In a large bowl, whisk together the flour, cocoa powder, baking powder, Sucanat, and salt. In a blender or mini food processor, process the flax seed until finely ground. Add the oil, maple syrup, and vanilla and process until blended. Pour the flax mixture into the dry ingredients and stir just until blended. Stir in the chocolate chips.

Scrape the batter into the prepared pan and spread evenly. Bake for 45 to 50 minutes, until the brownies are set. Set the pan on a wire rack and cool.

2 cups unbleached all-purpose flour

1 cup unsweetened cocoa powder

1½ tablespoons baking powder

1½ cups Sucanat (see page 24)

⅛ teaspoon salt

2 tablespoons flax seed

1 cup canola oil

1 cup maple syrup

1 tablespoon vanilla extract

½ cup dairy-free chocolate chips

VEGAN

BAKED APPLES WITH WALNUTS

Baked apples are a comforting, old-fashioned dish—simple to make and only requiring a few ingredients. To allow steam to escape and keep the apples from bursting, remove a strip of skin around the apple's stem end with a vegetable peeler. Serve these baked apples warm with Whipped Tofu Topping or tofu ice cream. The apples can be cooled to room temperature, covered, and refrigerated for 2 days. Reheat before serving.

SERVES 4

4   large apples, such as Northern Spy, Cortland, or Golden Delicious, with a strip of skin peeled from the stem end, cored

½   cup maple syrup

¾   teaspoon ground cinnamon

¼   cup chopped walnuts, toasted (see page 114)

1   cup apple cider

Preheat the oven to 350°F. Place the apples upright in a 9-inch pie pan or 8-inch square baking pan. In a small bowl, mix maple syrup and cinnamon. Spoon over and inside the apple cavities. Fill each apple cavity with walnuts, dividing them evenly. Pour the cider into the pan.

Bake the apples for 45 to 55 minutes, basting them every 15 minutes, until tender when pierced with a thin, sharp knife or cake tester. Serve warm.

··

WHIPPED TOFU TOPPING

1   pound soft tofu, drained

¼   cup maple syrup

1   tablespoon vanilla extract

This is a basic recipe for a tofu topping that can be used instead of whipped cream. You can flavor the topping with the addition of ¼ teaspoon of extract such as lemon, orange, or almond.

In a food processor or blender, combine all the ingredients and process until smooth. Transfer to a small bowl, cover, and refrigerate for 30 minutes before serving. Makes 2 cups.

VEGAN

GINGER-POACHED PEARS

SERVES 6 TO 8

Poaching is a simple but excellent way to prepare pears, particularly if they are too hard to eat raw. Here, the pears are simmered in red wine, which imparts a beautiful rosy blush to the fruit and makes a stunningly colorful dessert.

Peel the pears, leaving the stems on and taking off as little flesh as possible. Take a thin slice off of the bottom to make a stable base. In a large saucepan, combine the wine and orange juice. Add the pears and simmer gently until tender, about 30 minutes.

Transfer the pears to a shallow bowl or individual serving bowls. Add the sugar and ginger to the liquid in the pan. Bring to a boil and simmer until syrupy, about 5 minutes. Spoon the syrup over pears and garnish with strips of orange zest. Serve warm or at room temperature.

8 ripe but firm medium pears, such as Bosc or Bartlett

2½ cups dry red wine

1 cup fresh orange juice

½ cup sugar

2 teaspoons finely chopped crystallized ginger

Thin strips of orange zest for garnish

VEGAN

CHOCOLATE CHIP–GRANOLA COOKIES

The granola gives these cookies extra crunch and a chewy texture. You can also use chopped nuts instead of granola.

1¾ cups whole-wheat pastry flour

1 cup unbleached all-purpose flour

1½ teaspoons baking powder

½ teaspoon ground cinnamon

¼ teaspoon salt

1 cup maple syrup

⅓ cup canola oil

2 teaspoons vanilla extract

1 cup granola

1 cup dairy-free chocolate chips

In a large bowl, whisk together the whole-wheat and all-purpose flours, baking powder, cinnamon, and salt. In a medium bowl, mix the maple syrup, oil, and vanilla. Add to the dry ingredients and mix just until blended. Stir in the granola and chocolate chips. Cover and chill the dough for 15 minutes.

Preheat the oven to 375°F. Lightly grease 2 baking sheets. Drop the dough by heaping tablespoonfuls onto the prepared baking sheets, spacing them about 2 inches apart. Bake for about 14 minutes, just until the cookies are set. Set the baking sheets on wire racks to cool for 2 minutes. Transfer the cookies to the racks and cool completely.

MAKES ABOUT
20 COOKIES

CINNAMON-HAZELNUT BISCOTTI

The twice-baked Italian cookies known as biscotti are easy to make. A longer-than-average baking time yields a uniquely crunchy texture and also gives them an unusually long shelf life, making biscotti an excellent choice for gift-giving.

Preheat the oven to 325°F. Line a baking sheet with parchment or foil. In a large bowl, mix the flour, ¾ cup sugar, baking powder, 1½ teaspoons of the cinnamon, and the salt. In a medium bowl, whisk together the eggs, butter, and vanilla. Add to the flour mixture with the nuts and stir just until blended.

Turn the dough out onto a lightly floured surface and knead lightly 10 times. Place on the prepared baking sheet and shape into a 16-inch-long roll. Flatten to a ¾-inch thickness. In a small bowl, mix the remaining 2 tablespoons sugar and ½ teaspoon cinnamon. Sprinkle over the dough. Bake until firm, about 30 minutes. Set the baking sheet on a wire rack to cool for 10 minutes.

Using a serrated knife, cut the loaf diagonally into twenty-four ½-inch slices. Arrange the slices about ½ inch apart on the baking sheet, cut sides up. Bake for about 15 minutes, turning each cookie over halfway through baking, until crisp and golden brown on both sides. Transfer to a wire rack and cool completely. (Biscotti can be stored in an airtight container for at least 1 month.)

2½ cups unbleached all-purpose flour

¾ cup, plus 2 tablespoons sugar

1½ teaspoons baking powder

2 teaspoons ground cinnamon

¼ teaspoon salt

3 large eggs

2 tablespoons butter, melted

2 teaspoons vanilla extract

1 cup hazelnuts, toasted (see page 114), skinned, and chopped

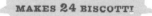

MAKES 24 BISCOTTI

CHOCOLATE-PEANUT COOKIES

For a wallop of chocolate and peanuts—and who doesn't love the combination?—try these cookies. Your kids will love them, and so will your dinner guests.

1½ cups unbleached all-purpose flour

2 teaspoons baking powder

½ teaspoon salt

1 cup maple syrup

¾ cup unsweetened cocoa powder

¾ cup vegetable oil

½ cup plain soymilk

1 tablespoon vanilla extract

2 teaspoons ground flax seed

½ cup dairy-free chocolate chips

½ cup chopped unsalted dry-roasted peanuts

Preheat the oven to 350°F. Lightly grease 3 baking sheets. In a large bowl, mix the flour, baking powder, and salt. In a food processor, combine the maple syrup, cocoa powder, oil, soymilk, vanilla, and flax seed and process until well blended. Add to the flour mixture and stir until well blended. Stir in the chocolate chips and chopped peanuts.

Drop the dough by level tablespoonfuls onto the prepared baking sheets, spacing them about 2 inches apart. Bake for about 15 minutes, until set. Transfer to wire racks to cool.

VEGAN

MACAROONS

These crispy yet chewy cookies are one of my favorite flavor combinations—coconut, walnuts, and oats.

Preheat the oven to 350°F. Spread the coconut and the walnuts on separate baking sheets. Bake the coconut for 5 to 7 minutes, stirring occasionally, until lightly toasted. Bake the walnuts for 8 to 10 minutes, stirring occasionally, until lightly toasted. Set aside. Lightly grease 2 baking sheets.

Put the oats into a food processor and process until coarsely ground. Transfer to a large bowl. Add 2½ cups toasted coconut and salt to the bowl. In the food processor, process the toasted walnuts to a paste. Add the oil, barley malt syrup, maple syrup, and vanilla and process until blended and smooth. Add this mixture to the dry ingredients and mix well.

Roll heaping tablespoonfuls of the dough into balls and roll each ball in the remaining ¾ cup coconut on the waxed paper. Place the cookies on the prepared baking sheets, spacing them about 2 inches apart. Bake for about 15 minutes, until the bottoms are lightly browned. Set the baking sheets on wire racks and let cool for 3 minutes. Transfer the cookies to wire racks and cool completely.

3¼ cups grated unsweetened coconut

1½ cups walnuts

1⅓ cups old-fashioned rolled oats

¼ teaspoon salt

2 tablespoons vegetable oil

⅓ cup barley malt syrup

⅔ cup maple syrup

1 tablespoon vanilla extract

VEGAN

MAKES ABOUT 30 COOKIES

RASPBERRY-LEMON GRANITA

A granita, unlike most frozen desserts, isn't smooth, but has a coarse texture consisting of ice crystals. The name comes from the Italian word grana, *meaning grainy. To get the right texture, stir the granita every 20 minutes. A fork is the best utensil to use for stirring because the tines can be used to break up the large ice chunks.*

3 cups water

1½ cups sugar

Zest of 2 lemons, removed in wide strips with a vegetable peeler

3 tablespoons seedless raspberry preserves

½ cup fresh lemon juice

½ pint fresh raspberries (1⅔ cups)

In a medium saucepan, combine the water, sugar, lemon zest, and preserves. Bring the mixture to a boil. Reduce the heat and simmer for 5 minutes. Refrigerate until cool, about 30 minutes. Stir in the lemon juice. Pour through a strainer into an 8- or 9-inch square metal pan. Discard the zest.

Hold a strainer over the pan and press the raspberries through it with the back of a spoon. Scrape the purée from the outside of the strainer into the pan. Stir the mixture until blended.

Place in the freezer. When the mixture starts to freeze, scrape the frozen sides into the center of the pan every 20 minutes with a fork. Cover the pan with foil and freeze for at least 8 hours, or until firm.

To serve, move the pan from the freezer to the refrigerator for 20 minutes to thaw slightly. Scrape the surface with a spoon and mound it into serving dishes, or use an ice-cream spade or scoop.

MAKES ABOUT 6 CUPS

BERRY TOFU ICE CREAM

MAKES 5 CUPS

You might be surprised to find that replacing the dairy products in homemade ice cream with soymilk and tofu gives you a frozen treat with the same rich, creamy quality and a lot less fat and calories.

In a blender or food processor, combine all ingredients and process until the mixture is smooth. Pour into an ice-cream maker and freeze according to the manufacturer's directions. Serve right away or freeze in an airtight container for up to 3 days.

VEGAN

INGREDIENTS

1   pound soft tofu, drained

2   cups frozen unsweetened berries, such as raspberries or strawberries

1   cup sugar

½   cup plain soymilk

2   tablespoons fresh lemon juice

1   tablespoon vanilla extract

⅛   teaspoon salt

MOCHA TOFU ICE CREAM

The rich, chocolaty flavor of this dairy-free ice cream will have everyone coming back for seconds—or even thirds.

1   pound soft tofu, drained

1   cup sugar

1   cup plain soymilk

½   cup unsweetened cocoa powder

2   teaspoons instant espresso

1   tablespoon vanilla extract

⅛   teaspoon salt

In a blender or food processor, combine all ingredients and process until the mixture is smooth. Pour into an ice-cream maker and freeze according to the manufacturer's directions. Serve right away or freeze in an airtight container for up to 3 days.

MAKES ABOUT 5 CUPS

PINEAPPLE-BANANA SORBET

The flavors of these two tropical fruits are delicious together.
The fresh pineapple gives the sorbet a wonderful, slushy texture.

In a saucepan over medium-high heat, stir together the sugar and water until the sugar is completely dissolved and the mixture is clear. Remove from the heat and let cool to room temperature.

In a food processor, combine the pineapple and banana and process until almost smooth. Add the lemon and orange juices and process until smooth.

Pour the mixture into a large bowl. Stir in the sugar syrup. Pour into an ice-cream maker and freeze according to the manufacturer's instructions. Serve immediately, or pack into an airtight container and freeze for up to 2 weeks. Before serving, let stand at room temperature for 10 to 15 minutes to soften slightly.

2   cups sugar

2   cups water

5   cups fresh pineapple chunks (1 large)

2   cups chopped banana (2 large)

¼   cup fresh lemon juice

¼   cup fresh orange juice

VEGAN

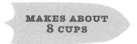

MAKES ABOUT
8 CUPS

chapter 10

ON THE TABLE

MEATLESS MENU PLANNING

Menu

Braised Root Vegetables

Grain-Stuffed Acorn Squash

Wilted Spinach Salad

Chocolate Majesty Cake

THERE

are several ways that you can approach
planning a meatless menu. One way, and
perhaps the most common for new vegetarians,
is to replace the meat that would ordinarily be on
your plate with something that is similar, such as a
meat analogue made from soy or nuts. There is nothing
wrong with this approach, but it does limit your choices.
Another, simpler approach is not to replace the meat and
instead to build your meals around a variety of whole grains,
legumes and beans, and noodles, plus a broad selection of
vegetables and fruits. High in complex carbohydrates, vitamins,
and minerals, these foods will fill you up and provide all the
fuel your body needs without over-loading your system
with protein, fat, and cholesterol.

It doesn't matter whether you're organizing a holiday
feast for twenty or just planning family dinners for
the week; with practice you'll soon be a menu-
making pro. Following are some suggestions based on the recipes in this
book to get you started.

MIDSUMMER MEAL

CORN AND POTATO CHOWDER
(PAGE 105)

PENNE WITH CAPONATA
(PAGE 164)

**MIXED GREENS WITH
LEMON TOFU DRESSING**
(PAGE 136)

PEACH UPSIDE-DOWN CAKE
(PAGE 278)

RUSH-HOUR DINNER

PENNE AND CHICKPEA SOUP
(PAGE 93)

ENGLISH MUFFIN MELTS
(PAGE 152)

SAUTÉED ZUCCHINI

WEEKEND BREAKFAST

BANANA-MANGO SMOOTHIE
(PAGE 51)

POTATO AND PEPPER FRITTATA
(PAGE 28)

**MAPLE-GLAZED PINEAPPLE WITH
MACADAMIA NUTS**
(PAGE 47)

TRATTORIA FARE

RICE AND ZUCCHINI SOUP
(PAGE 94)

EGGPLANT AND ARUGULA SANDWICHES
WITH HUMMUS
(PAGE 159)

RASPBERRY-LEMON GRANITA
(PAGE 296)

TAPAS PARTY

ROASTED EGGPLANT DIP
(PAGE 57)

SPANISH SPINACH DIP
(PAGE 59)

ROOT VEGETABLE CHIPS
(PAGE 67)

ROASTED POTATOES WITH TAPENADE
(PAGE 68)

CARAMELIZED ONION TARTLETS
(PAGE 72)

MARINATED OLIVES
(PAGE 84)

MARINATED GARLICKY MUSHROOMS
(PAGE 85)

COCKTAIL PARTY

BEAN DIP PROVENÇALE
(PAGE 60) **WITH PITA CRISPS**

PARMESAN TOASTS WITH
ROASTED PEPPER AÏOLI
(PAGE 69)

POLENTA CROSTINI
(PAGE 63)

TEMPEH SATAY WITH
PEANUT DIPPING SAUCE
(PAGE 74)

ZUCCHINI TRIANGLES
(PAGE 76)

ASPARAGUS WITH HAZELNUT VINAIGRETTE
(PAGE 70)

MUSHROOM PÂTÉ
(PAGE 61) **WITH CRACKERS**

BROCCOLI AND MUSHROOM BREAD
(PAGE 260)

BISTRO DINNER

ARUGULA AND PEAR SALAD
(PAGE 129)

ROASTED VEGETABLE TART
(PAGE 206)

GREEN BEANS WITH CARAMELIZED ONIONS
(PAGE 240)

SPRING LUNCHEON

CREAMY ASPARAGUS SOUP
(PAGE 103)

TUSCAN QUICHE
(PAGE 202)

CAESAR SALAD
(PAGE 126)

PICNIC

GAZPACHO
(PAGE 107)

VEGETABLE PESTO WRAPS
(PAGE 156)

SMOKY BEAN SALAD
(PAGE 119)

CHOCOLATE CHIP-GRANOLA COOKIES
(PAGE 292)

SOUTHWESTERN DINNER

GREAT GUACAMOLE
(PAGE 56)

NO-MEAT FAJITAS
(PAGE 196)

THREE-GRAIN PILAF
(PAGE 227)

REFRIED BEANS

BOOK-CLUB MEETING

APPLE COFFEE CAKE
(PAGE 46)

PECAN STICKY BUNS
(PAGE 48)

FRESH FRUIT SALAD WITH LIME-GINGER DRESSING
(PAGE 132)

CAPPUCCINO AND TEA

DIXIE DINNER

CURRIED SWEET POTATO FRITTERS
(PAGE 71)

JAMBALAYA
(PAGE 180)

EDAMAME SUCCOTASH
(PAGE 241)

BANANA BREAD PUDDING
(PAGE 286)

OKTOBERFEST

ARUGULA AND PEAR SALAD
(PAGE 129)

TEMPEH WITH BRAISED RED CABBAGE
AND APPLES
(PAGE 214)

MASHED POTATOES
(PAGE 220)

STEAMED BROCCOLI

ASIAN DINNER

SPINACH MISO SOUP
(PAGE 106)

THAI TOFU CURRY
(PAGE 195)

CRISPY PAN-FRIED NOODLES
(PAGE 232)

FRESH FRUIT CUP—
MANGO, PINEAPPLE, AND MELON

FRIENDS ON FRIDAY

MARINATED OLIVES
(PAGE 84)

PESTO PRIMAVERA PIZZA
(PAGE 252)

**MIXED GREENS WITH ROASTED GARLIC
AND BASIL DRESSING**
(PAGE 133)

FUDGY BROWNIES
(PAGE 289)

SUNDAY BRUNCH

BLACKENED HASH BROWNS
(PAGE 33)

TEMPEH "SAUSAGE" PATTIES
(PAGE 37)

FRUIT COMPOTE
(PAGE 50)

GREEK DINNER

BULGUR-STUFFED GRAPE LEAVES
(PAGE 82)

STUFFED BABY EGGPLANT
(PAGE 238)

**LENTIL SALAD WITH LEMON, MINT,
AND FETA**
(PAGE 113)

SNOWED IN

SPICED CHICKPEA SOUP
(PAGE 91)

BROCCOLI AND CHEESE CALZONES
(PAGE 158)

APPLE CRUMBLE
(PAGE 279)

BACKYARD BARBECUE

GRILLED PORTOBELLO CAPS

BRUSCHETTA WITH TOMATOES AND BASIL
(PAGE 62)

WARM POTATO SALAD
(PAGE 120)

CORNMEAL SHORTCAKES WITH
LEMON-BLUEBERRY COMPOTE
(PAGE 276)

BIRTHDAY DINNER

ROASTED RED PEPPER HUMMUS
(PAGE 58)

BRAISED ROOT VEGETABLES
(PAGE 237)

GRAIN-STUFFED ACORN SQUASH
(PAGE 194)

WILTED SPINACH SALAD
(PAGE 130)

CHOCOLATE MAJESTY CAKE
(PAGE 274)

HARVEST LUNCHEON

CURRIED BUTTERNUT SQUASH SOUP
(PAGE 98)

WHEAT BERRY WALDORF
(PAGE 114)

CARAMELIZED ONION FLATBREAD
(PAGE 258)

GAME NIGHT

NACHOS SUPREME
(PAGE 66)

CHIPOTLE-BLACK BEAN CHILI
(PAGE 198)

CHILI CORNBREADS
(PAGE 204)

HOLIDAY DINNER

CRANBERRY BISCUITS
(PAGE 271)

SAUTÉED MEDITERRANEAN VEGETABLES
(PAGE 234)

HERBED APPLE STUFFING
(PAGE 246)

PORTOBELLO GRAVY
(PAGE 247)

ROASTED VEGETABLE TART
(PAGE 206)

APPLE CRUMBLE
(PAGE 279)

BREAKFAST FOR DINNER

OAT SCONES WITH DRIED CHERRIES
(PAGE 43)

SPINACH-MUSHROOM OMELET
(PAGE 31)

FRESH FRUIT SALAD WITH LIME-GINGER DRESSING
(PAGE 132)

Resources

BEAN BAG
818 Jefferson Street
Oakland, CA 94607
800-845-BEAN (2326)
Beans and bean products.

**BOB'S RED MILL
NATURAL FOODS, INC.**
5209 SE International Way
Milwaukee, OR 97222
800-349-2173
www.bobsredmill.com
Grains, grain products, seeds, and beans.

BRIDGE KITCHENWARE
214 East 52nd Street
New York, NY 10022
212-688-4220
www.bridgekitchenware.com
Cookware and utensils.

COUNTRY LIFE NATURAL FOODS
P.O. Box 489
Pullman, MI 49450
616-236-5011
Soy foods by mail order.

DEAN & DELUCA
560 Broadway
New York, NY 10012
800-221-7714
Specialty foods.

DELFTREE FARMS
234 Union Street
North Adams, MA 01247
800-243-3742
Fresh and dried shiitake mushrooms.

DIAMOND ORGANICS
P.O. Box 2159
Freedom, CA 95019
888-ORGANIC (674-2642)
www.diamondorganics.com
Fresh and organic produce.

**GOLD MINE NATURAL FOOD
COMPANY**
1947 30th Street
San Diego, CA 92110
800-475-FOOD (3663)
www.goldminenaturalfood.com
Full-service whole-food supplier.

**GOURMET MUSHROOMS
AND MUSHROOM PRODUCTS**
P.O. Box 515
Graton, CA 95444
800-789-9121
Fresh and dried mushrooms.

THE KING ARTHUR FLOUR BAKER'S CATALOG

RR2, Box 56
Norwich, VT 05055
800-827-6836
www.kingarthurflour.com
Special bread and baking equipment and ingredients.

LUNDBERG FAMILY FARMS

P.O. Box 369
Richvale, CA 95974
530-882-4551
www.lundberg.com
Brown rice and brown rice products.

THE MAIL ORDER CATALOG

P.O. Box 180
Summertown, TN 38483
800-695-2241
www.healthy-eating.com
Soy foods supplier.

MAINE COAST SEA VEGETABLES

3 George's Pond Road
Franklin, ME 04634
207-565-2907
www.seaveg.com
Domestic and imported sea vegetables.

MELISSA'S WORLD VARIETY PRODUCE, INC.

P.O. Box 21127
Los Angeles, CA 90021
800-588-0151
www.melissas.com
Exotic and specialty fruits and vegetables.

MENDOCINO SEA VEGETABLE COMPANY

P.O. Box 1265
Mendocino, CA 95460
707-895-2996
www.seaweed.net
Sea vegetables.

ORGANIC PROVISIONS

P.O. Box 756
Richboro, PA 18954
800-490-0044
www.orgfood.com
Full-service whole-food supplier.

ORIENTAL PANTRY

423 Great Road
Acton, MA 01720
978-264-4576
Asian foods.

PENZEY'S LTD.

Brookfield, WI 53150
800-741-7787
www.penzeys.com
Herbs and spices for all ethnic cuisines.

SULTAN'S DELIGHT

P.O. Box 090302
Brooklyn, NY 11209
800-852-5046
www.sultansdelight.com
Middle Eastern and Mediterranean foods.

Index

TABLE OF EQUIVALENTS

The exact equivalents in the following tables
have been rounded for convenience.

LIQUID/DRY MEASURES

U.S.	Metric
¼ teaspoon	1.25 milliliters
½ teaspoon	2.5 milliliters
1 teaspoon	5 milliliters
1 tablespoon (3 teaspoons)	15 milliliters
1 fluid ounce (2 tablespoons)	30 milliliters
¼ cup	60 milliliters
⅓ cup	80 milliliters
½ cup	120 milliliters
1 cup	240 milliliters
1 pint (2 cups)	480 milliliters
1 quart (4 cups, 32 ounces)	960 milliliters
1 gallon (4 quarts)	3.84 liters

1 ounce (by weight)	28 grams
1 pound	454 grams
2.2 pounds	1 kilogram

OVEN TEMPERATURE

Fahrenheit	Celsius	Gas
250	120	½
275	140	1
300	150	2
325	160	3
350	180	4
375	190	5
400	200	6
425	220	7
450	230	8
475	240	9
500	260	10

LENGTH

U.S.	Metric
⅛ inch	3 millimeters
¼ inch	6 millimeters
½ inch	12 millimeters
1 inch	2.5 centimeters